INTRODUCING BUSINESS STUDIES

INTRODUCING BUSINESS STUDIES

SECOND EDITION

Joseph Chilver

MACMILLAN

First edition 1979
Reprinted 1982
Second edition 1984

Published by
Higher and Further Education Division
MACMILLAN EDUCATION LTD
Houndmills, Basingstoke,
Hampshire, RG21 2XS,
and London
Companies and representatives
throughout the world

ISBN 0 333 37113 5

Printed in Hong Kong

Contents

Preface

There is a basic area of study which is required in all business courses and it is this common core of commercial knowledge which has been collated here. Business Education Council courses remain a prime target for this new edition but the lecture notes have been extended for the benefit of secretarial students. These now cover the syllabus and course specifications for the Background of Business and the Structure of Business for Royal Society of Arts and London Chamber of Commerce and Industry examinations.

Although the characters and companies are fictitious, the case-study scenarios are based on real-life business situations.

My thanks are extended to the Macmillan Press for permission to reproduce a part of the illustration from pp. 12–13 of *Further Education College Catalogue 1983: Arts & Business Education.*

JOSEPH CHILVER

PART 1

INTRODUCTION

CHAPTER 1

An Introduction to the Case-study Concept

The four introductory chapters which follow have a dual purpose. They are directed primarily at the students, many of whom are becoming involved with case studies for the first time. They will need to have the techniques explained to them. But the introductory notes also have the purpose of indicating some of the underlying ideas in this particular text, for the benefit of tutors who play such a crucial role in any proceedings of this nature.

What is a case study?

In essence a case study is a description of a problem situation. After being told what the situation is, the participants have to decide what would be needed to produce a desired result. Take a very simple problem situation. You are walking along the bank of a river when you see a child in difficulties in mid-stream. What would you do? That gives us the sort of framework we need for a case study, but here we are concerned with business matters, and so we would need to find ourselves a problem set in a business context.

Here is an example. Claire and Carol are assistants in a store. One day Carol's boy friend comes to the counter and gives her a £1 note in payment for an inexpensive article. Carol gives him change for a £5 note and he goes away smiling. Claire cannot be certain what transpired so she says nothing. The next day Carol's boy friend appears again, and the performance is repeated. What should Claire do in these circumstances?

Here we have an embryo case study. We have something to think about. We have a problem to solve. And it is the sort of problem which might confront any of us – in one form or another – during our working lives.

Of course problems are not usually posed in such simple and direct terms. If we wish to simulate a real-life business situation, we need a lot more background information. In some case studies a mass of data is provided. In those we shall study here the information will be limited. That is because the prime objective is to develop the student's social and oral skills, and it does not require lengthy tracts to achieve this goal.

What is the purpose of case-study work?

By using case studies we try to bridge the gap which admittedly exists between classroom theory and business experience. We can never close the gap completely, but we can try to minimise it. By playing the roles of businessmen and women confronted with a real-life problem we can familiarise ourselves with the roles we shall be expected to play in due course. We can acclimatise ourselves to the business environment before we actually experience it. And we shall be better equipped to deal with authentic business problems when we are confronted with them.

With some banks young people who are about to become cashiers are sent to a training school. As part of their training they will spend time behind a mock counter. They will have real money in their tills. They will keep proper records, as their fellow trainees pretend to be customers, present them with cheques for encashment, or pay in sums of money to fictitious accounts. Mistakes are made by the rookie cashiers but they are easily rectified and no harm has been done. It is better to make a mistake in the training session than in the real-life situation. Indeed we learn by making mistakes. But it is a good thing if we can confine our most glaring errors to the classroom.

We are trying to achieve the same sort of objectives in our case-study exercises. We simulate a real-life situation so that students can practise their future roles – under the watchful eyes and ears of a sympathetic tutor.

Why is it necessary to develop oral skills?

Traditionally education has centred on the development of written skills. Educational processes have been geared to the examination system. Individuals have been judged academically solely on success at written examinations – apart from the occasional language oral. The value of this approach is undiminished, but the Business Education Council has decided to emphasise the value of group work and case studies, at least in its own courses. It is a wise decision because, while written skills are obviously an essential part of the armoury for young businessmen and women, much of their involvement at work is going to relate to face-to-face situations calling for a display of social and oral skills.

In business people have to be able to write letters and reports. They have to understand a wide range of techniques of one sort or another. But they also have to talk to clients and customers. They have to co-operate effectively with their work-mates, because all businesses are work *teams*. In school and college it is individual effort which is at a premium, but in business people depend very much upon each other. Group exercises which require personal involvement and oral contributions are therefore invaluable in any realistic training programme.

Indirect benefits to be gained

Historically learning has often been regarded as synonymous with listening. While one has to be prepared to listen to one's mentors in order to absorb knowledge and understanding, it can be tedious for students to attend one lecture after another with little opportunity of participating in the proceedings. The case-study approach will at least give students a chance to 'stretch their legs' mentally. It is a break from the normal teaching style, and if a change is as good as a rest the break from routine will be useful in itself. Furthermore everyone suffers from frustration in one form or another, and being able to offer ideas and criticisms during a lively debate can be very cathartic. Most people will experience the pleasure of a lively debate at some time in their lives. Why should we not be able to enjoy a discussion which is related to business affairs?

It is rather flattering when someone asks you what your views are – for the first time in your life. It is perhaps an acceptance of your maturity. Students who get involved in discussions like these may feel uncomfortable at first, because they are playing unfamiliar roles, but as they gain experience their confidence will grow, as will their skill. They should always bear in mind that a prime purpose of the exercise is to develop personality. The ability to speak well and easily to others is a worthy aim. Life is much more enjoyable if you can communicate effectively with other people. Someone with a pleasant rounded personality is likely to be well received anywhere. And personality can only be demonstrated through conversation.

Some of the most enlightened employers appreciate the value of staff who can work effectively with other people. As part of their selection process they put candidates to work on case studies. Performances are assessed and the results are included in the final selection data. The numbers concerned may be small at this stage, but anyone who has had experience in this sort of exercise at school or college has a distinct advantage. What is probably more important is that any candidate for a job normally goes through an interviewing procedure. Someone able to converse intelligently and without inhibition is bound to be judged more favourably than tongue-tied competitors.

CHAPTER 2

A Specimen Case Study for Analysis

Title of case study – 'Store Layout'

A new store is being opened shortly in one of the shopping centres of a well-known south coast seaside resort. It is planned to make the store operational in time for the next peak holiday period. Figure 2.1 represents a floor plan of the new store.

The store is to be divided into twelve different departments and, initially at least, in terms of floor space occupied these will be of equal size. There are fifteen possible departments, but only twelve of these can be set up because of the limited floor space.

Frank Sayers, Manager elect and presently Manager of the existing store, half a mile from the new site, has got two immediate problems to solve. In the first place he has to decide how the floor space is to be allocated to the various departments. In the existing store there are fifteen departments, but Head Office have decreed that the new store must not have more than twelve. The Store Manager has been asked to send a report to Head Office giving his recommendations.

The existing departments are as follows:

(1) Cosmetics – including wigs.
(2) Jewellery – including watches and clocks.
(3) Confectionery and ice-cream.
(4) Gardening.
(5) Leather goods and luggage.
(6) Stationery, books and records.
(7) Sports and games.
(8) Toys.
(9) Food and tobacco.
(10) Electrical fittings and hardware.

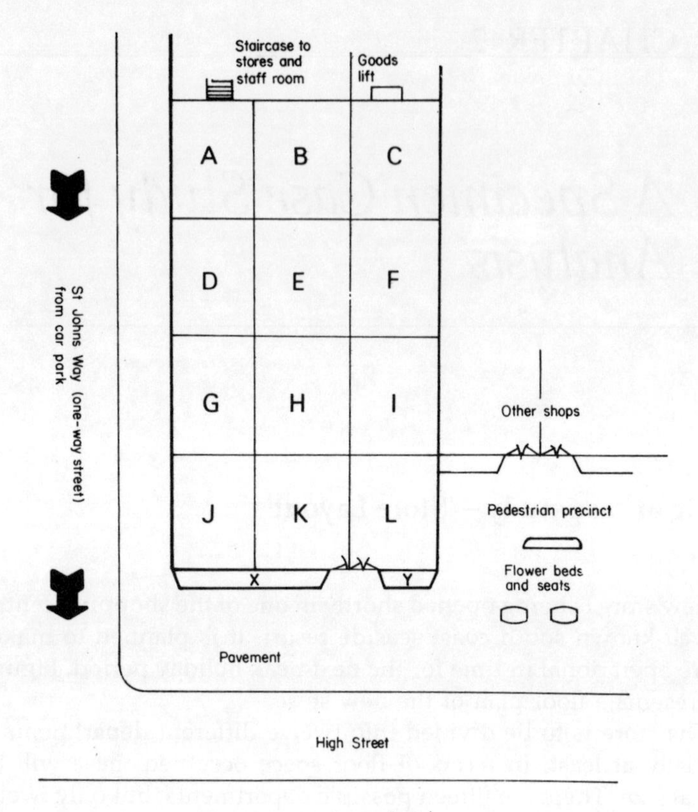

Figure 2.1 Store layout

(11) Ladies' wear.
(12) Men's wear.
(13) Children's and babies' wear.
(14) Shoes.
(15) Underwear and swimwear.

The second problem confronting Frank Sayers relates to advertising. He has to decide which of his wares will be displayed in the windows (X and Y on Figure 2.1), and also which of his wares to give priority to in the local press advertisements.

Your task

You are to represent a group of trainee managers and supervisors brought together by the Store Manager to discuss plans for the new store.

Which three existing departments do you think should *not* be allocated floor space in the new store?

In which floor spaces (marked A to L in Figure 2.1) should the remaining twelve departments be located?

	Department	*Floor space*
(1)	....	A
(2)	....	B
(3)	....	C
(4)	....	D
(5)	....	E
(6)	....	F
(7)	....	G
(8)	....	H
(9)	....	I
(10)	....	J
(11)	....	K
(12)	....	L

Which departments should be given the windows for display purposes?

Which departments should be given most press coverage through advertising?

Are there any other matters you think the Store Manager, Frank Sayers, should consider when he is drawing up his plans?

Analysis of the case study

This is a simple study which requires no specialist knowledge to enable participants to contribute to the discussion, yet the problem does need to be thought about. The siting of the departments and the need for publicity at the time of the opening of the new premises are vitally important, and there are no obvious answers to the questions posed.

A tutor will find the best students offering comments along the following lines.

WHICH THREE DEPARTMENTS DO WE JETTISON?

(1) Much will depend on the extent to which we cater for holiday-makers or locals. We should consider winter trade as well as

summer. We might get an indication as to how valuable winter trade is by comparing sales totals in June with sales totals in December in the existing branch.

(2) Whichever departments are seen as least profitable by the store manager would be favourites for closure, though figures could be misleading. A large department enjoying a specially favourable position in the existing store might show excellent returns, but so might a less-favoured department if given the same opportunities.

(3) A compromise solution might be possible where there were no blatantly unprofitable departments to dispose of. For example, 'Sports and games' might be combined with 'Toys', or 'Ladies' wear' could be amalgamated with 'Underwear and swimwear'. This would leave the store manager with more options than if he were to close departments completely. Another form of compromise would be to have a Gardening department in Summer, to be transformed into a Toys department to take advantage of Christmas trade.

(4) Some departments may be more valuable than any sales figures indicate. For example, ladies may come into a store to look at dresses, buy none, but stay to look at other items; or parents drawn into the store to buy their children ice cream will find themselves staying to look at other things.

HOW WILL THE FLOOR SPACES BE ALLOCATED?

(1) Goods which tend to be bought on impulse should be at the front of the store, so that people passing might be tempted to buy them: confectionery and ice cream, cosmetics and tobacco would be typical examples.

(2) If changing rooms were necessary so that people could try on clothes, 'Men's wear' and 'Ladies' wear' would need to be sited at A and B. Changing rooms could be made available at the rear. If they were put anywhere else, they would take up floor space. The goods lift probably makes C inappropriate for a clothing department.

(3) There should be a reasonable juxtaposition of departments, so that 'Sports and games' are close to 'Toys', 'Ladies' wear' to 'Babies' wear', and so on. This would help customers to find the goods they want more easily.

(4) Generally departments having window displays should be sited at the back of the store, so as to ensure that members of the public attracted into the store by the window displays have to look at a wide range of good before making their purchase. The same argument applies to goods advertised in the press. The maxim

could be described as 'Offer the customers something at a very favourable price so they will come to the store.'

Which department should have window displays?

(1) In brief whichever departments are able to display goods likely to attract most customers into the store. Many departments would be excluded simply because it is difficult to make an attractive display with their goods (consider 'Confectionery and ice cream' or 'Cosmetics').
(2) Combined displays showing 'scenes' would be attractive – the beach in summer, models wearing swim-suits, children in summer-wear playing with beach toys, travel lugguage in evidence, and all items neatly priced and available inside.
(3) Are there no windows facing out on to St Johns Way, or facing the pedestrian precinct? Some advantage could be taken of the flow of traffic from the car park, and the presumed flow of pedestrians to it.

Which departments should be given most press coverage?

(1) Different products would be attractive at different times of the year, for example dresses or gardening products in spring.
(2) Special purchases with exceptionally low prices would be worth advertising, particularly if they had wide appeal.
(3) Since it is Mums and Dads who read the newspapers, goods which appeal to them should be featured.
(4) Products with wide appeal should be selected because the aim is to get large numbers of people to visit the store.
(5) Some items can be displayed attractively in an advertisement while others do not lend themselves to this treatment. Compare, for example, furniture and confectionery.

General comments

There is a danger that a disproportionate amount of time is spent on some problems at the expense of others. The same thing can happen in an authentic business situation. So one should keep one eye on the clock as the discussion proceeds.

For one reason or another tutors might wish their students to consider points not raised in the case study. This problem can be overcome by adding further information in the form of an addendum.

The addendum technique

The additional data can be given to the students in the form of a hand-out, and in this way the tutor can extend the case in any direction required. For example, a tutor may wish to introduce some personnel problems into the store layout case study. This can be done by simply adding some additional features in the manner indicated below.

Addendum to the store layout case study

An additional problem facing Frank Sayers concerns the staffing of the new store. Some departments will have to be contracted while others will expand, and this is bound to cause friction among the managers and supervisors concerned. Some are already showing signs of stress.

One specific issue relates to Connie Meadows, the Floor Manager for Ladies' Garments in the existing store. She is a long-serving member of staff who is still not near retirement age, but her daughter emigrated to Canada some years ago and now Connie is preparing to join her. She and her husband have put their house on the market and as soon as they find a buyer they will be booking their passage.

Frank is sorry to be losing her because she is a key member of his staff. However, Frank can do nothing immediately. She has not yet handed in her notice. There are a number of aspirants for her post – some within the store, and some within the larger organisation. One of the hopefuls is Mrs Janet Gange, who has been with the firm since she left school thirty-three years before. She has been Assistant Floor Manager for the past seven years and there is a rumour circulating that she has already been promised the post. In fact the Store Manager has not yet made a decision, but he would like to know on what basis you think an appointment should be made. Should there be a public advertisement? Should the post be reserved for an internal upgrading? Should seniority be recognised? What other criteria should be used in the selection process?

When departments are closed there might be a need to make some existing employees redundant. How do you think this problem should be resolved? Should it be a case of last in, first out? How can unfairness be avoided?

It can be seen that by adding further information to the case study the tutor can introduce further flavour to the exercise and in doing so satisfy the needs of a particular group of students. The basic case is stretched in an appropriate direction. A tutor will graft on to the original details a superstructure which elaborates the original and poses a new set of problems. As a result the original material is made more flexible, the students are given a more comprehensive view of business, and the relevance of their present studies can be demonstrated.

Do we have to use names? Why cannot we just refer to the Store Manager rather than Frank Sayers? Why bother to give a name to the Floor Manager and her assistant? This is done quite deliberately. In business we deal with people. We deal with customers, storekeepers, managers, typists, telephonists, clerks, and so on, and they all have names. We are expected to use their names. And if we are attempting to simulate a real-life business situation we should get used to the idea of using names.

What do we do about tangential questions which we could ask, even though they are not referred to specifically in the narrative? For example, in the store layout case study no mention was made of a restaurant, yet surely there would be a need for a staff restaurant. And if a staff restaurant functioned, why not introduce a restaurant for the public? These questions are certainly not irrelevant, and could be put to management in real life. Obviously the Store Manager would consider the suggestion and evaluate it – if it were feasible. The best way of dealing with tangential problems would be to recognise them but not spend too much of the limited time in studying them.

A tutor will be aware that the laws of copyright forbid the photostatting or use of extensive tracts from a book without permission, but the use of addenda does not infringe copyright. We are simply adapting an existing case, by producing our own hand-out which is used in conjunction with the original material, to make it more useful to us.

CHAPTER 3

The Assessment of Individual Performances

When assessment is deemed necessary, the course specification for the British Education Council National Awards gives us clues as to how performances in these case-study exercises might be assessed. It states that the general objectives for Common Core Module 1 are to develop, *inter alia,* a student's ability to 'identify false argument; formulate rational arguments; respond flexibly to personal factors; engage in constructive discussion; ... understand the constraints and opportunities of group working' and 'respond constructively to the contributions of others'.

With these thoughts in mind guidelines can be developed, both to clarify for students the sort of approach which is expected from them, and to suggest to tutors the sort of behaviour to encourage – or discourage – as the case might be. The first group of factors below are proposed as favourable interactions – or positive scoring points. The second group indicate what are regarded as unfavourable or negative scoring points. We will look at the scheme in outline first, and then elaborate on it.

Positive scoring points

Contributions. Useful ideas, coherently expressed and relevant, made acceptable to the other members of the group.

Criticisms. Constructive disagreement – blocking someone else's proposal for a valid reason, without rancour and objectively.

Regard. There must be regard for the other members of the team – dynamism with politeness, support for someone else's good idea, recognising the need for co-operation.

Leadership. Pressure exerted to keep the discussion flowing – marshalling ideas, collating views which have been expressed, summarising progress to date, directing discussion to relevant areas.

NEGATIVE SCORING POINTS

Lack of involvement. Silence – no positive ideas or reactions to the ideas of others – equivalent to a blank piece of paper submitted for a written exercise.

Irrelevancy. Leading discussions into areas unrelated to the topic, or spending an undue amount of time on minor issues.

Adverse reactions. Irritation caused to others – counter-productive interaction, and lack of sympathy and support for others.

An explanation of the positive scoring points

All progress is achieved as a result of an exchange of ideas, and any business which lacks dynamism and drive and which fails to adapt to changing situations is doomed to early extinction. A business which is going to prosper is one which has a good flow of ideas – upwards to the chief executives, as well as downwards from them. A work-force which is devoid of ideas can never be as valuable as a thinking team of workers – in the long run anyway. Many of the best ideas are in fact very simple. They do not require genius to conjure them up. Subordinates can produce very useful ideas, and they ought to be encouraged to do so. Of course having an idea is one thing, but putting the idea across to others is another matter. The more practice a student has at conveying ideas, the better performance we can expect in a real business situation.

Many ideas sound good superficially, but for one reason or another they are impractical. For every 'ideas man' in a team of businessmen and women, it is useful to have another character whose feet are firmly on the ground. An admixture of vision and common sense are ideal in business, and the role of the 'blocker' is a useful one – so long as it is based on facts and not prejudice.

Most of the material possessions that surround us are the result of teamwork. Business is effected through co-operation. We need to persuade other people to do certain things – to buy goods or services from us, to indulge in activities with us which are mutually beneficial. In order to persuade other people to work with us, constructively and harmoniously, we need to win their support. In a free society this requires the employment of social skills. With the advent of works councils and other instruments of industrial democracy it is going to be increasingly necessary to have regard for others in the work team. The function of the educators should surely be to help their charges to fit easily into their future roles.

The leadership factor is not only related to student-led case studies. In tutor-led or free-rein group discussion there will be times when an individual will draw attention to the fact that the debate is losing direction, that the questions asked are not being answered, or that time is running out, and the group should be reaching conclusions by now. Similarly when someone attempts to collate or marshal the views which have emerged, credit should be given, so long as it has been done in a manner which is generally acceptable to the group. The objective in encouraging people to adopt a leadership pose is not only to inculcate leadership skills. By making an attempt to steer the debate and direct the proceedings, or even by watching and listening to others attempting to do so, a greater appreciation of the need and value of good leadership should develop.

An explanation of the negative scoring points

There are a number of reasons why members of the group do not get involved greatly, if at all, in the discussion. It may be that the role they are asked to play is unfamiliar to them. Has anyone asked for their opinion on a serious topic before? Because the experience is new to them, they will feel unsure of themselves. It will be even worse if they are sensitive, because they will fear being ridiculed by the group when their efforts turn out to be clumsy. Of course these are the very people the exercises are designed to help. It is better to make the mistakes in a training session than to make them in front of the person who can decide to promote you, or recommend you for a rise at the end of the year. But students cannot learn from their mistakes unless they are prepared to make them.

Another common reason for non-involvement is that a student has contributions to make but someone always makes the point first; or the student has an idea to put to the group but cannot fit it into the flow of discussion. This is most likely to occur when there is a lively discussion, or when there are dominant characters in the group. Before marking students down for lack of involvement, a tutor should try to give them opportunities to become involved, even though in a real-life situation they would have to stand on their own feet. One of the objectives of the exercises is to allow the future businessmen and women to find out how to get their ideas across the other people. The timing of interjections is an art which has to be learned through practice.

There is a danger that participants who want to do well will strive to get their points in first. This could leave little ammunition for those who are left, but this problem can be alleviated by giving credit to a participant who supports a useful idea proposed by another member of the group. If less spontaneous participants realise that the function of the group is not simply to put forward ideas, but also to select the best ones and expand on them, they may be encouraged to contribute – even late on in the discussion.

There is bound to be a degree of irrelevancy when a group first embarks on a course of case studies. It would be unwise for a tutor to clamp down too firmly or too quickly when a student seems to be drifting away from the point. For one thing this would have an inhibiting effect on the individual, and probably on the discussion generally. For another, expansive thinking is to be encouraged rather than discouraged. The dividing-line between irrelevancy and a completely fresh line of thought is sometimes hard to distinguish, and certainly in the early discussions a tutor should not be too restrictive, or punitive, in an assessment. As the group becomes more experienced, however, the tutor's standards should change. It should then be made clear to the group that irrelevancy is to be avoided in business discussions since it is time-wasting and therefore expensive, and that it is frustrating for the rest of the work team.

Some people are personable and get on easily with others. Some people are less popular. Some have a knack of irritating others, even when they are proposing something eminently reasonable. There is a pecking order with chickens, and a tutor will sometimes find the same sort of effect in a group of students. If a student does seem to face this problem, the tutor obviously has a duty to help in every way possible, but in the meantime a personality deficiency – or lack of social skill if you prefer – has to be acknowledged. Acknowledging the problem may be the first step required to overcome it.

Assessment

For those tutors familiar with marking schemes for written examinations, the scoring pattern would be similar whether the exercise is oral or written. But whereas one could re-read a phrase which does not make sense the first time, in an oral exercise to interrupt the flow of discussion would probably destroy it. This is what makes assessment of an oral exercise more difficult than its written counterpart. It would be possible to use a tape-recorder, however, and the play-back could be analysed critically by the whole group. It would be unwise to introduce a tape-recorder too soon, because it would be extremely inhibiting for some people, but it could be brought in when the group is more practised.

While every college using case-study discussion groups cannot be expected to have the same facilities, at the Dorset Institute of Higher Education we are able to let students watch themselves on video/television at least once on the course. It is a time-consuming operation, but invaluable whenever it can be done. The groups on these occasions have to be small, but one group can watch while the other group tackles a case-study in front of the cameras. The roles can then be reversed, with the first group watching while the second group goes into action with a second case. The whole group can watch the half-hour play-backs and comment critically.

Students will need to prepare themselves fairly thoroughly for this sort of exercise but the threat/promise of 'television exposure' is found to be a useful stimulant. The studio layout is simple enough (see Figure 3.1)

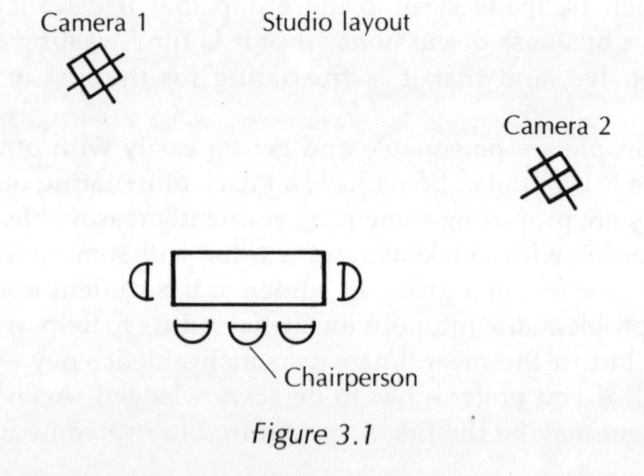

Figure 3.1

While any assessment attempted is likely to be based on impression, particularly in the early stages, experience indicates that the best students in these exercises will emerge clearly and unambiguously. They can be given an A grade without difficulty. Similarly there is not likely to be much controversy over the performances of the really weak students, who can be given an E grade – assuming a five-point scale or grading system. The tutor is then left to classify the remaining participants as above average (in which case they merit a B grade), below average (D grade), or average (C grade). While individual tutors might vary in their assessments, perhaps to the extent of one classification, the variation is not likely to be greater than occurs when written exercises are marked or graded. The marking scheme suggested, then, in line with BEC requirements is based on a five-point equidistant scale as follows:

A superior
B above average
C average
D below average
E very weak

A sixth grade – grade F – could be reserved for any student who makes little or no contribution to the group work, but the tutor will try to ensure that this category is never used.

One way of dealing with students who are shown up as very weak because of their lack of contribution is to give them a central role in a subsequent case study. This may well have the desired effect of ensuring that their grading is improved. Indeed, the threat of being given a central role in future proceedings is often enough to persuade laggards to improve their workrate.

A tutor may decide to give grades/marks for written work based on the case study, and ignore the oral performances as far as formal assessment is concerned, but if this happens there is a danger that the student will underrate the significance of the oral work. The Tutors should make known their views on individual performances so that students are given a feedback.

Where a group discussion of one sort or another is called for, as well as written work, a number of different methods of assessment are available:

(i) A grading can be given to both the written work and the oral contribution, say, a double grading for the written work and single grade for the oral (a set of grades BB and A would end up as B for the assignment – but BB and D would become a C overall and CC and A would become a B).

(ii) Less formally, but just as effectively, the assessment for the oral work can be included in the grading for the written work. The tutor can in effect say, 'this written work is of poor quality, but this student's oral contributions were of a high standard so I will compensate upwards'. Or 'this written work is of a high standard, but the oral contributions were negligible so I will compensate downwards'.

(iii) An overall grading can be given for the oral work during a session.

Whichever technique is used the objective is always to make students aware that learning to present arguments orally is a vital part of their training package. People in business cannot live by the pen/typewriter/word processor/computer alone. Their voices are also essential items of 'business equipment'.

CHAPTER 4

An Explanation of What Follows

The essence of the course which follows is basic business knowledge such as needs to be known and understood by anyone intending to find an interesting job in industry or commerce. One cannot begin to discuss business problems without some basic knowledge and the underlying course aims to convey certain data as a prelude to the group discussions. The lecture notes cover the syllabuses of a number of different courses, but this should not be surprising. Whether students are training to be secretaries or supervisors and managers in the retail trade or commerce generally, they will need to know how businesses are organised, the sorts of problems they face and the different roles people are called to play in the business world. Similarly workers in the nationalised industries or those employed by local authorities will find themselves involved with all types of private enterprises. The more they understand about all aspects of the business scene the more effectively they will be able to play their future roles.

This central core of studies is common for all business courses. In this text it is backed up by a series of case studies. Each set of lecture notes is followed by either a case study or some other assignment which is designed to test your understanding of the learning material.

There are two basic methods of integrating case studies into a learning programme. The tutor can either (i) start with the case-study discussion and then move on to a related lecture, or (ii) give a lecture on a specified topic and then apply the theory to a practical situation through a case study.

The springboard technique

One way of using a case study is as a springboard so that the students start off by discussing a problem that has been put to them.

Then, at the summarising stage, the tutor begins to elaborate on a particular aspect of the study, and blends it in to the next lecture in the programme. An example may be welcome, and if you refer back to the store layout case study in Chapter 2 you will see how logical it would be for tutors to move off the discussion centred on window-dressing and press coverage, and begin to discuss advertising generally. They would be able to refer back to the case-study situation from time to time if they found this useful.

Any of the case studies in this book can be used in this fashion.

The alternative approach

An alternative approach is adopted here generally (Parts 2 to 4 inclusive) and the case study is introduced at the end of a set of lecture notes. The case studies following the notes tend to be tangential in the examples given here, simply because they would represent no challenge if students merely had to regurgitate their lecture notes.

Thus the lecture notes on the EEC (Chapter 35) briefly outline the history and purpose of the Community. They mention one of the most interesting developments in the movement towards industrial democracy in Western Europe – namely works councils – and you are then invited to play the role of a group of work-people involved in the proceedings of such a council. It is a role many students can expect to play in real life in the not-too-distant future, which is why this particular case study was chosen.

The alternative approach might be seen as a case of first dealing with theories and principles and then applying these to a practical situation.

Integrative case studies

In Part 5 the case studies call for a working knowledge of more than one discipline. The cases are designed to show the interrelationship between the different modules (or subjects) in the general framework of a course. The multi-discipline approach may also reflect more accurately the sort of situation found in real-life business where subject boundaries are often different and/or less significant than in the academic world.

Other assignments

While the assignment which follows each narrative is most commonly in the form of a case study a variety of other assignments have been introduced. This is partly to offer a change of diet. Even though the case study is a prime vehicle for studying business – at any level – it is also true that a varied programme will be beneficial. It is for this reason that the case-study assignments have been interspersed with a deliberately varied range of other tasks. The twin objectives remain in mind – student participation and practical business applications.

Group discussion

There are a number of ways in which your tutor may organise the discussions. The commonest technique is for the tutor to lead the session, asking questions and drawing responses from the students. As students gain in confidence and experience they may be left increasingly to discuss the problems among themselves, simply reporting back to the tutor. Each tutor will find a method which is most appropriate for the particular group. However, experience with the case studies in this series has provided a format which produces good results in a wide variety of group sizes and course levels. This requires students to work in twos or threes. They discuss the problems in these small groups and then report their findings to the tutor and the main group. It is certainly one way of ensuring that everyone in the group is involved in the discussions. Another variation would be to ask each of the small groups to tackle a *different* case study. This would allow more cases to be covered in a limited time and might be a particularly useful ploy when coping with the respective trios of cases at the end of Parts 2 and 3, and the cross-modular cases in Part 5. The more senior the students the longer these discussions are likely to take. Whatever time constraints are imposed on the discussion the student should be aware of the constraints which exist in business. It can hardly be viewed as a successful discussion when one problem has been dealt with, but two problems remain disregarded.

Any written work may be dealt with separately. The general approach is to ask for written reports of one sort or another after the group discussion has been completed. This should generally help to raise the standard of written work.

Guidelines

Fairly detailed guidelines have been provided for each of the case studies. These aim to be stimulating rather than restrictive. Many ideas may emerge from discussion which are not mentioned in the guidelines. This is to be expected. However, the guidelines are part of the learning package and students should always refer to the guidelines at some stage of their study. They are an integral part of the course.

The guidelines do not immediately follow the case study because it is recognised that tutors will sometimes prefer their students not to refer to the guidelines while the discussion is proceeding. For that reason the guidelines have been removed to a final section in the book.

PART 2

ON THE THEME OF PEOPLE AND COMMUNICATION AT WORK...

CHAPTER 5

Basic Industrial Psychology

Why do people go to work? The obvious answer is that people go to work to earn money so they can buy all the things they need. What sorts of things do they need? Again the answer is fairly obvious. They want nice clothes, tasty food, enjoyable holidays, nice accommodation and all the other things which go with a high standard of living. We live in a materialist society and we tend to judge success and failure in terms of our material possessions. Whether this is how it should be is another question.

One of the complications is that all jobs are different in one way or another. They may require special skills or talents. Some jobs are more difficult to find than others and some jobs are more satisfying than others. So what makes a job satisfying? Perhaps we will begin to find the answer to that question if we look at a real-life situation through the eyes of a typical young secretary (see Figure 5.1).

Sallyanne is a secretary working in the offices of Avery & Jordan, a London advertising agency. She feels she has a reasonably good job, but admits 'it could be better ...'. What can she mean by that last remark? It could mean that she would like more pay but that goes without saying. Everyone would like more pay... especially if they do not have to work for it. Yet everyone who has been to work, even for a short time, will know there is more to a job than just pay. Indeed, if we look further into the situation in which Sallyanne finds herself we will find she is influenced by a number of different factors.

Salary and 'perks'

The salary is above average for secretaries in London and this was one of the attractions of the job initially. In addition Sallyanne receives daily luncheon vouchers (hence the 'perks' – short for perquisites). She was a little disappointed recently when the annual

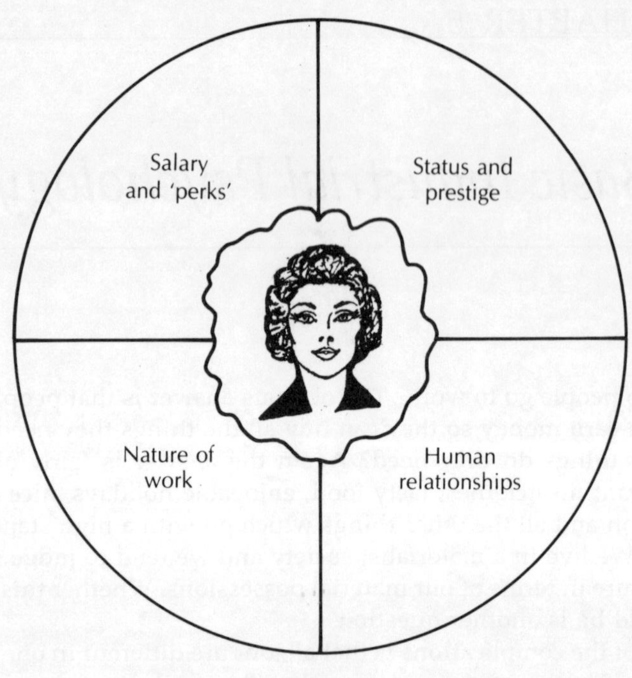

Figure 5.1

review of salaries gave her another £200 per annum on her salary while some of the others received £250 and the senior partner's secretary was given an annual increase of £400. The point to note is that people are concerned about what other people are getting as well as what they are receiving themselves. These are called 'differentials' and explain many of the stresses and strains which develop in business life. This concern over what other people have got is not limited to money. You might note the same sort of reactions when tutors return marked work. Most students are curious to know how well their neighbours got on.

Status and prestige

When Sallyanne joined Avery & Jordan she was given the post of secretary to John Stokes, the Office Manager. She found that there were girls in the typing pool who envied her the job. Why? For one reason she seemed to know a lot more about what was going on. And for another reason she was outside the control of the Pool Supervisor. This affected things like signing on in the mornings, the timing of coffee breaks and fitting in with holiday rotas. These apparently minor privileges gave a certain distinctive prestige to Sallyanne, but she was by no means top of the tree.

Each of the partners have a personal secretary and those attached to the senior partners are regarded with the highest favour. Of course they tend to get more pay than their counterparts, but this is not always the case. For example, the typing-pool supervisor earns more pay than any of the secretaries though her job is not highly regarded since she is seen in the role of a disciplinarian. Many of Avery & Jordan's clients are associated with the entertainments industry and are well-known figures. So, since the more important clients are dealt with by the senior partners, the latters' secretaries often meet the celebrities.

Sallyanne has noticed that the partners' secretaries tend to group together in the coffee room and, while she is free to join them, if she does so she has to do the listening rather than the talking.

Two of the partners are women, one of them quite young, but neither of them ever go to the coffee room or socialise with any of the office or secretarial staff. Sallyanne has heard that one of their secretaries is leaving shortly to have a baby. Sallyanne could apply for the post if she wishes and, although there would be no increase in pay for her, she would like to make the switch.

Such attitudes should not surprise us. It is not only in an advertising agency that jobs carry prestige or status quite apart from the monetary rewards that accompany them. Consider the following jobs. Assuming they carry the same salaries, which carry the greater prestige or status?

(a) a nurse or a wages clerk?
(b) a doctor or a dentist?
(c) an architect or a scrap metal merchant?
(d) a teacher or a lorry driver?
(e) an air hostess or a librarian?
(f) a receptionist or a waitress?
(g) a secretary who works for the BBC or one who works for the Bolton Brick Company?

Nature of work

Sallyanne finds some aspects of her work interesting while other aspects are boring. The mail tends to be routine, but Mr Stokes has made it clear he expects her to be his aide, helping him to do his job more efficiently and effectively. She seems to thrive on this responsibility. He keeps her informed on most of the happenings at Avery & Jordan and she likes 'feeling in on things'. The one job she finds really tedious is the filing. Copies of all letters – incoming and outgoing – have to be put into the customers' files. She knows the work is vital and tries hard to concentrate, but letters do occasionally get into the wrong file. It can be very embarrassing when there are important customers on the other end of the telephone expecting you to know what has been going on. This is one of the problems with boredom. When people get bored they make mistakes. In the circumstances Sallyanne would be advised to spend no more than twenty minutes at a time on this task. In that way the mistakes would be minimised.

If instead of working in an office Sallyanne had been on a production line in, say, a cosmetics factory, she might have found herself sitting at the same machine for eight hours a day filling plastic containers with foundation creme at the rate of one every two seconds (a so-called two-second work-cycle). Ever since Adam Smith in the eighteenth century explained the advantages of specialisation the emphasis has been on increasing productivity by breaking down work into shorter work-cycles. This is the idea behind mass-production techniques which have so increased our industrial output and given us such a high standard of living. Unfortunately they have also brought some rather mind-numbing tasks for our workers. Some would say it is the price we have to pay for our material prosperity.

Pehr G. Gyllenhammar, President of the Swedish motor manufacturers Volvo, crystallises the problem faced by both employers and employees in a modern industrial society:

> By its nature, routine factory work has no correlation with what we seem to offer people in the educational system. Until they are eighteen or so, students are encouraged to learn about ideas, sciences, history, literature, languages, art, and music and to develop some related skills as well .... Then from eighteen ... to sixty five, we expect them to do exactly the same thing for eight hours a day.... Creating educated automatons is unacceptable if you view people as adults who can develop in a number of directions – as human beings with enormous potential. Given this view, which I hold strongly, it is cruel to the individuals and wasteful to society to expect people to spend more than half their waking hours each day without stimulus of any sort, simply acting as efficient machine-tenders. (*People at Work*: Reading, Massachusetts, Addison-Wesley, 1977)

Human relationships

Sallyanne gets on well with the Office Manager. The relationship is based on a mutual respect rather than a liking for each other. Mr Stokes praises her when she does a good piece of work and generally appreciates her efforts. The encouragement and support gives Sallyanne confidence and helps her to do well. Her Manager also takes an interest in her progress, and she knows he would listen to her if she went to him with any problems. This is very different from the case of her friend, Janet, who is in the typing pool. Janet does not get on well with the Supervisor, who is always reprimanding her in front of the other staff.

Sallyanne gets on well with most of the clerical staff. There is a limited amount of socialising outside of work, but there is a friendly atmosphere in the office. If there is an overload of work they tend to share the burden and generally act as a team. At a more personal level, they seem genuinely interested in each others' affairs.

According to the American psychologist, A. H. Maslow, people have certain needs which they are striving to satisfy. As one need is satisfied we find another need has taken its place. The basic needs are related to food and clothing and material things generally. But people also have social and ego needs. They generally prefer the company of others and this might explain the way we live in family units, the development of towns and the numbers of clubs and associations there are in our society. Maslow saw the needs as falling into a fairly predictable pattern (see Figure 5.2) and you will note the centrality of the social needs. People will do much to obtain and retain the affection and respect of those around them. Indeed, if we are honest with ourselves this is what life is really about. Even though we see money as the driving force in business we may well ask why people want more money when they are neither cold nor hungry. Could it be that we are trying to impress other people with our material prosperity?

According to Maslow, when we have convinced others that we are worthy of their respect we need to convince ourselves. The ego is related to a feeling of self-importance. Are we of any consequence? Are we satisfied with our performance in life?

There are important implications for business. If people are balked in the drive to satisfy their needs they are likely to become aggressive. Anti-authority attitudes might emerge which would result in reduced efficiency (or lower productivity). Bearing in mind that workers can only enjoy higher standards of living if goods and services are provided, any aggressive actions (such as strikes) could lead to a reduction in productivity and hence to a fall in the standard of living.

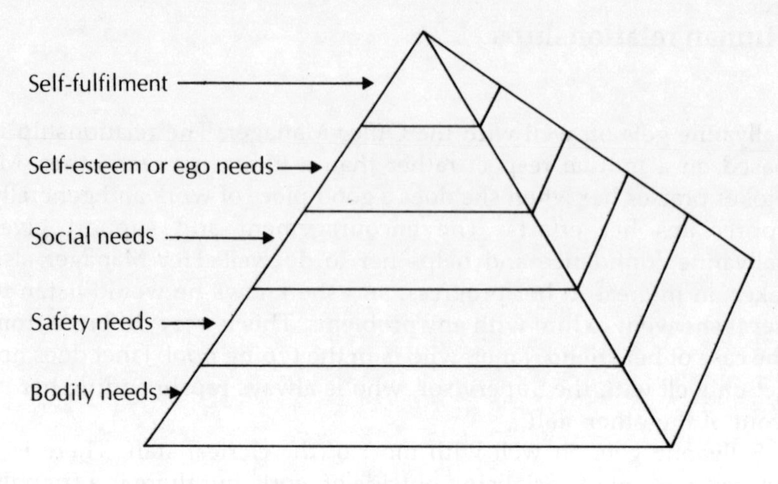

Figure 5.2

The hygiene-motivation theory

Another American psychologist, Frederick Herzberg, produced a theory that people have two different sets of needs. The hygiene needs are those such as physical working conditions and the working relations which exist between management and staff. Why 'hygiene'? If illness is to be avoided, attention has to be paid to hygiene, but if good health is to be achieved something more positive is called for. If the so-called hygiene needs are neglected in the work-place work-people will be dissatisfied and their performance will suffer. But paying attention to these needs is not enough. The motivation needs such as the need for responsibility and a sense of achievement are also vital if the best possible performance is to be obtained from the work-force. People at work want to feel that they are improving themselves and developing. Herzberg talks of 'personal growth'. The two sets of factors are summarised below:

Hygiene factors

1. The goals of the organisation should be broadly in line with those of the staff.
2. Managers and supervisors should be technically competent.

Motivation factors

1. Achievement – the satisfaction derived from work well done.
2. Recognition – the appreciation of efforts which have been made – adding to one's self-esteem.

Hygiene factors	*Motivation factors*
3. Remuneration has to be seen as 'fair' compared to what can be obtained in similar occupations elsewhere.	3. The work itself – can be so interesting that it can be pleasurable though challenging.
4. Interpersonal and social relationships need to be satisfactory.	4. Responsibility – people normally respond positively and favourably when given responsibilities.
5. Working conditions and working environment have to be acceptable.	5. Advancement in the form of actual or hoped-for promotion can motivate staff to greater effort.

The first application of this theory was to the work of secretaries in the Registrar's Department of Bell Telephone, one of the largest corporations in the world. The jobs were redesigned to include more responsibility and interest and as a result performance and efficiency were greatly improved. Other firms thereafter sought Herzberg's advice and the technique he propounded became known as 'job enrichment'.

Case study – Job Factors

A London-based insurance company are advertising for staff for a new office which is to be opened shortly. You have applied for one of the posts and have been offered an interview at their head office. The personnel officer has sent you the following form and asked you to complete this and bring it along when you attend for the interview. When you have completed the form compare the results in your group.

An optional assignment

Consult a selection of people in various jobs and ask them how they would complete the form. Try to ensure you have taken a cross-section of age groups and sexes. Examine the results and draw conclusions where possible.

The Buttress Insurance Company
Northgate

Candidate's name ....

You are asked to consider ten features of a job as listed below. Which features appeal to you most? We would like to know your order of preference. Please write the figure 1 in the right-hand column against the feature which appeals to you most. Write the figures 2 against the second most attractive feature. And so on, unitl you have ranked all ten features in order of importance.

Feature	Order of importance
(a) A challenging and responsible post	
(b) Security and a good pension	
(c) Working in a friendly group	
(d) Working for a sympathetic and appreciative manager	
(e) A job with promotion prospects	
(f) A job with above-average pay	
(g) Interesting work	
(h) Working for a company which provides a valuable service to the community	
(i) Average pay with a shorter working week	
(j) A job which calls for meeting a variety of people	

CHAPTER 6

The Personnel Department

If you apply for a job in a large concern your application will be received and considered by staff in the Personnel Department. The first representative of the business you are likely to meet will be a Personnel Officer. Yet, recruitment and selection are but one of the tasks undertaken by the personnel staff as you will see from Figure 6.1 below:

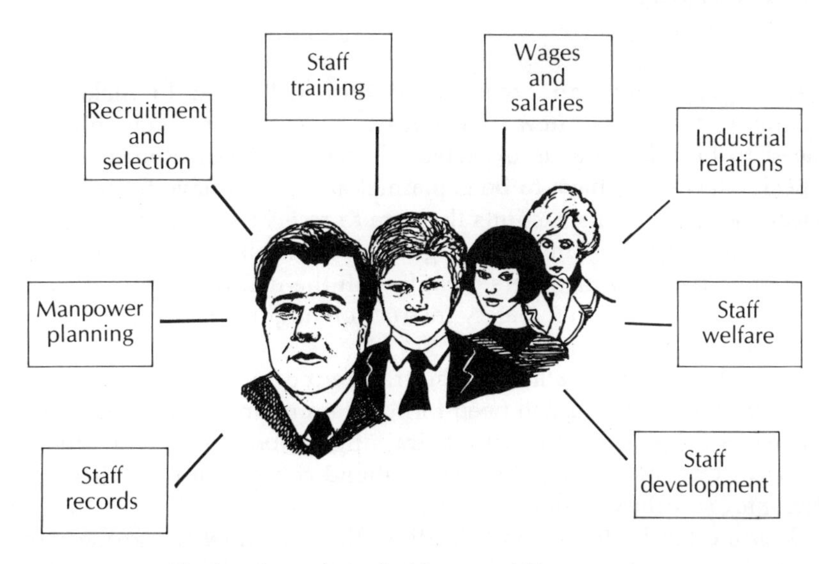

The functions of a typical Personnel Department

Figure 6.1

The personnel function relates to the employment and management of people. Where an organisation is large enough to merit specialist personnel staff they will assume the responsibility for providing staff for the various departments in the business. However, the responsibility for day-to-day control of staff will rest with the managers and supervisors to whom staff have been allocated. Thus it can be seen that all executives have some form of direct involvement with the personnel function.

Recruitment and selection

This will be the topic for the next chapter but at this stage the distinction might be made between recruitment, which aims to provide a pool of persons who are available to serve the organisation, and selection which aims to sort out the best of the candidates applying for the posts.

Staff training

When people join an organisation they will need to make the acquaintance of their new colleagues and workmates. They will also need to be told what is expected of them in detail. Routines and specific tasks will have to be explained and it will have to be made clear the types of instructions they are to receive and who is to give them instructions. Many firms organise a formal *induction programme* to familiarise new members of staff with the nature of the business and their roles within it. Safety instruction might well be included in the induction programme.

From time to time staff will be transferred to other departments and/or other jobs and will need formal training in order to make the switches. The firm may run a training school to provide these services or staff may be allowed to attend colleges or other institutions for so-called off-job training.

It will often be the responsibility of the Personnel Department to provide instruction manuals setting out detailed routines where these need to be followed by staff.

Wages and salaries

Personnel will normally be responsible for payment of wages and deduction of taxes, etc. They will maintain wage records and play a role in developing fair pay structures throughout the organisation.

Industrial relations

There will be times when the interests of employers and employees are diametrically opposed, as when a pay claim is being pursued. The Personnel Department may play a vital role as a bridge between the two sides of the conflict, representing management as they do, but also having close links with the work-force. They may be entrusted to negotiate with trade unions and/or shop stewards, and will take part in joint consultation, sitting on works councils and welfare committees.

Staff welfare

Canteen services, lighting and heating, health and personal hygiene, first-aid facilities and accident prevention fall under the purview of the Personnel Department. While for the individual, counselling services might be provided so that an employee facing problems, whether at work or at home, is able to approach specialist personnel staff for advice on a wide range of domestic and personal problems.

The department has a responsibility for the general health and welfare of the work-force and for the provision of a satisfactory working environment.

Staff development

People in a business organisation will invariably have talents and potential which could be developed to their own advantage and for the benefit of the firm. With this in mind personnel officers may interview staff periodically to discuss personal goals and progress achieved. At such interviews advice can be given on career development generally, while opportunities are also given to air grievances.

To help staff identify with the organisation and share the firm's goals staff magazines and/or news sheets may be produced and circulated. These will normally be provided free of charge and staff will be encouraged to contribute.

Staff records

The application form completed at the recruitment stage may be the first document in the individual's staff records. This is usually the basis of the contract of employment required by law. In the case of staff with executive potential more detailed records may be kept, giving reports of progress from supervisors and managers, and indicating academic success and other material facts. Other records handled by the Personnel Department will include:

(a) Time and attendance records – required when wages are based on hourly rates and where overtime is payable.

(b) Earnings-record data – required by the tax authorities to show wages paid to each employee and the tax deducted (Pay As You Earn/PAYE). Each employee will be given a code determining the amount of tax to be deducted.

(c) Pay slips – issued to each employee will show the amount of pay and details of deductions such as tax and National Insurance contributions.

(d) Payroll – a summation of wages listing names of the employees and basic details of the payments made to them for the week (or other period).

Manpower planning

The overriding function of the Personnel Department is to ensure that a work-force with *appropriate skills* is available in the required *place,* at the required *time* and in the required *numbers* in order to perform the tasks needed to achieve the organisation's targets. Planning by definition entails anticipation. What is required from the work-force over the coming year(s)? What changes will occur in the demands for staff? What needs to be done to ensure that these changing demands within the organisation can be met?

The starting-point in the manpower plan is to compare the present situation with that envisaged in the Strategic Plan for the company. Recruitment can be adjusted without difficulty except for the possi-

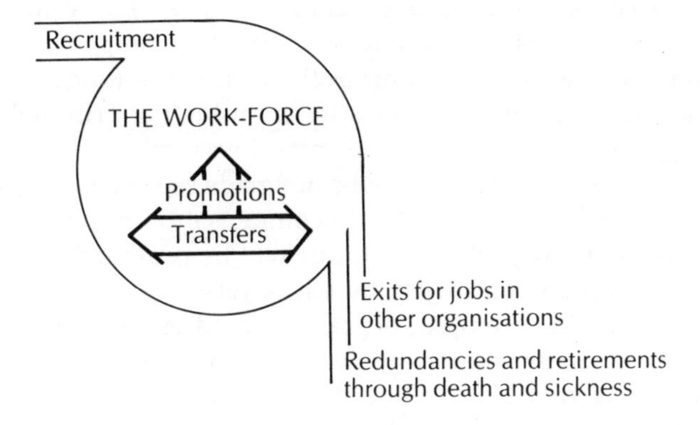

Figure 6.2

bility that certain specialist skills might be in short supply at a particular time. Exits are likely to fall into a predictable pattern so that one knows, for example, that 12 – 15 per cent of staff between the ages of 20 and 30 will leave the organisation within the time-span. Retirements and deaths can be assessed with fair accuracy. Training, transfers and promotions can then be geared to the organisation's requirements. Changing technologies are likely to provide the major elements of uncertainty.

And while manpower planning seems to concentrate on forecasts of future staffing requirements in terms of numbers the quality of staff is also an issue, as is the motivation and morale of the work-force.

Legal requirements

The Personnel Department will need to ensure that various legal requirements are complied with including those under the Employment Protection (Consolidation) Act 1978 as amended by the Employment Acts of 1980 and 1982. Problems might arise under the following headings:

(a) *Dismissal* – employees must receive a written statement setting out the terms and conditions of their employment. The statement will include a job title which could be relevant if the employee is subsequently dismissed for refusing to do something different. The contract accords the employee certain rights. For example, any employee who is dismissed may be entitled to compensation where the dismissal is wrongful, unfair or the result of redundancy. Claims for unfair dismissal will be heard by an Industrial Tribunal. It is for the employer to prove that the dismissal was fair.

(b) *Redundancy* – employees who are made redundant as a result of reorganisation, etc., are entitled to compensation under the Redundancy Payments Act, 1965. The funds will be provided partly by the central government and partly by employers.

(c) *Discrimination* – employees can seek redress where discrimination is proved under either the Sex Discrimination Act, 1975 or the Race Relations Act, 1976. While discrimination is often difficult to prove, the principles behind these laws are clear-cut. It is illegal to refuse jobs or promotions to people simply because they are born of a particular sex or race.

Employers appearing before Industrial Tribunals to justify their actions will be expected to have complied with the Codes of Practice drawn up by ACAS (Advisory, Conciliation and Arbitration Service) which deal with disciplinary practice and procedure.

Under the Health and Safety at Work Act, 1974 a system has been set up whereby a series of regulations and approved codes of practice can be developed to ensure that the highest standards of safety will be applied to work situations. It becomes possible to bring in criminal prosecution (an unlimited fine and/or a two-year prison sentence) where there is a breach of duty either towards employees or others who come into contact with the enterprise. But there is also an onus placed on employees to take reasonable care of themselves and others.

Notwithstanding the more recent legislation the principal legislation affecting offices remains at this stage The Offices, Shops and Railway Premises Act, 1963. Among its provisions are:

S. 5 'No room shall be overcrowded ...' essentially 40 square feet or 400 cubic feet per person.

S. 6 'A temperature of less than 16° Centigrade shall not be deemed, after the first hour, to be a reasonable temperature while work is going on.'

There shall be....

S. 7 'Adequate supplies of fresh or artificially purified air....'

S. 8 'Suitable lighting, whether natural or artificial ... glazed windows and skylights kept clean and free from obstruction.....'

S. 9 'Suitable and sufficient sanitary conveniences ... at places conveniently accessible ... clean and properly maintained....'

S. 10/13 'Accessible washing facilities ... running hot and cold water, soap and clean towels....'

S. 48 'Notice sent to the appropriate local authority where an accident causes loss of life or disables any person for more than three days from doing normal work....'

Case study – The Staff Welfare Programme

Mentmore (Warmair) Ltd is a company which has developed a new form of underfloor heating. It operates from five different factories scattered throughout the London area. The company has made substantial profits over the past three years, and is continually expanding the scope of its operations. In a gesture of appreciation to their staff the Board of Directors have donated a sum of £50 000 for general staff welfare, leaving it to the company's Staff Social Committee to determine how the funds are to be utilised. However, the Board added the rider that they hoped the funds would be used with 'the essential unity of the company in mind'.

The breakdown of the work-force shown in Table 6.1 will no doubt explain the reason for the Board's rider.

Table 6.1 Staff of all grades (by age)

	Male			Female			
	−21	21–40	+40	−21	21–40	+40	Totals
Chadwell Heath (East London)	617	504	315	212	208	215	2071
Stratford (East London)	36	46	121	272	185	157	817
New Barnet (North London)	212	185	42	186	112	65	802
Peckham (South London)	64	28	71	84	33	112	392
Camberwell (South London)	29	45	36	147	68	24	349
	958	808	585	901	606	573	
Totals		2351			2080		4431

The Staff Social Committee have been meeting over the past three months and have now drawn up a short-list of projects they favour. These are listed below, together with the estimated cost of each.

(1) *Provision of changing rooms and club house.* There is a small sports ground adjacent to the factory at Chadwell Heath. There is a

football pitch, a cricket pitch and two tennis hardcourts, but apart from an inadequate and dilapidated timber hut there are no changing facilities. This scheme includes provision for a brick-built club house with changing rooms and a small refreshment annexe. It also provides for the replacement of certain outworn equipment.

The company football club run three football teams and one cricket team, with support for them coming mainly from the Chadwell Heath works.

Total cost is estimated at £25 000.

(2) *Purchase of holiday chalets on the south coast.* This scheme involves the purchase of six cedar-clad timber chalets on a plot of freehold land extending to approximately $\frac{7}{8}$ acre. The site is close to the sea and also to the amenities of the nearby town. The committee plan would be to give sick and deserving members of the company a holiday or convalescent period 'according to their needs'.

It is suggested that whenever there were vacancies free holidays would be offered to the longest-serving members of the staff, with a maximum of two weeks for any person.

Total cost is estimated at £40 000 but this would be increased by a further £12 000 if an adjoining cottage were to be purchased for residential staff. If a caretaker and nurse (husband and wife) were provided on site the guests would be obliged to pay sufficient to meet this expense.

(3) *Provision of facilities for producing a company staff magazine.* An office would be required and the Directors have agreed in principle to a store-room at the Peckham factory being used without charge. The expenses would be incurred in purchasing printing equipment, wall partitioning and paper supplies. The objective is to print a weekly news-sheet and a quarterly magazine. Editing and printing would be done by existing staff on a voluntary basis. Staff at Peckham are reputed to have the necessary expertise.

Total cost of setting up the equipment is estimated at £15 000. It is suggested that the running costs thereafter would be covered by advertising revenue. A number of local firms have already indicated a willingness to buy space on a regular basis.

(4) *Purchase of a social club at Chadwell Heath.* Next door to the factory at Chadwell Heath there is a Labour Club which is now selling its premises. The plan is to take over and modernise the buildings. There would be useful kitchen facilities, three smallish committee rooms and a large hall capable of seating up to 400. A bar would be provided and the profits would be expected to provide for the bulk of the outgoings.

There are already a number of clubs and societies which are active in the company, and meeting-places would be available if this building were to be purchased. Groups which have indicated they would benefit from the availability of premises include the Shop Stewards Committee, the Aquarist Society, the Amateur Dramatic Society and some younger workers who would like to organise regular discothéques.

Total cost is estimated at £52 000. A further £50 000 would be required for modernisation.

(5) *Purchase of radio-transmitting equipment.* While there are some legal technicalities to comply with before this scheme could come to fruition, it has got a lot of support from the younger female elements in the various factories. The objective is to provide a disc-jockey programme allowing for record requests and messages to be received in the five factories simultaneously. The studio would be situated in the store-room previously mentioned in (3) above. The room would not be large enough to accommodate both projects. If one scheme is adopted the other is excluded for lack of available space.

The system envisaged is second-hand but reputedly in good order, and 2000 records of varying vintage are included in the purchase price, but it has been suggested that the staff would provide their own records when requesting items for the programme. Management have agreed to a maximum one-hour session each morning and a maximum 1½-hour session each afternoon, but these would not be relayed to the offices or the administration block at Headquarters, where there is a total staff of 156.

Total cost is estimated at £28 000.

Your task

Play the role of the Staff Social Committee and, on the evidence available here, select the projects you consider worthy of support.

CHAPTER 7

Recruitment and Selection

An organisation will need to recruit staff from time to time for any or all of the following reasons:

(i) to replace staff who are leaving,
(ii) to bring in vital skills which are otherwise lacking, and
(iii) to apply additional human resources to operations where it is intended to expand the business.

The recruitment and selection procedures will vary according to the type of staff in question, but a typical employment procedure is shown in Figure 7.1.

Recruitment

The post becomes available. There is a consideration of the work which has to be done and the type of person who would be able to do the job effectively. A *job description* is drawn up indicating (a) the job title, (b) the location, (c) the detailed duties associated with the job, (d) the equipment to be used, (e) supervision given or received, and (f) any special features of the work. A *job specification* can then be drawn up setting out the qualities to be looked for in candidates for the post. These would include references to characteristics such as (a) education and experience required, (b) initiative and judgement called for, (c) physical effort needed for the tasks, (d) resposibilities involved, and (e) any special qualities required. Some personnel departments combine the job description and personal profile, but essentially there is a formal job analysis. After this it will be possible to design a suitable advertisement inviting candidates to apply for the post.

Of course an advertisement will be unnecessary if it is decided to offer the post to someone within the organisation. Where the post

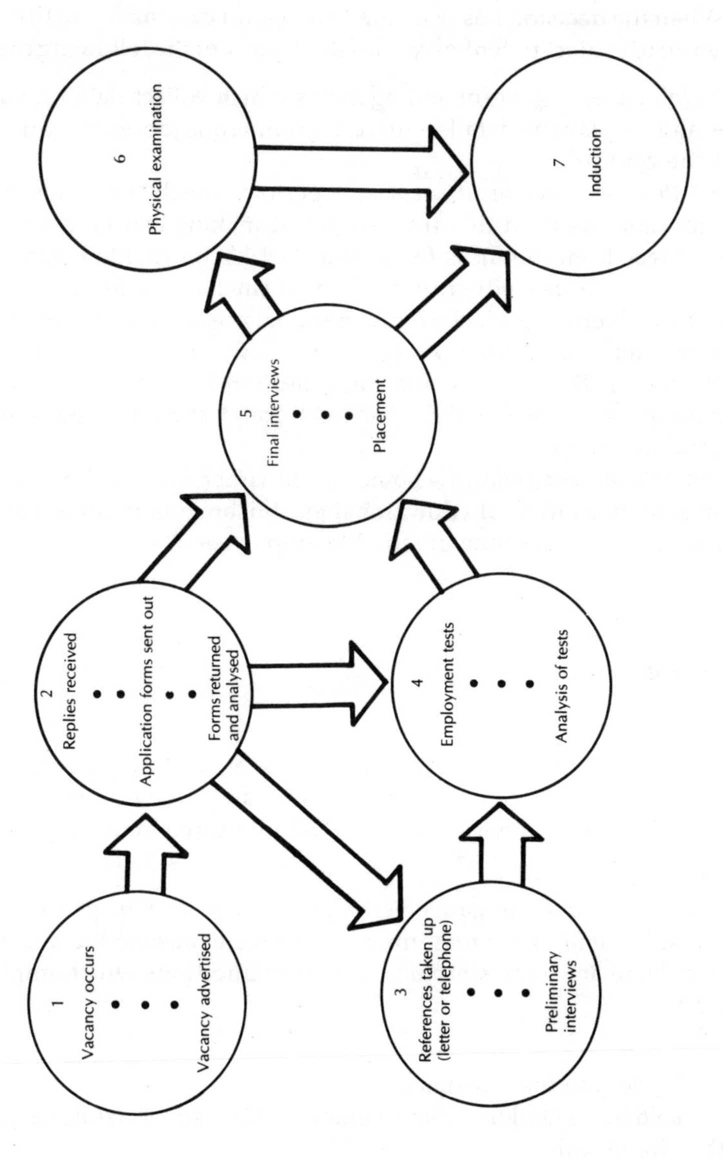
1
Vacancy occurs
Vacancy advertised
2
Replies received
Application forms sent out
Forms returned and analysed
3
References taken up (letter or telephone)
Preliminary interviews
4
Employment tests
Analysis of tests
5
Final interviews
Placement
6
Physical examination
7
Induction

Figure 7.1

can be offered as a promotion to an existing member of staff this would serve as an encouragement to staff generally. However, if the best person available is to be employed it will be necessary to advertise the post.

When the decision has been made to recruit externally the firm may attempt to contact potential candidates by any of the following means:

(i) *Jobcentres* – government agencies which collect data on vacancies and display the details – there are numerous jobcentres throughout the country.

(ii) *Private employment agencies* – perform much the same role as the jobcentres except that they are profit-making concerns normally taking fees from the firms for whom they have provided staff.

(iii) *Newspapers* – either in the form of small ads in local newspapers or in advertising blocks in the national press. Advertisements for senior staff will normally appear in newspapers like the *Daily Telegraph* or *The Times*, while unskilled/semi-skilled labour, being generally less mobile, will be reached through the classified columns of local newspapers.

(iv) *Schools and colleges* – some of the larger firms will send their representatives to local educational establishments in an attempt to ensure an adequate flow of suitable employees.

Testing

When candidates have applied for a post some vetting procedure will be necessary to determine which, if any, are to be offered employment. The testing devices available fall into three main categories:

(i) *Intelligence tests*
These are designed to gauge verbal, numerical or perceptual ability. Invariably some sort of reasoning is required to answer the questions posed. Here are some simple examples of questions which might be included:

(a) Verbal
Underline the odd-man-out.
soldier   sailor   sportsman   stranger   storekeeper

(b) Numerical
Insert the missing number.
2   4   .   16   32

(c) Perceptual
Complete picture no. 4 in Figure 7.2.

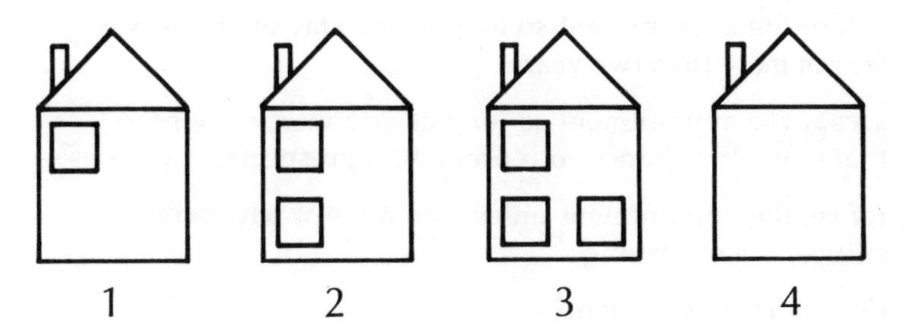

Figure 7.2

(ii) *Aptitude tests*

While qualifications will give some indication of talents and abilities, a would-be employer will often wish to assess the candidate's actual or potential skill in relation to a particular task. Thus, where the nature of the work is such that manual dexterity is called for, an appropriate practical test might be devised whereby differently shaped pegs have to be fitted into matched holes in a pegboard. By contrast a candidate for the post of a copy typist in a solicitor's office might be asked to reproduce a corrected draft from the sort of material shown in the brief extract here.

> This is the last will and testament of me Gladys Garfield of Manor House Manor Drive Crutchley Winstanton in Yorkshire I revoke all former wills and appoint my brothers Robert Louis Stewart and David Stewart to be the executors of this my will I bequeath the following (1) to my cousin Sylvia three thousand pounds (2) John White six hundred pounds and (3) Alison Jamieson £50.

Where word processors are to be used rather than typewriters it would be simple enough to adapt the test to such equipment.

(iii) *Personality tests*

These are less common than intelligence and aptitude tests partly because of the difficulty of measuring personality traits in artificial situations. They are likely to take the form of questionnaires in which the applicants are asked to give their responses from a given range of options. For example:

> If you were asked to take up an appointment overseas in the company's service would you
>
> accept the appointment without hesitation? ☐

accept the appointment so long as the stay overseas was for not more than two years? ☐

accept the appointment so long as you were convinced that it would enhance your promotion prospects? ☐

refuse the appointment unless the rates of pay were sufficiently rewarding? ☐

refuse the appointment? ☐

(Tick the box following the response which comes closest to the answer you wish to give.)

Interviews

Although some employers do not use tests as part of the selection process, they almost invariably interview applicants before offering them employment. One of the principal aims of the selection interview is to see how the candidate compares with the profile set out in the job specification. The ideal candidate will match the profile precisely. In a typical situation the interviewer will be considering:

(i) The physical appearance of the candidate. The dress and visual impact will be of special significance where the employee will represent the firm to members of the public and/or clients.
(ii) The confidence and general demeanour of the applicant. While brashness is generally unwelcome, a positive and pleasant personality is likely to be an asset in any business.
(iii) The ability of the prospective employee to communicate effectively.

The interview is a useful device for testing social and verbal skills.

On the one hand the interviewer will be able to clear up any lingering doubts about the candidate's suitability for the post, and on the other hand the interviewee will be able to seek further information about the nature of the job and/or the firm. Before the final selection takes place, candidates are sometimes introduced to their future managers or supervisors. The assumption is that the manager would have the right to veto the appointment.

The *planned* interview aims at getting the candidate to talk about certain topics upon which the interviewer wants further information. This may relate, for example, to the candidate's previous work experience, domestic situation or attitude to work. The *patterned* interview, by contrast, uses the same series of questions for all candidates. This ensures some sort of consistency in the selection process and gives equal opportunities to all the applicants. The *stress* interview is used to test a candidate's ability to control emotions in a stressful situation.

Legal aspects

When someone is employed the firm must supply them with a written statement setting out the main terms and conditions of employment. To accord with the Employment Protection (Consolidation) Act, 1978, this statement must be provided within thirteen weeks from the starting date.

It is illegal to discriminate against anyone in respect of employment on grounds of sex or race (Sex Discrimination Act, 1975, and the Race Relations Act, 1976).

Case study – The Short List

It is called the Ellerton Boyle School of English. It is situated in a well-known seaside resort on the south coast, and it caters for students from all over the world who wish to improve their English. The students are found accommodation in the locality and attend school throughout the year. The school is looking for a new member of staff and the following advertisement was placed in the local newspaper:

> THE ELLERTON BOYLE SCHOOL OF ENGLISH
> We require a highly qualified secretary, aged 19–28 years, for a responsible post as Secretary to the Executive Director. Our requirement is for someone who has excellent shorthand and is a fast, accurate typist. The applicant will be expected to work on own initiative and give a great deal of time and energy to the tasks assigned. Excellent pay and working conditions are offered. Please write to The Administrative Officer, The Ellerton Boyle School of English.

There were over forty applicants for the post, and the seven most likely candidates have been interviewed by the the Administrative Officer and the Deputy for the Executive Director. The Executive Director is presently in Rio de Janeiro organising a course for Business English which it is hoped to run next summer. He has agreed to allow his colleagues to select a short-list of four candidates. They are then to send out the brief biographical details to Brazil and he will make the final selection. The details he receives are as follows:

Candy Wenzel – age 24 – currently secretary to Claims Manager in local insurance office. 5 'O' levels including French and English Literature. Rather quiet and reserved, but well-spoken and neat in appearance. Recently married a local teacher in a primary school. Previous business experience – two years as shorthand typist in a stockbroker's office, and eighteen months in the offices of a local authority. Reason given for leaving present employment – 'I have been working in the insurance office for nearly four years now, and I just feel like a change'.

Shorthand and typing speeds have been tested by the Administrative Officer and he finds them 'more than adequate' for the post in question.

Hobbies are horse-riding and tennis.

Jane Cavanagh – age 20 – currently personal secretary to the Chairman of a hotel and entertainments group of companies. She has been in three jobs since she left the local college of commerce two and a half years ago: 'I just haven't found the right job yet', she says. Passed 7 'O' levels at school and has since added an 'A' level in Spanish to her English and Spanish passes at 'O' level. Shorthand and typing speeds are 'just about adequate for the post'.

She turned up for the interview wearing a rather colourful trouser suit which put off the interviewers originally, but she has a pleasing appearance and a likeable personality.

Has no particular hobbies.

Katrina Velasquez – age 21 – has recently completed a year's course in Advanced English at the Ellerton Boyle School of English in a neighbouring resort. Plans to stay in England for another two years to perfect her English. Father is Spanish and mother is German. Katrina speaks both languages fluently. Apart from working in her father's business in Madrid for six months, she has no previous business experience.

Her shorthand and typing are 'outstandingly good', but she admits she prefers talking to people rather than doing office work.

The Administrative Officer feels that she is only taking the job because her boy friend is attending the school.

Sylvia Daley – age 30 – the American-born wife of a Director of a large printing and publishing firm in the area. Has two small children aged 5 and 8. Has not worked for nine years, but has maintained her shorthand and typing skills while helping her husband from time to time. Her secretarial skills are considered 'adequate for the post in question', and both interviewers agree that this candidate has a very pleasant and confident personality. She does not speak any foreign languages but has an H.N.D. in Business Studies in addition to her secretarial qualifications.

Features of the job not disclosed in the advertisement

The secretary will take instructions from the Executive Director, deal with telephone calls during his absence, control his engagement diary and organise a filing system for his voluminous correspondence (at the moment the letters are simply filed according to the date of their receipt). During the Executive Director's frequent trips abroad she will be expected to deal with his mail and sign routine letters on his behalf.

Your task as a group

On the evidence available reach a consensus as to which of the four candidates would be best suited to the post in question.

Do you see any problems which the successful candidate might have to face when she takes up her appointment?

Note

Under the Sex Discrimination Act, 1975, the advertisement had to be worded so that either males or females could apply for the post.

CHAPTER 8

Remuneration

Some jobs require skills which can be acquired very quickly. For example, it would take no more than a few minutes to learn to use some of the machinery on mass-production lines. Such jobs are suitable for unskilled workers. Other jobs call for substantial skill and relatively few people possess the necessary talents or experience. So we can expect to find some jobs paying more than others. The pilot of a jumbo jet could be expected to earn more than the aircraft's steward and the supervisor in a typing pool could be expected to take home a bigger pay packet than the telephonist.

Within any organisation it is necessary to develop a fair pay structure so that monetary rewards produce the desired effect on the work-force. There are two dimensions to the problem. First, the pay offered to the various employees has to be sufficient to stop them leaving the firm to work elsewhere. Then, it is necessary to ensure that each member of staff receives a level of pay which is fair in comparison with the pay received by the firm's other employees.

Job evaluation

One way of attempting to establish a fair pay structure within an organisation is to introduce a job-evaluation scheme. Each job is analysed on the basis of the job description and placed, in terms of pay, in a proper relationship to other jobs in the organisation. The evaluation may take the form of (a) ranking or (b) point rating.

(a) *Ranking*

Jobs are ranked in order of difficulty and complexity. So, in a banking branch we might find jobs ranked in the following order:

1. Branch Manager
2. Manager's Assistant
3. Securities Officer
4. Cashier
5. Manager's Secretary
6. Clerk

The pay structure will reflect this rank order. However, there is no attempt to calculate fair differentials as between the jobs. Should the Manager's secretary earn much more than one of the clerks? How much more? What should be the difference in pay between a securities officer and a cashier?

(b) *The points system*

Each job is analysed in relation to a number of factors. These might be classified under the following headings for a range of jobs in an industrial undertaking:

1. *Skill*
   Experience needed
   Education required
   Manual dexterity
   Special training
2. *Responsibility*
   For equipment
   For material
   For people
   For costs/revenue/profits
3. *Effort*
   Lifting of weights
   Working in awkward positions
   Pushing/pulling
   Concentration required
4. *Conditions*
   Excessive heat/cold
   Dirty work
   Dangerous work
   Unsocial hours

A committee might be used to evaluate the various jobs and the job of storekeeper might be assessed along the following lines:

		Points rating	*Maximum points*
Skill	experience	4	10
	education required	6	10
Responsibility	for material	13	15
Effort	concentration	10	15
	working in awkward positions	3	10
		36	

The storekeeper's job having been allocated 36 points can now be compared to those of a frame fitter and an arc welder which scored 34 points and 58 points respectively. Assuming that each point is counted as worth 2.5p per hour the result in terms of hourly wage rates for these three jobs would be:

	Points	*Hourly wage rate (in addition to basic rate)*
Storekeeper	36	90p
Frame fitter	34	85p
Arc welder	58	£1.45

Job evaluation at a national level

There would be obvious merits in introducing a national rational pay structure on the basis of job evaluation. In this way the job of a coal-miner would be equated with that of a teacher, the job of a bus driver equated with that of a teacher, the job of a bus driver equated with that of a shop assistant, and so on. The problem of devising a national scheme would be enormous, but such a scheme has been operating in Sweden for many years and has helped to bring industrial harmony to that country. And national pay structures are standard practice in the communist world, of course. Indeed, in Red China there is a continuing discussion on whether to retain the existing five levels of pay or to introduce one level of pay for all workers.

In Britain both employers and trade unions seem to favour free collective bargaining although this brings with it an endless succession of industrial disputes over pay claims.

Payment by results

This may entail payment by unit of output as opposed to payment by the hour regardless of the amount of work done. However, a fair time allowance is now commonly calculated by time-study engineers who work out how long each piece of work should take. Allowance is made for rest pauses, fatigue and interruptions. The essence of such a system is that where the task is performed in less than the standard time the worker will still be credited as if he had worked the standard time. Take the case of James, a garage mechanic. During the course of one hour at work he performs three tasks with standard minute values of 20, 45 and 15 minutes respectively. Instead of being paid for one hour he will be credited with 80 minutes' work at the appropriate rate of pay.

Merit increases *v.* flat rates

Many firms link pay increases to performance appraisals. Workers who attend regularly, produce outstanding work and are generally co-operative receive additional increments of pay. Sometimes progress to higher levels on a salary scale is provisional on satisfactory performance. Trade unions frown on a situation where some workers are treated differently from others and they generally aim at achieving a rate for the job (so-called flat-rate payments).

Job classification/grading

This is the system used in many large offices. A number of different grades are established and the various jobs are allocated to one or other of these grades. The Institute of Administrative Management suggest a basic eight-grade classification. Grade A is reserved for tasks which require no previous experience and are either very simple or closely directed. While the top-category grade H is reserved for tasks which call for professional knowledge (university degree or final professional qualification) extensive exercise of initiative and judgement, or the supervision of twenty or more clerical staff.

The merits of job grading are that it simplifies staffing problems and provides employees with a promotion ladder.

Salary scales

These are designed to reward loyalty and an employee's salary is increased annually over a certain span of time. The additional amounts are described as increments. In the example below during a seven-year period the salary increases from £5000 to £7400 in steps varying from £200 to £600. Additional increments to a maximum of £1000 can be given for outstanding merit (see Figure 8.1).

Note that the larger increments in the normal scale are given in the early years. Such a scale might be described as front-loaded. What would be the purpose of this feature? And why are the merit increments so devised?

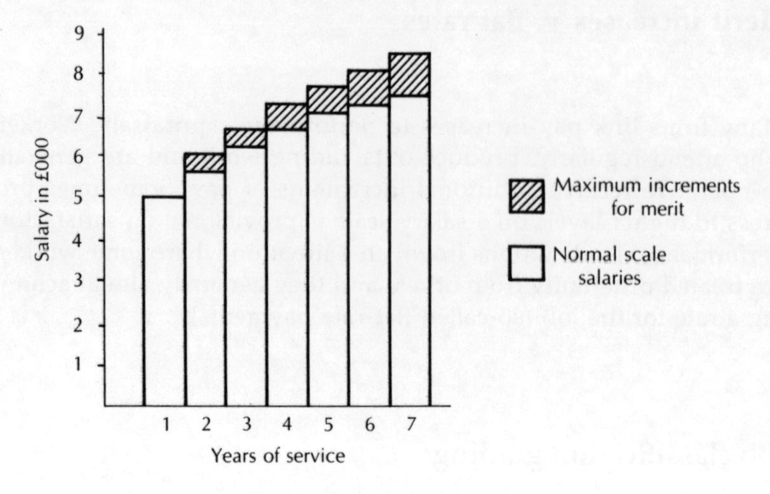

Figure 8.1

Fringe benefits

Organisations in the private sector particularly offer their employees a wide variety of 'perks' (perquisites) often as a device to overcome the effects of government restraints on pay increases and heavy taxation on earnings. Among those on offer might be:

(i) Company cars – a substantial proportion of all cars sold in Britain are purchased by organisations for the use of their employees.

(ii) Low rates of interest on mortgages for the purchase of houses.

(iii) Sports and social facilities (see case study on page 41).

(iv) Luncheon vouchers, subsidised travel and discount on purchases.

(v) Assistance with school fees – particularly valuable when the job necessitates travel abroad and children are sent to boarding school.

(vi) Profit-sharing schemes – whereby employees are allowed to share in the success of the business.

(vii) Co-ownership schemes – whereby employees are given the right to acquire the shares of a company on favourable terms.

Case study – The Upgrading

Three years ago Philip Smallwood was given a first managerial appointment. He was made manager of a small country branch near York, and the bank for whom he works was obviously pleased with his performance because he has now been appointed manager of the York branch. He has been in his new post three weeks and is now facing his first awkward staff problem. There are four young cashiers in his branch, all of whom are on the same grade for salary. The previous manager has been satisfied enough with their work to recommend them all for an upgrading. However, the District Manager has not approved this course of action. He has returned the recommendations – to Philip Smallwood of course – indicating that 'in order to be fair to the staff in other branches in the district, it is only possible to accept two upgradings from the branch at this time'.

Philip's personal knowledge of his cashiers is very limited at the moment, and he has to rely very heavily on other people's judgements to cope with this problem. He appreciates only too well that whoever he chooses for promotion he is going to be left with two rather disconsolate young cashiers to contend with.

All Philip has to go on is a set of notes left by his predecessor. They give essential details plus the comments made to the District Manager when the recommendations were submitted.

Daniel Pope (19 years of age) has been cashier for the past year. He joined the bank three years ago. The previous manager's comment: 'Rather quiet and reserved with customers. A little slower than average, and there are sometimes small errors in his till. He studies hard for his professional examinations and has done extremely well to date.'

Annette Burden (21 years of age) married recently, joined the bank 3½ years ago, and has been cashier for three years. The previous manager's comment: 'Although she has no intention of taking the professional examinations, she is very popular with the customers. She has a pleasing appearance, dresses very smartly, speaks well, and has not made a mistake of any consequence since she first went on the till.'

Stella Cavanagh (24 years of age) is unmarried, a graduate in languages at Leeds University, and has been in the bank for one year – the last nine months on the till. There is a special note from Staff Department explaining the gap which exists between the time she completed her university course and the time she joined the bank. Apparently her mother became seriously ill just before she finished at university and Stella had to stay at home to nurse her. Her mother has since died. The previous manager's comment: 'A very satisfactory first year. I feel she finds her cashier's job a bit beneath her dignity, but she performs her duties well. She is intending to study for her professional examinations within the coming year.'

Martin McAlpine (24 years of age) joined the bank 4½ years ago, and has been cashier for the past two years. This is Martin's second branch. He was transferred here six months ago from Peterborough. The previous manager's comment: 'He has recently started studying for his professional examinations again. He had given up at one stage because of some disappointing results. Has a pleasant personality, but has made one error of £90 – a short – in his till.'

Philip consulted with his Assistant Manager, Douglas Critchel, who contributed orally:

> They're all quite good. We're lucky to have such a good team of junior cashiers. I've had to reprimand Annette for being late a few times. And Stella was off sick for a couple of weeks in the summer, which was a bit awkward. Oh! and there was that cheque that McAlpine paid which should have been referred. The account's in credit now, but it was a near thing. We threatened to charge it to McAlpine's own account if we lost the money. That was a laugh really because McAlpine's account has a nil balance for half the month. Oh! and his wife is having another baby – quite soon now I think.

Questions

(1) What does the group think about this situation? Which members of staff should the manager recommend for promotion?
(2) What would be the effect on the staff who felt they had been overlooked?
(3) Do you think banks need to be especially careful in the selection of their staff? Why?
(4) Can you think of other organisations which would need to bring in factors other than skills and qualifications when selecting staff?

CHAPTER 9

Labour Turnover

When people leave the firm that has been employing them the loss can be described as 'labour turnover'. Some might imagine that this loss of staff represents a minor problem, but they would be wrong. One does not just bring in new workers to replace those who have left. It is because the problem is a serious and expensive one for the employer that an attempt is made to monitor the rate of turnover. A simple formula for calculating the rate is:

$$\frac{\text{number of workers leaving in a given period of time}}{\text{average number of workers employed during the period}} \times 100$$

Example for the group to consider

Apex Engineering had 3903 workers on its pay-roll on 31 March. By 30 September the number of workers had increased to 4097. During the calendar year 803 workers left the organisation. Was this an improvement on the previous year, when the following figures pertained?

31 March 3734 30 September 3866
(exits by staff during the year = 785)

Work out the figures individually but compare your answers. If this represents a deterioration, how could it be accounted for? Together draw up a comprehensive list of possible explanations. Which of these exits could be indications of poor management, and which are beyond the control of the firm?

The cost of labour turnover

(1) *The period of initial/internal training*
Staff have to be allocated to train new workers. Safety procedures and normal routines have to be explained. Meanwhile the staff allocated find their own work disrupted, if not halted completely. And it is usually the better and more experienced staff who are used for training purposes.

Mistakes are bound to be made in the early stages. Materials are wasted. Machines are sometimes damaged.

There is also the likelihood of social friction during the time when new staff are settling in. The learning process involves a barrage of questions and verbal explanations which can become tedious for both parties. The new staff have to learn as quickly as possible the sort of behaviour which is expected from them. The existing staff will weigh up newcomers to determine whether they represent any sort of threat. Any frictions that arise are almost certainly going to be counterproductive.

(2) *Advertising for new staff*
Block advertisements in newspapers and magazines can be very expensive, though it is as cheap to advertise for sixty new staff as for one.

In a seller's market it may be necessary to offer a higher level of pay to attract new recruits, but the higher pay will have to be passed on to existing workers too. The firm is likely to be in competition with other firms for scarce labour – especially skilled labour.

(3) *Administrative costs*
Interviews will take a minimum of twenty minutes. In a typical case four candidates may be interviewed for every one employed. Staff leaving are also interviewed in many firms. Interviewing rooms take up valuable space. Personnel Officers have to be paid, and Line Managers have to spend time consulting and conferring. If selection tests are used on candidates, the tests have to be compiled, marked and collated.

There is bound to be correspondence. Hundreds of applications for a job may be submitted. They all have to be vetted. Candidates invited for interviews may have to be compensated for travelling expenses, perhaps for hotel expenses too. When someone is offered employment, tax, pay and personnel records will have to be set up.

(4) *Unsettling effect on rest of staff*
When someone leaves the organisation he or she invariably gives

glowing accounts of the new job. It is better paid. There are all sorts of extras or perks. There is more freedom. Other staff listen and become restless themselves. They begin to look around for another employer too. Loss of interest is contagious.

Figure 9.1 shows the productivity of an individual during a typical career with a firm.

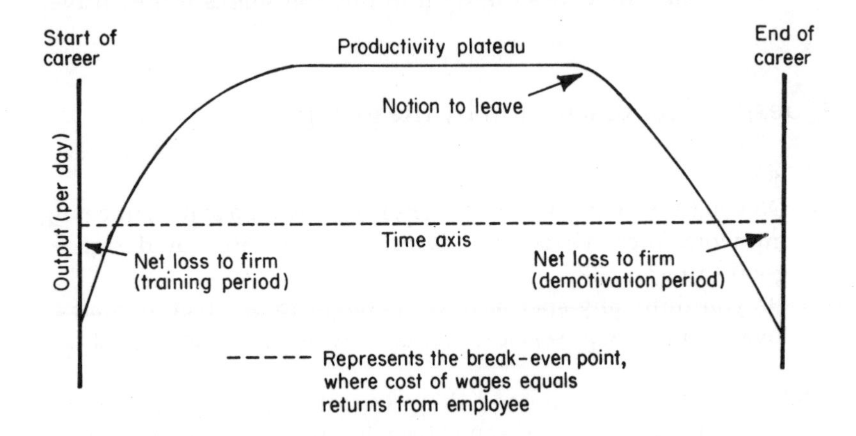

Figure 9.1

Ways of reducing labour turnover

Many people will leave an organisation because they are bored with the work. Others will leave because they fail to get on well with their work-mates or managers. So among the remedies will be those which attempt to deal with these problems:

(i) *Careful recruitment and selection* will ensure that the people who are employed are suited to the work they are given. If work is very boring it may be more appropriate for part-time workers or those with low aspirations.

(ii) *Job rotation* is a technique by means of which workers change jobs with each other from time to time. It may help to relieve boredom and can also be part of a training process. Managers will find it is useful when staff can be switched to other jobs in order to cover sickness and holidays.

(iii) *Job enrichment* involves the redesigning of jobs to make them more interesting – or less boring. A simple example would be where a filing clerk is also asked to deal with incoming telephone calls. People are likely to respond positively to increased responsibility.

(iv) *A share option scheme* gives employees the right to buy a certain number of shares in the future at the present price. This is a valuable option if the price of the company's shares goes up in the meantime. Key staff will be encouraged to stay because they lose the right to buy the shares if they leave.

Questions for discussion by the group

(1) Do you think a firm would benefit from having a stable, unchanging work-force? Or is a steady turnover of staff – by design – a good thing?
(2) Do you think any special rewards ought to be given to staff for loyalty and long service? What sort of rewards would you advocate?
(3) Do you think it is a good thing from the individual's point of view to stay with the same firm for the whole of his or her working life? Or is it better to gain a wide experience with a variety of firms?

Case study – Rewards for Loyalty

Carl Berger, Chief Executive of Apex Engineering, wants to reduce labour turnover, and realises that one way to do this would be to show his appreciation to workers who stay with the company. He has had discussions with his Personnel Manager, and together they have drawn up six different schemes which are now being put to the workers' representatives on the firm's Works Council for discussion. The schemes are as follows:

(1) *Luncheon vouchers*
These would be for use in the company canteen which is run on a 'cost-covered' basis. Blue vouchers would be issued to those workers with five to ten years' service, and these would entitle the holders to a 30 per cent reduction on all canteen prices. Red tickets would be

given to anyone who had worked for more than ten years with the company, and would entitle the holder to a 50 per cent reduction.

(2) *Holiday scheme*
At the end of every third year of continuous service, every member of staff who has not reached executive status becomes entitled to a free two-week holiday for two at a well-known holiday camp. This is in addition to the normal holiday entitlements.

(3) *Long-service bonus*
For anyone who has not reached executive status, their weekly pay packet will be increased by the following sums – related to their length of service. The bonuses will only be paid when there are no absences for any reason during the week in question.

£1 extra per week after three years' service.
£2 extra per week after six years' service.
£3 extra per week after ten years' service.

(4) *Staff shares*
For every five years' service members of staff would be allocated 100 Ordinary shares of £1 each in the company – they would be charged a nominal sum of 5p per share to meet the legal requirements, but the shares are presently standing at £2.50 and pay an annual dividend of 20 per cent.

(5) *Staff sickness scheme*
This proposal offers the staff two kinds of benefit:
(i) Up to a total of £1000 to meet hospital fees for all employees and any of their immediate family requiring hospitalisation.
(ii) A sliding scale for sick pay – based on length of service:

Up to two years' service	nothing
After two years' service	full pay for one month
	half pay for two months
After 5 years' service	full pay for three months
	half pay for six months

(6) *Badges*
Shop-floor workers might display sew-on badges in the form of the company crest after they have been with the company for more than two years. The crests would be sewn over the breast pocket of overalls – each department having a different colour badge.

The group's task

Carl Berger now asks you, playing the role of the workers' representatives, to select one of the schemes from the first five offered. If there is no consensus, take a vote on the proposals. The sixth proposal is an independent one, and he simply wishes to know whether you think this is a good idea or not.

When you are studying these proposals you might consider whether there are any alternative proposals you would like to suggest to the Chief Executive.

CHAPTER 10

Morale

The morale of the work-force is reflected in their mental attitude towards work and by their enthusiasm for the roles they have been given to play. While morale, as a term, is usually associated with troops and armies, it is appropriate to refer to the morale of the work-force since the members of it are in a competitive situation: some organisations will prosper, others will perish. Morale is often the crucial factor which determines the organisation's fate.

If morale is so important, what can be done to improve it and make the work-force more effective? First, we must decide what damages morale in the organisation, and then we must be prepared to take corrective action. As a prerequisite, however, we must attempt to find a method of assessing the level of morale in an organisation. We cannot begin to discuss the effect of certain things on morale until we can find a method of evaluating morale.

A number of methods are available for assessment, but in most cases the evaluation will not be quantifiable. Consider the following channels for providing a feedback on the levels of morale within the organisation.

Line managers

The person best suited to gauge the morale of an individual in the organisation is the individual's line manager or immediate supervisor. The line manager's contact with subordinates is normally continuous, and it should be possible to find out a great deal about their changing moods and attitudes. This will be especially true when line managers listen to their subordinates as well as give them instructions.

Personnel department

Personnel Officers, in their roles as counsellors, should gain some insight into the prevailing attitudes of the staff with whom they come into contact. Organisation members who are interviewed periodically by these officers will express their grievances to them. Employees may say things to the Personnel Officer which they would not dare say to their own managers. Conversely, the weakness of these contacts is that they are spasmodic and often superficial.

Joint consultation

Workers' attitudes should also emerge during the course of meetings with management representatives. Such meetings include works councils, meetings of joint committees, and the regular confrontations with trade-union officials and shop stewards. It remains necessary for management representatives to distinguish between trivia and significant grievances which indicate a decline in the level of morale.

Labour turnover

If the number of people leaving an organisation is rising, the most likely explanation is a fall in morale. Of course there are other possible explanations. It could be, for example, that the age structure of the work-force is such that there are a large number of retirements at a particular time. The problem with using the rate of turnover as an indicator of morale is that exits may take place long after the damage has been done. It may be some months after a worker has decided to leave before he can find another post.

Absenteeism and productivity

The rate of absenteeism and the level of output are further likely barometers of morale. As regards absenteeism, it will need to be borne in mind that true reasons for absence are often going to be disguised by employees; and on the other side of the coin, an influenza epidemic will take its toll regardless (or almost regardless) of the level of morale in the organisation.

Like labour turnover and absenteeism, productivity is measurable. There is a time lag, however, and pressure-orientated management can achieve an increase in productivity at the same time as morale is crumbling. By the time performances are beginning to show a decline, management may have a thoroughly demoralised work-force on their hands.

I.Q. tests

A deterioration in the quality of the work-force might be detected by sampling the I.Q.s of the organisation members. If the average I.Q. is falling, the implication is that the organisation is suffering a loss through having a less intelligent work-force at its disposal. This test is likely to be more relevant to managerial levels, where the work is challenging, than to rank-and-filers whose work requires limited skills anyway.

Job-attitude surveys

A modern method of measuring attitudes which is gaining favour is the census of opinions or job-attitude survey. It is based on the same principle as the Public Opinion Poll. A questionnaire is devised, either for a sample of members (random or stratified), or for the whole of the organisation. The questionnaire will require a respondent to place a tick in the box by the side of the answer which for him or her is considered the most appropriate response. A few examples follow to give the general drift of the questionnaire:

(1) How well do you get on with your work-mates?

A	Very well	☐
B	Quite well	☐
C	Satisfactorily	☐
D	Not very well	☐
E	Very badly	☐

(2) How do you think the company treats its employees?

A	Very well	☐
B	Better than most	☐
C	About average	☐
D	Not very well	☐
E	Very badly	☐

(Note that the possible answers to each question are at equally graded intervals. The questions must be unambiguous, easily understood and easily answered.)

An index of morale

An *avant-garde* suggestion is to produce an index of morale which would operate on the following lines. Let us suppose that, on 28 June, we distributed a hundred questionnaires (containing perhaps twenty questions such as those above). They are completed and returned by 1 July. It is essential that the respondents are not inhibited in dealing with the questions, so they are not asked to put their names on the questionnaire. Arrangements are made for completed forms to be returned to the Personnel Department through the internal mail using pre-addressed envelopes specially provided.

The next stage is to score each response according to the marking scheme:

$A = 5 \quad B = 4 \quad C = 3 \quad D = 2 \quad E = 1$

Thus if a respondent ticked box *D* in response to the first question, indicating his lack of rapport with his fellow employees, a score of 2 will be recorded. A total score will be calculated for each respondent. The scores of the 100 respondents are added together and, let us say, the total is 4000. This now becomes the base for an index (i.e. 4000 becomes 100). At the end of a set period we do a similar exercise with another sample of 100 employees. If the total score for all respondents is then 3800, the new index number becomes:

$$\frac{3800}{4000} \times 100 = 95$$

Too much should not be read into changes in the index without reference to other indicators of morale.

The index of morale could be used to quantify morale, and give managerial performance another dimension: not only is management expected to achieve physical and financial targets, it is also required to pay attention to the level of morale in different departments.

Questions for group discussion

(1) What specific problems would you expect to find in an organisation suffering from low morale?
(2) What do you think causes low morale in an organisation?
(3) When you have diagnosed the causes, what remedies could be applied?
(4) Why do you think large organisations are more likely to suffer from low morale than smaller ones?
(5) Is a worker entitled to anything more than wages from his employer?

Group task

Working as a team, prepare a twenty-question job-attitude survey which could be used for an index of morale, if required. The survey should cover such points as pay, working environment and job satisfaction.

The company in which you are operating is Fennex (Switchgear) Ltd, a light-engineering firm producing components for the car industry. The Personnel Department have broadly categorised the work-force on the lines indicated in Table 10.1. The essential difference between technicians and machine operators is that the former are skilled or semi-skilled, while the latter are unskilled. As you will see, the work-force is spread over two medium-sized factories and a small one.

Other relevant details are:

(i) 50 per cent of the sales and clerical staff are female, as are 20 per cent of the machine operators – otherwise the work-force is wholly male;
(ii) 82 per cent of the work-force are members of the Transport and General Workers' Union;
(iii) The headquarters of the company is at Birmingham.

Table 10.1 Fennex (Switchgear) Ltd work-force

	Birmingham	Shrewsbury	Four Oaks
Executives	317	32	14
Sales and clerical staff	483	35	22
Foremen	242	84	18
Tecnicians	825	958	87
Machine operators	1637	980	12
Storekeepers	97	25	13
Total work-force	3601	2114	166

Questions

(1) How would you organise the survey? Be as specific as you can.
(2) On what basis would you distribute the questionnaire?
(3) What problems would you expect to find in organising the survey?
(4) How would you overcome these problems?
(5) What would be the value of the survey as you have designed it?

CHAPTER 11

Communication

Communication involves the transmission of ideas, feelings and attitudes. It represents an interchange of thoughts on a particular subject. Many people would imagine that it is easy to communicate, but that is patently not the case. Inadequate communication leads to many divorces, not a few strikes, and even to international conflicts on occasion. It is certainly a major problem in life generally, and in business particularly. The point is that business units tend to get larger and larger, in order to achieve economies of scale, and larger businesses have more communication problems than their smaller counterparts.

The problems involved in communicating even simple ideas might be highlighted if the group perform a simple experiment, going carefully through each of the stages indicated:

(i) The tutor extracts three pictures from magazines. The pictures should be as varied as possible, for example a scene with people, inanimate objects, perhaps a face (other than someone who is well known).

(ii) Place the first of the pictures on a desk in front of the group – but screened from them. No one other than the tutor should know anything about the picture at this stage.

(iii) Now one of the members of the group is to be invited to sit at the desk in front. Studying the picture which remains hidden from the rest of the group, this person can spend up to five minutes describing the picture in detail, after which he (or she) rejoins the group.

(iv) The tutor now temporarily removes the picture – keeping it hidden from the group.

(v) A second person from the group is now invited to sit at the front desk. This time the picture is placed so that the whole group can see it – *except* for the person sitting at the front desk.

(vi) The person in front has heard the first person's description of the picture. Now he (or she) can describe again to the group what has been previously heard. The group can determine whether the picture is being described accurately.

(vii) Repeat the exercise with the second and third pictures – using different 'victims'.

If any of the group are artistically inclined, they might try to draw the pictures as they are described – in outline at least. Their interpretations could then be compared with the originals.

Having completed the experiment you will no doubt appreciate the suggestion that failure to communicate effectively is a basic fault in human relations. Because feelings and attitudes are conveyed inaccurately and insensitively, pressures build up for marital breakdowns, industrial unrest, even war. In fact communication is a central problem in life – and always will be (see Figure 11.1).

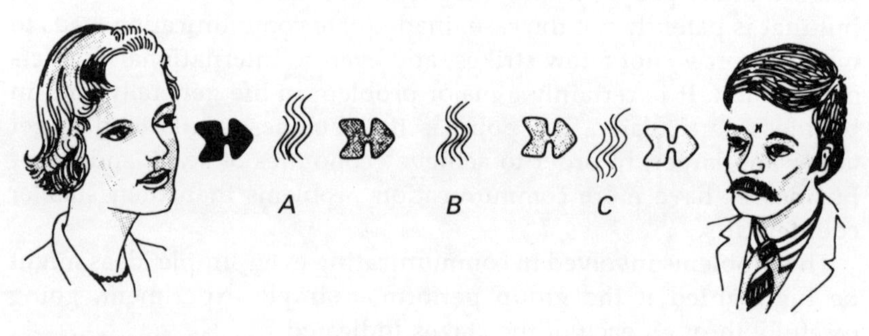

Distortion Barrier A	*Distortion Barrier B*	*Distortion Barrier C*
(1) Difficulty of choosing words	(1) Use of intermediaries	(1) Inability to comprehend
(2) Limitation of vocabulary	(2) Distractions, including noise	(2) Lack of interest
(3) Lack of effort	(3) Distance	(3) Emotional blockages

Figure 11.1

Some thoughts on communication

(1) It is one thing to have an idea and quite another to express it clearly and unambiguously. Many of our frustrations arise from our inability to convert our thoughts into appropriate words.

(2) You can talk eruditely to someone, but if that person's 'receiver' is switched off, the communication is ineffective.

(3) Some of the distortions are deliberate – if subconscious. Thus the sender will sometimes misinform the receiver rather than suffer a bruised ego.

(4) The grapevine is the informal method of communication by means of which rumours and misunderstandings occur when

there is a communications vacuum. Some newspapers thrive on sensationalism and distortion of the facts. The grapevine often has the same sort of appeal. Occasionally untruths are deliberately fed into the grapevine – by those who wish to take advantage of the situation.

(5) Feedback will improve the effectiveness of a communication. Subordinates will be able to clarify their manager's instructions by asking questions.

(6) If it is difficult for one person to communicate with another in a face-to-face situation, how much more difficult it must be for top management to communicate effectively with tens of thousands of shop-floor workers, or for a government to do the same with a population of many millions.

(7) While we have concentrated on oral communication, the problems of written communication are essentially similar. Written instructions are sometimes ambiguous – sometimes misinterpreted by the reader. And how often are items on a notice board ignored? Communication in organisational hierarchies needs to flow in three directions: downwards, upwards, and laterally.

(8) Communication in organisational hierarchies needs to flow in three directions: downwards, upwards, and laterally.

Case study – Pidgeon Savage Lewis

When John Forrester, the Personnel Manager of Crosby (Electronics) Ltd, walked into the executives' dining suite he knew he was going to have a rather gruelling session. The Managing Director, Mark Salmon, was in one of his bad moods and John soon found out why. It appeared that Mark had given 'clear instructions' about the way a new work-flow was to be organised in the Cross-Switching Department, but when he made a personal inspection he found a number of departures had been made from his instructions.

'It's almost bound to happen, you know', said John.

Mark stopped eating and waited to hear what was coming next.

'There was a study done by Pidgeon Savage Lewis – some American consultants – a few years ago', said John, as he glanced down the menu. 'They found that 30 per cent of communications were lost at every level of management. There are five levels of management in most organisations – as there are here. 30 per cent at each level – that means that there is only one-fifth of the communication left by the time it reaches the shop-floor.'

'Is that so?'

For a few moments the conversation halted while John told the waitress what he wanted to eat, and then Mark Salmon demonstrated why he had been made Managing Director.

'Sounds interesting, John,' he reflected, 'what ideas have you got for improving communications here? I'd be grateful if you could give me a report on it as soon as you can.'

John was sorry he had not had beer and sandwiches at *The Duke of Denmark*, as he usually did on a Friday.

Question for the group

What sort of ideas do you think might have gone into John Forrester's report?

Task for the group

When you have discussed the possibilities, draft a brief report which you think the Personnel Manager might send to the Managing Director.

CHAPTER 12

Committee Meetings

When a manager calls his subordinates together this is termed a 'command meeting'. Such a meeting is commonplace in business and the manager can use the occasion to:

(i) consult with his subordinates;
(ii) solve problems with their aid;
(iii) instruct them; or
(iv) simply give them information.

However, there are times when normal channels of communication are inappropriate, and that is when we can expect to find committees set up. But there is a basic difference between a command meeting and a committee in that the former is very much the agent of the manager calling the meeting, while the latter is a democratic device.

A committee is a specified group of people to whom the members of an organisation entrust certain tasks. The committee will comprise a chairman, a secretary and specified members. The Chairman will conduct the proceedings in accordance with an Agenda which is circulated before the meeting takes place. The Secretary will keep a record of the proceedings in the form of minutes. Under no circumstances can voting on any matter take place unless a quorum – or minimum number of members – is present. What constitutes a quorum will be laid down in the instructions setting up the committee.

A motion is the term applied to a proposal which has been put forward by one of the members for consideration at a meeting. It usually takes the form 'It is resolved that....' Every motion or proposal has to be proposed (or 'moved') formally and seconded by another member of the Committee who is prepared to support it. If no seconder is forthcoming, the motion fails.

The resolution is passed if a majority of the members present vote in favour of the proposal. The Secretary then records in the minutes that 'It was resolved that....' All the committee members, including the minority, share the responsibility for the decision. The only way a member can evade responsibility is by resigning.

It can be noted how the committee concept is part of our way of life. In politics we have the notion of collective Cabinet responsibility for decisions which are reached in much the same way as any committee makes decisions. In business we have the Board of Directors, who constitute a committee elected by the shareholders. And in our social lives we find committees appointed to run our tennis clubs, our professional associations, our social clubs and almost every other organisation with which we are likely to become involved. One can see the committee as an instrument of democracy because in every committee the principle of 'one person, one vote' applies.

The effectiveness of any meeting depends on the ability of the Chairman to control the proceedings without dominating them. Each member should be given the opportunity to make a contribution to the debate without allowing too much time to be wasted. The Chairman is expected to be impartial, even though strong views are held on the subject under discussion.

Many committees are conducted on a less formal basis, but the pattern of procedure outlined above is generally followed. There are obvious advantages in knowing how a meeting is going to be conducted and what is going to be dicůssed. Similar benefits attach to the recording of the main trends of the discussions – and the decisions reached. (The merits and demerits of committees are listed in Table 12.1)

In business you may come up against four different types of committee:

Executive committees

These are formed primarily to promote *action*, for example a factory production committee. It would have as its members representatives from the production side of business, but also members representing sales, research, design and costing. Such a committee would aim at co-ordinating the efforts of the different departments in the business.

Table 12.1 Merits and demerits of committees

Merits	Demerits
(1) Everyone is given an opportunity to contribute ideas	(1) Decisions may be weak as a result of compromise
(2) There is a deep-rooted democratic tradition that people have a right to say in things which affect them, and if a decision is reached by consensus it is more likely to be accepted	(2) A number of people will have to listen to things which do not interest them, and this can be very time-wasting, even frustrating
(3) Idea exchange is of benefit to everyone – progress *depends* on the exchange of ideas	(3) While each member has an equal say in the proceedings, he or she does not necessarily have an equal *stake* in the outcome (this is one of the fundamental problems in a 'one person, one vote' type of democracy)
(4) Other people's problems can only be understood when we know about them	(4) There may be a development of cliques – at the expense of objectivity
(5) Fewer mistakes are likely, since each suggestion is talked around and viewed from different angles by different people	(5) The proceedings may be dominated by a single individual or one small group

Advisory committees

The object here is to obtain expert consideration of problems and plans. The committee formulate recommendations as opposed to instructions. Whenever a non-executive committee such as this offers suggestions to the person or group it is set up to serve, the proposals may be accepted or rejected.

Liaison committees

A number of groups may be involved in a project without being linked in the normal chain of command. The liaison committee is formed to study areas of mutual concern. Its function is essentially to ensure co-ordination of activities.

Ad hoc committees

These are set up to cope with 'one-off' or non-recurring problems. For example, a committee might be formed to look into the causes of a recent outbreak of unofficial stoppages in a particular factory.

Questions for the group to consider

Have any of you been involved in committee meetings yet? If so, what are your feelings about them?

Role play – Complaints Committee

You represent the members of a Complaints Committee set up by the Chief Executive of the Joshua Smart Retail Stores Group. Your function is to advise the Chief Executive on how he should deal with customer complaints which fall outside the range of those normally dealt with by branch managers. The Group operate through a large number of supermarkets spread out over the whole of the south of England.

First, you are asked to elect formally a Chairman for the proceedings, and then to elect a Secretary who will keep a record of the proceedings for submission to the Chief Executive, Jonathan Smart, in due course.

The following complaints appear on the agenda paper and require your specific recommendations:

(1) A Mr McAlister bought an electric lawn-mower for £82.25 from the Reading branch. He did not use it for three months after purchase but when he did the motor broke down. It was under guarantee with the manufacturers so the machine was returned to them, and after a long delay it was sent back to him. As it was the autumn by then there was little need to use the mower. But in the spring the motor broke down again almost the first time it was used. Mr McAlister wrote to the manufacturers immediately and when he got no reply he took advice from a solicitor. Eventually he discovered that the manufacturers had gone into liquidation, and it seems unlikely he will ever get any redress for the faulty lawn-mower. He recognises

that Smarts do not have any legal obligation but feels we have a moral obligation to either replace the machine, or refund the purchase price.

(2) A Mrs Foy was apprehended by a store detective leaving our Norwich store. The police were called but there were no goods in her basket which had not been paid for, though there was a tin of tuna which had a price label of 26p covering the original label for 66p. Mrs Foy claimed she picked up the can innocently, unaware that someone had put another price label on it. In the circumstances no charges were made, though the store detective is convinced Mrs Foy did steal goods from the store. She feels there must have been an accomplice and does recall a young child being with Mrs Foy at one stage.

The manager of the Norwich store has now received a letter from Mrs Foy claiming that she has been so ill as a result of the incident she has had to have three days off work. She is claiming reimbursement for this loss, and will put the matter in the hands of a solicitor unless she gets a satisfactory reply from the store.

(3) A few days before Mr Crampthorne and his wife were due to go on holiday they purchased a jar of mussels from our Southend branch. After eating the mussels they both became ill with food poisoning. They have approached the manager of the store and explained how their holiday was spoiled through their illness, and he has reported the case to Head Office because he feels they have genuinely suffered. He had another complaint about mussels about the same time and disposed of half a dozen jars which had become tainted.

In view of the special role of this committee it is suggested your secretary prefixes your resolution with the words 'It is recommended that ...' when sending in the report to the Chief Executive.

CHAPTER 13

Trade Unions

What part do unions play in the business world? Perhaps they can be left to put their own case. In *Hands Up for Democracy*, a booklet published by the Trades Union Congress in May 1983, the role of the unions was explained in the following terms:

(i) The unions bargain with employers about pay, hours and working conditions; about the way that wages are paid; about allowances, extra payments; and about retirement and pension arrangements.
(ii) They work with employers to increase productivity, to sort out problems of work and to make industry more efficient.
(iii) They try to ensure that their members get the rights they are entitled to, including sick pay, maternity pay, and time off for union duties and training – and they negotiate for improvements beyond the legal minimums.
(iv) They protect workers against unfair disciplinary action or dismissal.
(v) Where lay offs or redundancies are threatened they negotiate with the employer to protect their members.
(vi) They give advice to their members at work, help with problems and represent them if they have difficulties with their employer.
(vii) They press employers to make sure safety standards are maintained.
(viii) Where accidents happen they negotiate, or even go to court, in order to obtain compensation for their members.
(ix) They fight against racial or sex discrimination against individuals or groups of workers.
(x) They fight for equal pay for women.
(xi) They try to ensure that part-time workers receive fair treatment.
(xii) They provide individual benefits, legal advice on problems at work, representation at tribunals, advice in times of difficulty.
(xiii) Workers acting together, through trade unions, can achieve much more for themselves and for their families than they ever could if they tried to go it alone against a powerful boss.
(xiv) Through their unions they can have a say in what is going on, an influence on the running of their workplace – their pay and conditions at work.
(xv) Through unions and the TUC, presssure can be brought on the Government on a whole range of subjects that matter to ordinary people.

Types of union

The earliest unions were the *craft unions* which were formed to limit the number of new entrants to the trade. Printers organised to control entry of apprentices by 'chapels' as early as the seventeenth century – *c.* 1683. Other early examples were the Gold Beaters (1777), Brushmakers (1778), and the London Bookbinders (1784).

Later, *general unions* developed which marshalled the ranks of the unskilled and the semi-skilled. They depended, not on the special skills of their members, but on their size. They developed an interest in politics to improve the lot of their members. Examples of general unions include the Transport and General Workers Union and the National Union of General and Municipal Workers.

In the United States and elsewhere there has been a tendency to develop *industrial unions* – one union for one industry. All workers in a single industry are organised regardless of the types of work or skills involved. Examples in Britain include the National Union of Mineworkers and the Iron and Steel Trades Confederation. There is a variation in Japan, where unions are *company-based* – there is one union for each company.

The appeal of the unions to workers

Within a few years of starting his job the typical worker reaches an effective wage ceiling. From then on there is only one way in which he can improve his pay – through the pressures exerted by his union.

Problems facing the unions

The unions are crisis-orientated, by which we mean the typical member only becomes interested enough to attend branch meetings when an emergency develops which is going to affect him personally. Meanwhile those with political axes to grind, i.e. those with extremist political views, might have moved into positions of influence in the union. They could control the communications system at the time of the crisis – using the situation for their own ends.

Another problem facing the unions is the distance from the shop-floor, where the grievances arise, to the union headquarters, where the full-time staff are sited. By the time the branch secretary has communicated with headquarters a small problem could have developed into a serious one. It is because of these shortcomings in the union's communications network that the shop steward has assumed so much importance in many firms.

The shop steward

The union officers are involved in the affairs of a national union, but the shop stewards operate in the particular factory where they are employed. The shop stewards often take a different line to the official union policy, and this in part explains the fact that there are so many unofficial or 'wildcat' strikes in British industry.

The shop steward is elected by a show of hands from his fellow trade unionists in his particular shop. His functions include recruiting members, collecting subscriptions, representing his fellow workers who have grievances and seeing that agreements entered into between management and unions are carried out.

Of course the situation varies from factory to factory and from union to union, but the problems outlined here are typical.

In some people's eyes there is continuous war being waged between management and workers (through their unions), and Table 13.1 provides a list of weapons both sides can use against the other.

Is it fair to describe the situation in military terms? What is the cardinal feature of war? That people get hurt? Do people get hurt in these situations? Innocent parties? How?

Note that the 'battle' is ritualised. Each side takes certain stances. Each side tries to call the other's bluff. Each side starts off in an extreme position and gradually eases towards an acceptable compromise.

Table 13.1

Workers	Management
(1) Withholding or threatened withholding of labour – strike action (official or unofficial)	(1) Mass dismissals or threat of same
	(2) Closure or threatened closure of plant
(2) Work to rule – or 'go slow'	(3) Automation

Questions for the group to consider

(1) Do you think unions cause strikes or avert them?
(2) Would there still be unrest in industry even without the unions?
(3) To what extent, if any, would you like to see the unions' powers curbed? Or extended?

Scenario – Motor-car Assembly Plant

The scene is set in the rather austere canteen of a motor-car assembly plant in the Midlands. Two young car workers are sitting at a table in the corner – talking animatedly. They are joined by an older man with grey hair and a lined face.

Steve: Hello Ted. This is Brian I was telling you about. He's just joined the company. He's been blowing his top because he's had to join the union. [He turns back to his companion.] This is Ted Mullard, our shop steward. You can tell *him* your troubles now.

Brian: Nothing personal Ted. I've nothing against the unions, but I don't like being told I've *got* to join one.

Ted: Well, you see Brian it's a closed shop. You can't get a job here unless you've got a union card.

Brian: I know that. And I've got my card. I thought this was a free country.

Ted: Listen Brian. In the bad old days there used to be some of us who paid our subscriptions – and quite a few people who rode on our backs. They were glad enough to accept the increases in pay our union got for them, but they kept their hands in their pockets when it was time to pay the union subscriptions.

Brian: What about the extremists though. They just use the rest of us as fodder.

Steve: That's what I was trying to tell you Brian. The trouble is none of the moderates are interested enough in the union to take office – present company excepted, Ted.

Ted: There's a lot of work involved if you do the job properly.

Brian: Well, I shan't be attending any meetings. You can lead a horse to water but you can't make it drink.

Ted: That's the trouble, Brian. The more people who think like that the easier it is for the militants to take over. The only time you fellows get interested in the union is when there's a crisis, and then you get upset when you find the union's been taken over by a lot of hot-heads who only want to stir up trouble. The union is a democratic institution, you know. You have a vote the same as anyone else – if you want to use it. If you don't like the way the union is run, change it!

Questions

(1) What are your views on this conversation?
(2) What do you think Brian should do if his work-mates decide to go on strike?
(3) What changes would you like to see in the situation generally?

CHAPTER 14

Industrial Unrest

> Where they [the workers] have become merely components in the production system, they have, during their working lives, lost their identity as individuals. This they feel, and underlying many strikes is a protest against this unnatural environment. If the society in which they live does not provide them with compensation for their loss of identity, there are social consequences as well (from John Newton's Presidential Address at the 101st Trades Union Congress).

One of the most disturbing features of our society is the general lack of harmony in our industrial relationships. This is in spite of our increasing affluence and the protection of the Welfare State. For most people the evidence of unrest is seen in an apparently endless succession of strikes which cause inconvenience, damage and disruption far beyond the area of discontent.

When there is industrial unrest such as a strike the adverse effects are widespread, for example:

(i) Management suffers a damaging loss of production and profits. Any set-back can make all the difference between success and failure in a highly competitive international market.

(ii) Long-serving and skilled workers have a considerable stake in the business and stand to lose in the same way as management and business owners in the event of the failure of the business. If the firm closes down, contracts its production, or even fails to expand as much as it might, the skilled workers and long-servers suffer particularly.

(iii) The customers of the firm or industry at home find their own production disrupted as supplies are terminated. Unfulfilled contracts and losses of future orders may damage them gravely even though they are not party to the dispute.

(iv) Overseas customers also suffer, and look for alternative and more dependable sources of supply. Exports fall in both the short and the long runs.

(v) Foreign investment is discouraged – much of which could provide work for Britons.

The problem for the workers is to recognise that their short-term and long-term interests may differ. They are not alone in finding it difficult to distinguish between the two. It is a problem facing governments, companies and individuals too. For example, you can probably appreciate that what gives you short-term pleasure may well give you long-term pain.

It is arguable, of course, but one could say that when coal-miners succeed in forcing up their wages, they force the coal industry to contract. As the result of an 'overpriced' product many mines may be closed down which would otherwise have stayed in operation.

A further hazard for the workers is that, as a result of 'overpricing' their labour, the workers may force management to change their capital-labour input ratios. In other words, where labour units are expensive, management may find automation profitable. Those people remaining in employment may benefit, but the 'wage fund' would be reduced. (Containerisation on the Docks might be an example where worker militancy produced this sort of effect.)

Workers will understandably wish to optimise their returns, and they can do this by ensuring that:

(i) Justice is obtained for them – individually and collectively – through their trade unions.

(ii) The national cake – from which they take their cut – is made as big as possible. This will involve (a) increasing output, (b) avoiding industrial stoppages, and (c) recognising that national interests often coincide with long-term sectional interests.

Management also has responsibilities. If it wishes for long-term profit maximisation, it will have to ensure that:

(i) workers are treated fairly and with dignity;
(ii) grievances are dealt with expeditiously;
(iii) the two-way flow of information between management and workers is maximised;
(iv) workers are allowed to become more involved in the making of decisions;
(v) they understand the workers – in the same way they understand technical processes and valuable machinery and equipment;
(vi) workers are valued.

How does the group view these ideas?

Of course strikes are only one way in which industrial unrest is caused. Discontent is also expressed through people staying away from work (absenteeism), people leaving their jobs (labour turnover), and people not working hard or well (low productivity and shoddy work). These other forms of industrial unrest are likely to be far more damaging than strikes, but the public generally equate unrest with strikes.

Do you think boredom is in some way connected with strikes? Do you think workers who are bored may be more inclined to strike than those who have interesting and satisfying jobs? Is it that boredom and frustration are relieved by aggressive acts such as taking strike action?

Do people go on strike to get more pay? That is the reason often put forward. Do you think strikes would stop if workers received more pay? Or do you think strikes have got something to do with 'keeping up with the Jones's'?

To get things in perspective we should remember, perhaps, that in some countries there are no strikes. That could mean workers have found happiness and contentment in these other societies. It could also mean that they do not enjoy the same freedom.

General questions for the group to consider

(1) How do you think industrial relations could be improved?
(2) Is a conflict between the 'two sides' in industry inevitable?
(3) Throughout the above, reference has been made to 'management' and 'the workers'. Where would you draw the dividing-line between the two groups? Is the Superintendent Cleaner 'management' or is he a 'worker'? Who is 'management' and who is 'worker', then?

Case study – The Medicine Man

Don Strachey is the recently appointed Industrial Relations Manager for Duvalier (Agricultural Machinery) Ltd, which operates in the West Midlands. The factory in Stafford employs 1320 workers (32 per cent of whom are women), while the main works at Stoke employs 2650 workers (12 per cent of whom are women).

Industrial relations at the works are abysmal, as evidenced by the statistics Don has been studying. During the last year:

(i) absenteeism has been running at an average of 19 per cent;
(ii) 26 per cent of the workers have left the company (labour turnover);
(iii) 28 676 working days were lost as a result of industrial stoppages.

He has been considering a number of possibilities for improving the situation. He has consulted with his Managing Director and the principal unions involved at the works, and as a result he has now a number of options open to him, any or all of which might help to improve industrial relations at the two factories:

(i) A generous profit-sharing scheme can be offered to the workers whereby 20 per cent of all net profits made by the company is shared out equally between all who were working for the company in the previous twelve months.

(ii) A good attendance bonus of £5 per week (average wages in the factories are £108.35 per week) can be offered as an alternative to any worker who does not miss a day at work during a particular week. One of the problems facing Don in connection with this alternative is how to deal with the occasional times when there is a short working week (when there are Bank Holidays, for example).

(iii) An offer of a place on the Board of Directors can be made to a nominee of the trade unions representing workers at the plant in the hope that this would be seen as a conciliatory gesture and would provide a useful means of communication between the Board and the work-force.

Questions for the group

(1) What do you think of these proposals? Do you think they would improve industrial relations in the works?
(2) Which of the two financial alternatives do you think the Industrial Relations Manager would prefer, and why?

CHAPTER 15

Resistance to Change

We live in a *constantly* changing world. Few things are unchanging. This is partly the result of rapidly advancing technology, and partly the result of natural processes. Oil is discovered in the North Sea and a declining economy is buttressed – until the oil is used up, or a new fuel makes oil obsolete. The birth rate falls, and the demand for prams – and teachers – declines. A television star appears on the screen with a weird hairstyle – and overnight everyone is rushing to change their appearance. And without any help at all from man, the coast changes its shape through erosion, continents 'drift' and the universe evolves.

An organisation's policies and structures have to be flexible if it is going to meet changing conditions, but changes are inherently resisted by both workers and managers. Why? Because people like to feel secure, and they prefer familiar procedures which they have come to understand and live with. So one of the basic problems confronting business organisations is resistance to change – throughout the whole work-force.

In order to minimise resistance to change managements will need to know (i) why there is resistance to change, and (ii) what can be done to overcome it.

Reasons for resistance

(1) *Economic factors*

Fears of redundancy are often linked with the introduction of new machines or work-flows. New systems mean new job evaluations and new pay structures. Everyone in the organisation is concerned with 'differentials' not simply with how much they earn but how much more they earn than others – and vice versa of course.

(2) *Resentment to new orders*
Any changes must increase the number of orders given, if only initially. It is understandable that additional controls will be resisted. New and unfamiliar lines of communication will be developed. Statuses will change. New management/subordinate relationships will have to be stabilised. In many cases one group of people will be initiating changes (the Headquarters' experts), while another group will be implementing the changes (the line managers).

(3) *Inconvenience and disruption*
A worker is likely to fight against the assignment of extra duties. New procedures have to be learned. Changing work-patterns also disrupt relationships. Patterns of co-operation and leadership are revised and have to be relearned. Work-groups may be broken up so that friends are separated. It becomes necessary to confront new situations and new faces.

(4) *Uncertainty*
Workers know what their present situation is. They do not know what the new one will be. Uncertainty is always a threat. A time of change is likely to be a time when rumours circulate. When workers do not know what is going to happen, they will speculate.

(5) *Union co-operation*
In many cases it will be necessary for management to seek the support of the unions if changes are to be effected. The unions, for their part, will be concerned to ensure that the interests of their members are protected. Management will be required to explain to the unions the need for change. They will also have to indicate how the changes are to be effected. The unions will then work through the implications for their members and will only accept changes if these are not seen as detrimental to the work-force.

Overcoming resistance to change

Having decided what causes resistance to change it becomes necessary to apply the appropriate remedy. In the same way a doctor diagnoses the cause of an ailment and then prescribes the medicine for a cure. The following methods are available:

(1) *Financial incentives*
Maintenance of earnings may be guaranteed, and redundancy fears may be allayed by confirmation that there will be no loss of

employment as a result of the changes. This may sound an expensive expedient, especially when the purpose of most changes is to use resources (including labour) more economically. But it would be possible to run down the work-force by allowing natural wastage to take its toll. For example, if labour turnover is 20 per cent, within two and a half years the work-force could be reduced by 50 per cent simply by not replacing workers who leave the organisation.

(2) *Exerting supervisory pressure*
If a manager has built up a fund of goodwill with his staff, he may be able to lean on them heavily during the period of the change without any adverse effects. It could be seen as a short-term remedy for a short-term problem.

(3) *Trial basis*
Changes may be introduced tentatively. Note that if a change is introduced for a trial period of, say, six months, at the end of the trial period the very forces which militated against change will now resist reverting to the original system.

(4) *Small-scale changes*
If small-scale changes are delayed, the necessity for change will intensify until major innovations are called for. It may be wise for management to encourage a continuous state of change so that a situation of change will be normal – and acceptable.

(5) *Two-way communication can be improved*
Management can give more information about proposed changes. It can be prepared to answer questions and to listen to the workers' grievances. Union approval should be sought well in advance. Bargaining may remove many obstacles: 'We would be willing to guarantee there will be no redundancies if you are prepared to accept 50 per cent women on the new machines.'

(6) *Participation*
If management allows the workers affected by the changes to participate in the making of the decisions, they will find resistance dissolving and workers accepting the innovations more willingly. Similarly, if workers are given a stake in the company, say in the form of stocks or shares, they will be more inclined to accept changes which benefit management, since any benefits resulting from the changes will be shared.

Case study – Glenfew Construction

Last month the Board of Directors of Glenfrew Construction Co. Ltd, a subsidiary of the Scottish Property Corporation, purchased a lease for a new office block in Bath. They are now preparing detailed plans for the removal of their existing Head Office in Balham, south-west London, to the new site in eighteen months' time.

Patrick Donovan, Glenfrew's Personnel Director, has the responsibility for organising the transfer of the Personnel Department to Bath, where they will have the whole of the fourth floor at their disposal, with a total floor space of 4000 square metres. The Personnel Director is considering introducing landscaping (or open-floor planning) for the new office at Bath, and partly as a training and selection exercise for you (a group of trainee managers), he asks you to prepare a report for him. He wants to know specifically (i) what problems you anticipate, and (ii) what you would propose to do to overcome these problems.

Designate one of your number to keep a record of your deliberations so that you can draft a report – collectively – in due course.

The only other information available is indicated below:

Age and sex breakdown of staff in Personnel Department

	under 20	20 –29	30 –39	over 40
Male	6	18	37	28
Female	35	14	5	3

At present the Personnel Department is operating from temporary premises, and all forty-two Personnel Officers have their own offices – though these are usually shared (see Figure 15.1 for top hierarchies of the department).

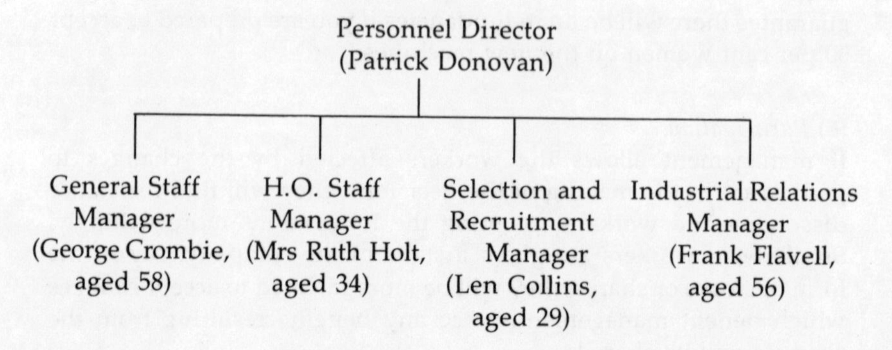

Figure 15.1 The organisation structure of the Personnel Department

The construction company have a largely mobile labour force which is required to move to any part of the country where a new project is undertaken, though in Glenfrew's case the work is concentrated in the Midlands and Home Counties. However, large numbers of new workers have to be recruited whenever there is a major job taken on. The Head Office staff have not needed to be mobile generally, but most of the Personnel Officers are out visiting sites as part of their normal work-load.

You are asked to prepare a formal report for Mr Donovan within the course of the next week.

A further question for group discussion

The North Sea oil finds will boost Britain's economy for many years to come, but the oil deposits are finite. Within our lifetimes the oil supplies will begin to dry up. At that time Britain's economy can be expected to take a downturn. The standard of living of its people will begin to fall. What do you think a government could do now to alleviate the problems which are likely to arise at that time? Would you give the same sort of advice to the oil-rich desert sheikhdoms which face the same problem – perhaps a worse one – in the long run?

CHAPTER 16

Further Case Studies on the People Theme

A. *The Holiday Rota*

A new Records Office was brought into operation by Ambidex (Toys and Games) Ltd last year. The office is situated at Slough and staff were drafted in from other offices in and around London. A number of new staff were taken on. These were generally less-experienced staff and school-leavers.

John Davies, the Office Manager, was aware of a number of teething problems in the new office. One of these problems concerned holiday arrangements for the staff. Some holidays were arranged by staff before they were transferred, and while existing arrangements were honoured last year, the Manager aims to avoid a recurrence of the ensuing stresses and strains. He wishes to produce a system which is seen to be fair. As a starting-point he has asked the staff for their views. He imposes just two constraints:

(1) only two people can be on holiday in any one department/section at the same time; and

(2) he reserves the right to vary any system that is proposed by the staff.

He has already had early feedback from some members of staff:

Sophie Calhoun (45), Senior Clerk in the Statistics Department: 'I shall have to have my holiday with my husband – or he will be divorcing me'.

Alan Kilbride (19), a Grade I clerk in the Mailing Section: 'I had to have my holiday last year in September. If I can't have a holiday at the proper time I shall leave'.

Sylvia Bratton (26), a Grade I clerk in the Documents Department: 'Drawing lots would be the only fair way'.

Ken Beaumount (56), Supervisor in the Accounts Department: 'It should be according to length of service. The longest-serving person in each department should have first choice. The newest arrival should go to the end of the queue. Or it should go to the most senior in rank.'

What factors do you think should decide who gets first choice? Draw up the rules for the holiday rota which seem fairest to all concerned.

Can you see any other way in which the manager might overcome these problems?

An analysis of staff in the records office

(1) by age and grade (grade indicates levels of responsibility)

Age	Grade I	Grade II	Senior grade	Supervisor	Totals
Under 21	11	6	2	0	19
21–40	4	12	4	1	21
Over 40	2	6	6	2	16
					56

(2) by length of service and department

Service	Accounts Department	Documents Department	Statistics Department	Mailing Section	Totals
Under 1 year	11	9	3	8	31
1–5 years	5	2	8	1	16
Over 5 years	6	1	2	0	9
					56

B. *The Liverpool Warehouse*

In a large warehouse in Liverpool dealing with the mail-order business, the General Manager, Sam Grimshaw, has been having disciplinary problems with the largely female work-force. The business operates by way of a glossy magazine which shows a wide range of goods in attractive settings. The magazine is sent to housewives throughout the country who act as agents by collecting and collating orders from their neigbours, relatives and friends. The agents receive a commission on their sales, or a discount on their own purchases.

Sam Grimshaw has asked his Deputy General Manager, Janice Anderson, to produce a report on absenteeism and lateness among the warehouse staff. When the statistics become available they make disturbing reading for Grimshaw. The document he sees is reproduced as Table 16.1.

'This is terrible,' says Grimshaw to his deputy, 'what are we going to do about it?'

'I haven't made my mind up yet,' says Janice Anderson, 'I had no idea things were as bad as this. I'm going to ask some of the senior staff what they think is at the root of the trouble.'

Most of the workers in the warehouse had already got wind of the report on absenteeism and lateness. If Janice Anderson could have heard some of the comments she would have found them rather illuminating:

Emma Wright (aged 23, dispatcher) – 'We clock on and if we're late we lose half an hour off our pay. *We* lose. Why should *they* worry? They're saving money. If I'm late by five minutes they get twenty-five minutes work out of me for nothing!'

Joyce Abercrombie (aged 42, dispatcher) – 'I'd like to see them get three kids off to school and a husband off to work without ever being late!'

Tom Griffths (aged 56, porter) – 'Well it's the women, isn't it? They don't think about work the same as a man does!'

Ken Brandon (aged 30, supervisor) – 'I know the problem with some of my girls. They come in by bus. If they catch an early bus it gets them in half an hour too early, and if they catch the next one it only just gets them in on time if they're lucky.'

Syd Willoughby (aged 48, accountant) – 'It's a wonder they haven't thought about giving people a good time-keeping bonus. That would do the trick. If they come in late or miss a day off, they lose their bonus.'

Connie Phillips (aged 25, typist) – 'Why haven't we got a proper Personnel Department?'

Questions for the group

(1) What are your views on this situation?
(2) What ideas do you have which might help to solve the problems for the General Manager?
(3) What sort of functions would be performed by a Personnel Department in this organisation?

Table 16.1 Absenteeism and lateness for last year

		Days absent during year*	Days late during year†	Average number of workers during last twelve months
	Females			
	Dispatchers			
(i)	under 20	738	2 746	36
(ii)	21–40	3 077	10 884	196
(iii)	over 40	186	195	23
	Storekeepers			
(iv)	under 20	911	3 304	46
(v)	21–40	562½	1 592	22
(vi)	over 40	85½	94	13
	Clerical staff			
(vii)	under 20	456	207	27
(viii)	21–40	32	144	9
(ix)	over 40	1½	0	3
	Supervisors			
(x)	all ages	723	1 746	35
	Males			
(xi)	Porters	23	53	10
(xii)	Supervisors	22½	17	8
(xiii)	Accountants	6½	26	5
	Totals	6 824½	21 008	433

* 2 half-days' absence = 1 whole day's absence.
† Late = more than ten minutes late (morning or afternoon sessions).

C. *Office Discipline*

David Rowan is one of the less-experienced Branch Managers with Topex Finance Ltd, but the Directors recognise his potential and have high hopes that he will emerge as one of their most talented executives. Topex provide finance for members of the public wishing to buy goods on hire-purchase, and specialise in the area of caravans, motor-cars and commercial vehicles. They are part of a large group of companies which deal in insurance and banking business generally.

Topex operate from fifty-six different branch offices around the country, and David is in charge of the Romford office. He took up the appointment six months ago.

David has a staff of seventeen. There are seven girls under 20, two older women in their late forties, and the remainder are males with a fairly even spread of ages between 18 and 50. David's second in command, John Travers, is a long-serving employee of the company who has suffered from ill health over the past two years. Before John's illness he was manager of the Romford branch and it was a much busier branch than it is now.

Within the past ten days an inspection team, headed by Donald McCulloch, the Chief Inspector for the Group, have reported on an extended visit they paid to David's branch. The report indicates that they found the standard of work in the office was 'below standard', though part of the explanation for this could be found in the fact that a number of the staff are below the quality usually found in the company. The inspectors' report draws attention to four particular areas of concern:

(1) The standard of dress among the younger people in the office leaves a lot to be desired. Some girls come to the office in slacks or jeans. None of the younger men wear collars and ties for work. Although there are no company rules on dress, and each Branch Manager is left to set his own standards, the inspectors felt that members of the public who meet junior staff in face-to-face situations will gain a bad impression of the company in the Romford office.

(2) On a number of occasions customers were kept waiting a long time for information when they telephoned the company. Furthermore, staff generally tended to be rather off-hand when they dealt with customers on the telephone.

(3) There is a considerable degree of conflict between, on the one hand, the two older women (who have both worked within the Group for over twenty years), and, on the other hand, a clique of younger staff. The inspectors feel this 'running battle' is having a detrimental effect on the staff as a whole.

(4) When the inspectors arrived unannounced on the first day of the inspection, eight of the staff arrived more than ten minutes late. On subsequent days the inspectors kept a careful and unobtrusive eye on times of arrival. While punctuality improved, there were still a number of persistent offenders, particularly among the young females.

Your task

You are asked to discuss the problem and consider possible solutions together, looking at the situation from (i) David's point of view, (ii) the company's point of view, and (iii) the staff's point of view.

When you have completed the discussion you are asked to draft a suitable response from David to the Chief Inspector, who has now returned to the head office.

PART 3

ON THE STRUCTURE OF BUSINESS

CHAPTER 17

The Forms of Business Organisation

Trading by definition involves interaction between two or more people. Whether we are talking about the manufacture and/or sale of goods (tangibles) or the provision of services such as banking and insurance (intangibles), the relationships between people dealing with each other need to be clearly structured. This is true within the business when we need to know who is responsible for different functions; instructions will need to be given and orders will have to be obeyed if things are to get done. It is also true that relationships have to be structured between a business and those with whom it deals. What sort of business are we dealing with? What legal remedies are available to us if things go wrong? Much will depend on the legal classification of the business in question, the main forms being shown in the diagram below:

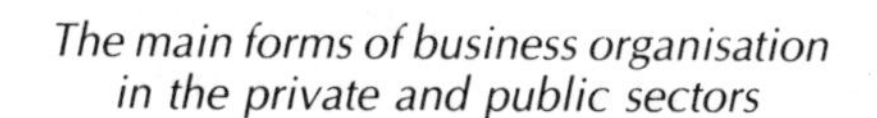
The main forms of business organisation in the private and public sectors

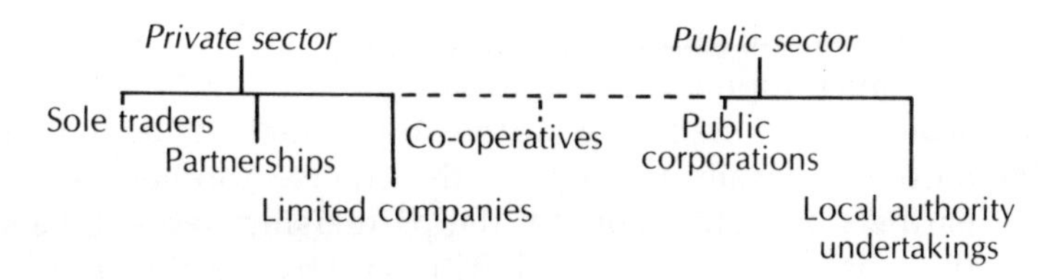

The sole trader

This refers to a person who has set up in business on their own account. A lot of retailers (shopkeepers) are sole traders because it is possible to start your own business with quite a small amount of capital. Very often they buy goods on credit. By not paying for them immediately they gain time to sell the stock before they have to settle their account.

Sole traders make their own decisions. They decide what sorts of goods they are going to sell (or what services they are going to provide). They select objectives for the business, choose their work-force and determine pricing policies. If the business makes a profit this belongs to them (subject to any tax on the profits which are payable to the Collector of Taxes). If the business makes losses the proprietor has to bear them.

The main danger for sole traders is that they are liable to be made bankrupt if they are unable to meet their commitments (i.e. to pay their debts). It is not only their business assets which would be used to meet these debts. Their personal belongings would also be at stake. Business people who are made bankrupt stand to lose their cars, their jewellery, their houses and indeed virtually all their personal possessions.

Partnerships

When two or more people join forces in business the relationship is described as a partnership. If the partners are wise they will execute (sign) a Deed of Partnership setting out in detail their rights. This would reduce the likelihood of damaging disputes. Apart from any provisions in a deed of partnership relationships between partners are governed by the Partnership Act, 1890. For example, in the absence of agreement, profits are shared equally between partners no matter how much capital they contribute.

One of the major pitfalls of a partnership is that any action taken by one partner is legally binding on the others. Another danger is that all partners are fully liable for the partnership debts. Like sole traders their liability is unlimited. This is why we find the partnership form of business concentrated in areas such as retailing, insurance broking and the professions, where large amounts of capital investment are not required. Any partner may dissolve the partnership at will and the partnership will be dissolved in any case on the death of one of the partners.

Sometimes a partner provides capital but does not become actively involved in the management of the business. Such a partner is described as a dormant or sleeping partner, but remains fully liable for the debts of the partnership.

The limited company

When the proprietors of a business form a limited company they acquire the benefit of limited liability. Then they stand to lose only their stake in the company and cannot be compelled to meet the company's debts from their personal assets. The safeguard of limited liability will mean that the company will find it easier to raise funds because the investors' personal assets will not be at risk.

A company has a legal personality distinct from that of its shareholders. It can own land and other property, sue and be sued, enter into contracts and borrow money from others, with certain restrictions. The *Memorandum of Association* is the document which sets out the company's constitution and governs its relationship with outsiders. One of its principal clauses is the so-called objects clause which sets out the activities the company is to pursue. If the company undertakes activities beyond those prescribed in the Memorandum these will be regarded as *ultra vires* (outside the powers of the company). The *Articles of Association* regulate the company's internal management. They deal with the appointment and retirement of directors and the rights of the various shareholders, etc.

When a company invites the public to subscribe for (buy) its shares it becomes a public limited company and stricter legal rules apply. Such companies are recognisable by the letters plc after the name. Many such companies will have their shares quoted on the Stock Exchange (e.g. Lloyds Bank plc and Trusthouse Forte plc). When the name of the company is followed by the word Limited or the initials Ltd it is an indication that the company is not seeking funds from the public.

Figure 17.1 below shows the main sources of funds available to a limited company.

Co-operatives

There are over 200 retail co-operative societies in Great Britain and Northern Ireland and they account for approximately 7 per cent of Britain's total retail trade. Anyone can become a member of a retail co-operative society by buying one share (usually £1). Each member then has one vote for the annual election of the Committee of Management. This committee is responsible for the appointment of senior staff who control the day-to-day administration.

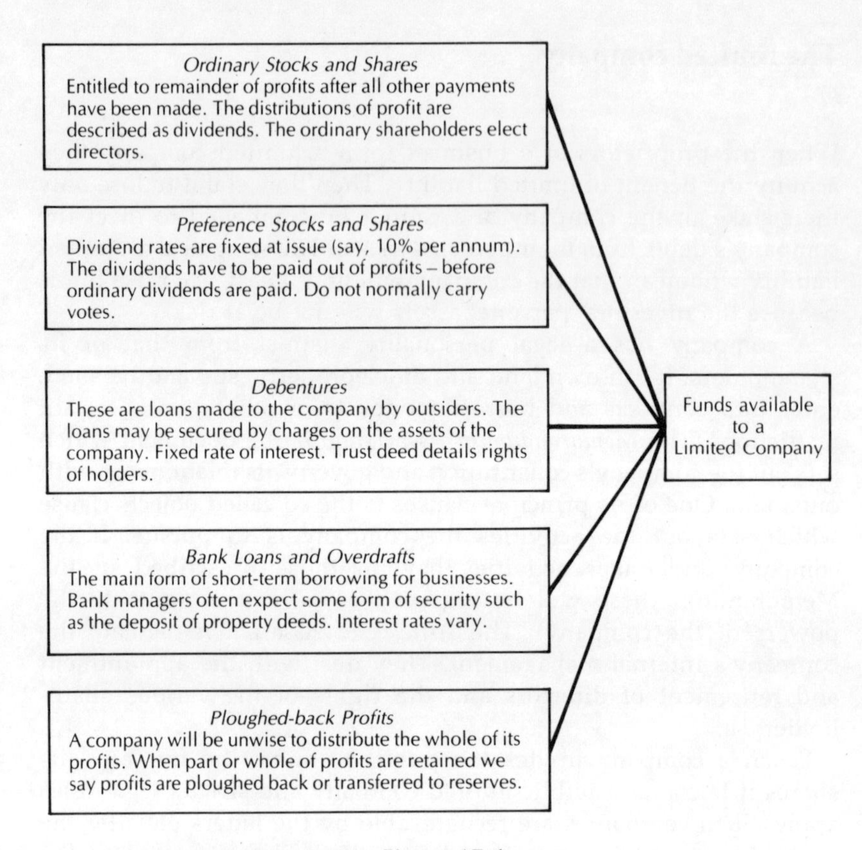

Figure 17.1

Each society is independent of others and operates in a particular town or district, but all the retail societies purchase supplies from the Co-operative Wholesale Society where possible. They provide the CWS with capital according to their size and receive dividends in proportion to their purchases. The CWS runs its own farms and factories and is also involved in the banking and insurance business.

Customers in the retail stores are usually given stamps in proportion to their purchases and books of stamps can be encashed or deposited in a share account. This system allows the co-operative stores to compete fairly effectively with the cut-price supermarkets. Any profits are used to maintain and expand the society's operations and to support various social, educational and political aims. The first co-operative store was opened in Rochdale in 1844 and there was from the beginning an attempt by consumers to obtain goods more cheaply by eliminating the middleman in the chain of distribution.

The political objectives remain to this day and the co-operative movement is affiliated to the Labour Party.

Retail co-operative societies are governed by the provisions of the Industrial and Provident Societies Acts 1893/1961. The liability of members is limited and a maximum shareholding of £1000 is imposed by the law, though some societies fix lower limits.

Producers' co-operatives marketing the products of their members are common in various parts of the world and one of the manufacturing co-operatives set up in recent years was the Meridian Motor Cycle workers' co-operative, established with state aid when the original company ran into financial difficulties.

Public corporations

In Britain some industries, such as coal, electricity, gas and the railways, are owned and essentially run by the state. These are the so-called nationalised industries.

The public corporation which controls a nationalised industry is created by Parliament and must act within the parameters laid down by the appropriate legislation. In 1946 it was the Bank of England Act which transferred the capital stock of the Bank of England to the state, and in the same year the Coal Industry Nationalisation Act established the National Coal Board.

When the state takes over a firm or an industry the essential mechanics are simple enough. The Treasury, acting on behalf of the government, usually compensates the existing shareholders by allocating to them government stocks of an equivalent value. In the case of the takeover of the Bank of England compensation was such that the former shareholders received the same return from the government stock as they previously received from their Bank of England stock. Of course the procedures can be varied to suit different situations.

The nationalised industries exist for the same purpose as any privately owned business. They provide goods or services for which there is a demand. But where the Chief Executive in the private sector will be responsible to his Board of Directors, and they in turn will be answerable to the shareholders, in the nationalised industry the Chairman will be responsible to the appropriate Minister of State – who in turn is responsible to Parliament.

The purpose of bringing undertakings into the public sector of the economy is to ensure that they are subject to political control. But control can be exercised in other ways. For example, the government, through the Treasury, can buy shares in any company – and, if desired, sell them later. In the meantime the government is able to exercise all the rights of a shareholder. It can also offer subsidies in one form or another to ailing companies – and in so doing impose certain constraints on their future policies.

The proponents of nationalisation would no doubt emphasise that it eliminates wasteful competition and that the policies for industry can be integrated with the national economic programme. Economies of scale become possible. There are also socio-political considerations. In making a decision the state can bring into account additional criteria, i.e. factors which are non-monetary. For example, if it is looking at the possible closure of a railway branch line, because it costs more to run than it brings in revenue, it can take into account the effect closure would have on the lives of the people in the area. The state would have to pay out unemployment and welfare benefits, and these extraneous costs would be brought into the deliberations. The entrepreneur, by contrast, would select the option which gave him more profits (or less losses) regardless of the effects outside the business.

The opponents of nationalisation would no doubt argue that a reasonable degree of competition positively induces efficiency. Since the nationalised industries are in monopolistic positions they could be quite insensitive to the needs of the consumers. Furthermore, the industries can cover their costs quite simply by raising their prices, so it is impossible to assess performance adequately.

Under a system of free enterprise entrepreneurs are enabled to marshal economic resources and use these with a view to making profit. In other words they determine the nature and extent of society's output of goods and services. Their only constraints are their own limited resources and the need to make profit. Thus entrepreneurs are forced to regard the markets they serve and generally attempt to cater for the needs of the consumers. In the same way that a politician has to concern himself ultimately with the votes of the electorate, the entrepreneur has to react to the 'votes' of the people in the market-place who either buy or reject what he has to offer them.

A question remains: What happens to the profits made, by the nationalised industries on the one hand, and the entrepreneurs on the other? First, let us remove any emotiveness about the term 'profit'. We can consider it here as the difference between the inputs of resources and the outputs of products or services. If there is no surplus, there is nothing in the Exchequer to spend on things like education, defence and social welfare. So profits, or surpluses, in this sense are essential in any system of production.

Any profits made in the public (nationalised) sector are usually ploughed back into the industry, though they could in theory be used to reduce prices, or as funds for the Treasury. In the private (free-enterprise) sector the bulk of profits are also ploughed back into the business, but sizeable portions are paid out to shareholders and to the Treasury (as taxes).

Questions for the group

(1) What are your views on nationalisation? Are there any industries you think ought to be nationalised? Why? Are there any industries which ought to be denationalised? Why? And how could they be privatised.
(2) To what extent does the fact that many free-enterprise companies are multinational corporations affect the arguments in the narrative?
(3) How would you judge the performance of (i) a nationalised industry, and (ii) a private firm?
(4) If the Channel Tunnel were to be built, do you think it would be best left to the government or to private enterprise?

A project for the group

Split up into sections. Each section should choose one particular nationalised industry. Find out all you can about it. Draw up a report – as a team effort. Come together again later and exchange ideas and reach conclusions.

Local authority undertakings

Throughout the country various local authorities conduct enterprises for the benefit of local inhabitants. They may run a bus service, museums, car parks, public restaurants, etc. The local ratepayers stand to gain or lose according to the standard of the service and the trading results. The undertakings will be managed by local government officers and council committees, but professional managers will be appointed to assume day-to-day responsibility for the operations.

Case study – Japanese Seaweed

Poole Harbour is reputedly the second largest natural harbour in the world, flanked to the east by the holiday resort of Bournemouth, to the west by the beautiful but sparsely populated Purbeck Hills, and to the north by the historic town and port of Poole. Poole and Bournemouth are essentially one conurbation. The population is in the region of 250 000, but in the summer season there is a large influx of visitors from all over the world. Bournemouth's prosperity has largely been built up through the hotel industry. Poole also has many attractions for the tourists, not the least of which is the ample expanse of sheltered water in the harbour which offers anchorage to a multitude of yachts and motor-cruisers of all types.

The Harbour Commissioners are greatly concerned because a certain variety of sea plant life, commonly known as Japanese Seaweed, has been found within the confines of the nearly landlocked harbour. The weed is notoriously fast-growing and clogging and has played havoc in other parts of the world. The Commissioners see the weed – potentially – as an impediment to commercial sea traffic, an annoyance to anglers, bathers and amateur sailors, and even an eventual health hazard, if masses of rotting seaweed take over the harbour area (there is about seven miles of coastline) (see Figure 17.2).

The Commissioners have evolved a contingency plan involving the use of a dredger, but this is acknowledged as an excessively

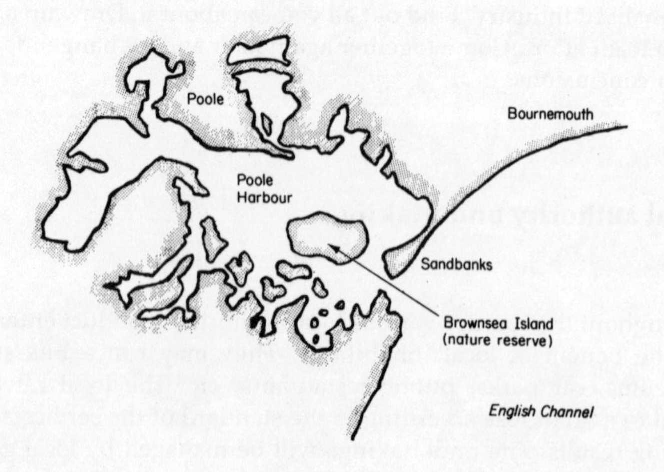

Figure 17.2

costly measure in itself. However, the suggestion has come from a local businessman that he would undertake to 'harvest' the seaweed and convert it into fertiliser for farmers and gardeners. He points out that his scheme would:

(i) remove the obnoxious weed from the harbour;
(ii) create employment for the local population; and
(iii) provide the Commissioners with a handsome sum of money (figures have not yet been quoted).

The local authorities would be very interested in the problem since public amenities are being affected. They would also be closely involved with planning permissions which may be required before any building programmes can be started. Local authorities can indulge in commercial activities where these are likely to serve local interests, and they may wish to become involved in this situation.

For group discussion

(1) What do you think of the idea proposed by the businessman?
(2) What problems would you anticipate?
(3) Can you conjure up any better ideas – from the authorities' viewpoint?
(4) If the businessman's idea was taken up by the authorities, what specific steps would he have to take to bring his plans to fruition? (Keep a careful record of the steps that would be considered necessary.)
(5) How do you think the public's interests would be best served in this situation?

CHAPTER 18

Organisation Structures

In Figure 18.1 you will see an extract from the organisation chart of a fairly typical manufacturing company. It shows the relationship between the Board of Directors and the company's senior executives.

The *Board of Directors* is the chief policy-making body in the company. The Directors are individually elected to the Board by the shareholders. It is the Board who fix the objectives for the company and appoint senior executives, including the Managing Director, to achieve the goals which have been set. The Board meet regularly, perhaps once a week in the case of a company like Kelwyn Fireworks Plc. Some Directors, such as the Managing Director and the Sales Director, will have day-to-day administrative responsibilities in the company, while others will be non-executive brought on to the Board to add a variety of expertise to the deliberations.

(Note that most Articles of Association require a Director to hold a minimum number of shares in the company. This is to ensure that Directors have a financial stake in the success of the company.)

The *Company Secretary* is the administrator for the Board of Directors and is responsible for the company's compliance with legal requirements.

The *Managing Director* is the Chief Executive. He is both leader of the management team and a member of the Board of Directors. He bears the main responsibility for the management team's efficiency and the harmony of purpose in the company generally.

The *Purchasing Manager* in Kelwyn Fireworks will be responsible for buying the raw materials required for making fireworks. He is answerable to the Managing Director, and has his own team of subordinates (the Warehouse Manager for one).

The *Works Manager* is in charge of firework production. While he is on the same level of the hierarchy as the Purchasing Manager and the other senior executives, it does not follow that he receives the same salary – or exercises the same influence. It may well be that 90 per cent of all the staff employed by Kelwyn Fireworks work in the

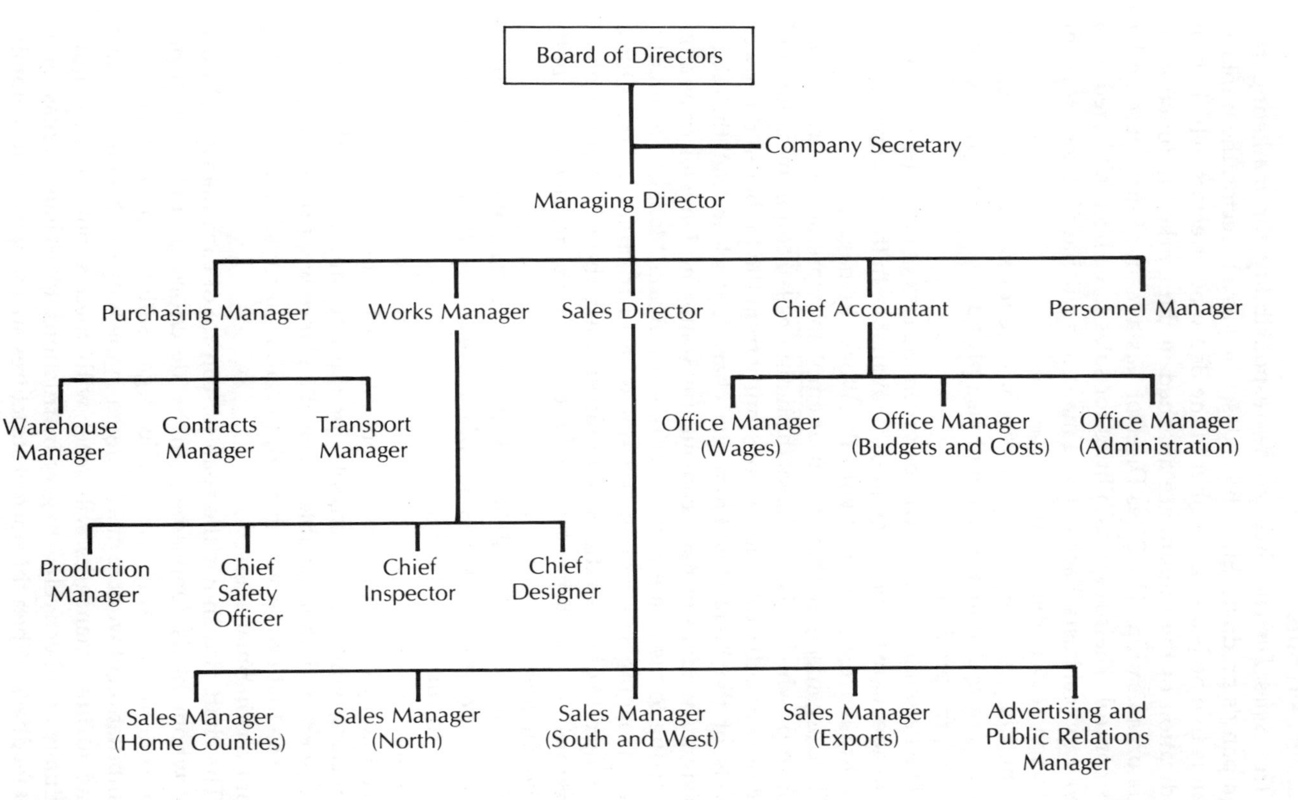

Figure 18.1 Kelwyn Fireworks PLC

factory and are therefore directly or indirectly under the Works Manager's control.

The *Sales Director* has prime responsibility for marketing the company's products. Since he is described as a Director, the implication is that he is also a member of the Board of Directors, which is an indication of the importance attached to the marketing function in this organisation. The Sales Director has a team of managers under his control. Their responsibilities for sales have been allocated on a geographical basis. Each of these managers will have his own team of salemen answerable to him.

The *Chief Accountant* will be responsible for keeping the financial records of the company. He will also play a key role in costing and pricing the products.

The *Personnel Manager* will be given the task of ensuring that there is an adequate supply of manpower available. In this example he will need to liaise a great deal with the Works Manager.

The organisation chart is an attempt to express the formal relationships which exist. It shows the main lines of communication and the flow of authority and responsibility from the higher to the lower levels of the hierarchy. From the chart it is clear that the Chief Designer would normally consult the Managing Director only after referring to his immediate superior – the Works Manager. Similarly, the Managing Director would not give instructions to the Office Manager (Administration) without keeping the Chief Accountant informed – otherwise he would be creating problems for both subordinates.

Of course names will be linked with the managerial positions indicated on the chart, and one of the uses to which the chart can be put is to illustrate the ages of the top managers. Assume that all positions occupied by managers over 60 are indicated in red, those occupied by executives over 55 but under 60 in blue – and so on. The Directors, who are responsible for the appointment of the senior managers, will then be able to see at a glance what plans need to be made so that executives of the right calibre are available to take over from retiring managers.

The chart also shows the span for control of each manager. Those for whom he is reponsible can be described as his work team. Viewed in this way the whole organisation can be seen as a combination of work teams arranged in the form of a hierarchy. From time to time managers will meet with their subordinates – individually or collectively – to give instructions, to exchange ideas, or to get feedback. When the normal structures are inappropriate, committees may be set up to supplement or even supersede these lines of communication and command.

As an organisation grows in size it will be necessary either to broaden the spans of control, or to introduce new levels of management. A structure is described as 'tall' when there are many layers of management between the lowest and highest levels in the company, and 'flat' when there are few layers. When a structure is tall problems are likely to arise as a result of the extended lines of communication. A flat structure will not have this defect, but might create problems related to co-ordination and control.

Line *v.* Staff

When an organisation is divided into departments such as in the case of Kelwyn Fireworks the structure is called a line organisation. A major merit is that the role, responsibility and authority of each departmental manager is clearly defined. However, in a large organisation the line manager is often able to draw on functional expertise both within the department and outside it. Consider, for example, the role of the Production Manager in relation to the personnel function in the fireworks factory. The Production Manager might have personnel officers on his team of sub-managers and supervisors. The placement of these officers on his staff would be logical because the bulk of the company's work-force would be located on his production lines. They would obviously play a crucial role in interviewing new employees and counselling existing workers. The problem for the Production Manager is to determine how far to be guided by the experts. What happens, for instance, when there is conflict between the advice offered by the specialists and the instructions coming from his line manager (i.e. the Works Manger). An example would be where the Personnel Department are pressing for a reduction in labour turnover while the production side are calling for increased output to cope with the upturn in seasonal demand. The personnel officers attached to the Production Manager's team would also have their problems. While they would receive their orders from the Production Manager, their interest and loyalties would be divided. Their long-term prospects are likely to be closely tied up with the Personnel Department and they will not want to displease their functional manager.

Line and staff organisation, whereby specialists are attached to the teams of the line managers, is prevalent in large-scale businesses in spite of the problems it brings with it.

The design of the organisation is the prime responsibility of the Chief Executive. In the case of Kelwyn Fireworks this would be the province of the Managing Director.

Questions for the group to consider

(1) If the company were contemplating a large-scale advertising campaign, which of the executives would you expect to find involved in the deliberations? Which media do you think they would use?
(2) How do you view the roles of non-executive directors who do not have administrative responsibilities, and may be directors in a number of companies? What sort of experts would you expect to find on the Board of this firework company?
(3) What would you see as the special risks involved in this business? What safeguards would you recommend?

Case study – Kelwyn Fireworks Plc

You are asked to play the roles of the various senior executives shown on the organisation chart (Figure 18.1) for Kelwyn Fireworks Plc. The manager has called you together to discuss two problems with which he is confronted.

Problem 1
The Board of Directors have asked him to look into the possibility of finding a site for a new factory outside London, where the existing works are situated. The intention is to close down the present factory in due course.

The Managing Director wants to know what sort of factors you would like him to bear in mind when he is assessing potential sites. Do you think there are certain parts of the country which would be more appropriate than others? Does it have to be a single-storied factory?

Problem 2
The Managing Director is greatly concerned at the downward trend of sales of fireworks over the past few years. The trend is similar for other firms, but the Chief Executive wants to know of any ideas you might have for raising the levels of sales of fireworks, or even for switching into other products. The Sales Director has agreed with the Managing Director that this meeting should have wide-ranging discussion on possible developments in order to collect as many ideas as possible.

CHAPTER 19

Production

Production can be defined as the activity which converts raw materials into manufactured goods. There are those who would suggest that the manufacturer produces goods which he then tries to sell. Others would say the manufacturer anticipates the needs of the public and then produces goods which will satisfy those needs. The truth generally lies somewhere between these notions.

The first stage is likely to be the designing of the product. For example, at Kelwyn Fireworks there may be plans to develop a new set-piece display for functions where simple messages can be incorporated such as 'Happy Birthday Kevin' or 'Good Luck Joanna and Ross'. The possibility of lighting up a sponsor's name has also been considered as a useful sales ploy. Before moving to the drawing-board the Chief Designer will no doubt confer with the Sales Director. What sort of market is being aimed at? What sort of price limitations are there? What is the target date? The Production Manager will also need to be consulted. What would it be possible to produce given the existing resources? What redeployments would be required? The Chief Accountant (or the appropriate Office Manager) would be consulted over the costings of the project and the Purchasing Manager and the Chief Safety Officer would no doubt be brought into the discussions at one stage or another.

When the designs are approved and a prototype has been produced and tested satisfactorily the project will pass over to the Advertising Manager to organise advanced publicity and to the Production Manager to start making up the set-pieces. Any of the following methods of production may be selected:

Job production

With this type of production the work is carried out to the specific requirements of the individual customer. Labour costs are likely to be high, both because greater skill is called for and because more time will have to be spent on executing the order.

Mass-production (or flow-line production)

This is only suited to large-scale operations. Large numbers of more or less identical units are in continuous production. There is little or no individuality in the product and workers perform short work-cycles. The same actions are repeated again and again every few minutes, or even seconds. The work-force tends to be unskilled or semi-skilled apart from the engineers, who set up the line and maintain it. Most mass-production lines will be computerised to some extent. The tendency is increasingly towards robotic production where machines are designed to perform the repetitive operations previously requiring human involvement. When orders for the products fall below the level of output it is usual to produce for stock rather than reduce output. This is done to save costs.

When the products are liquid, such as petrol or fruit juices the terms 'process production' or 'continuous-flow process production' are used to describe this type of operation.

It was the eighteenth-century Scottish economist, Adam Smith, who first advanced the benefits to be gained through the division of labour. To increase productivity, work is broken down into smaller and even smaller sub-processes. The advent of mass-production techniques has given the industrial world its high standard of living though it has also brought a number of social problems in its train. Work on mass-production lines can be quite stressful for the rank-and-file workers.

Small-batch production

This is called for when there are orders for a significant number of similar items. Subsequent orders follow but with slightly different specifications. A batch of one design will be followed by a batch of another. One of the problems for the manufacturer is to decide what is an economic run. It may not be possible to minimise costs per unit on the production runs required by the customer. But dare the manufacturer run the risk of holding stocks for which there is a limited demand?

The different types of production are represented diagrammatically below:

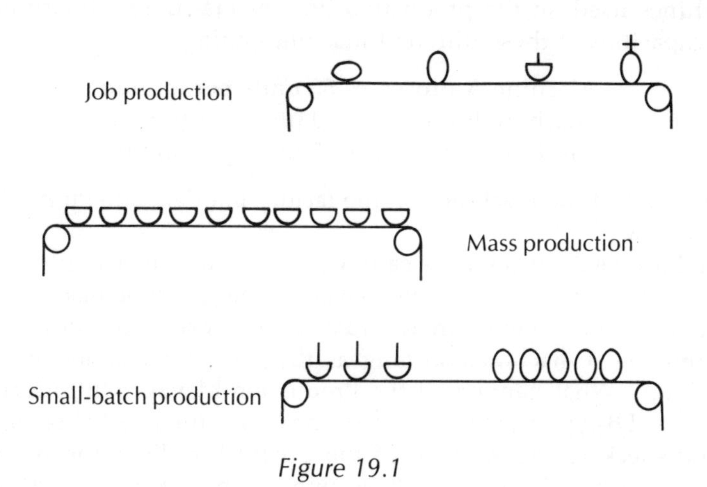

Figure 19.1

Factory layout

The layout of the factory will depend to a large extent on the production methods employed. Mass-production methods require a *flow-line layout*. Production lines will be laid out so that the machines will deal in sequence with the products as they are processed. By contrast, when there is job or small-batch production all the machines performing the same operations will be clustered together, perhaps even located in separate production shops. But in the layout of the machinery and the planning of the work-flows certain basic principles will need to be applied:

(i) the raw materials will travel the shortest distances possible during their making-up process;
(ii) handling (including loading and unloading) will be minimised to keep labour costs as low as possible.
(iii) there will be a logical and identifiable flow of work through the factory from entry as raw materials to exit as finished goods;
(iv) safety precautions will be taken with a view to eliminating accidents of every sort.

Bottlenecks

One of the problems likely to confront any production manager is that the various machines in the factory will have differing production capacities. Thus at Kelwyns there may be three different machines used on the production line for maritime/military flares, the capacities of these different machines being:

Machine A processes 50 units per minute
Machine B processes 60 units per minute
Machine C processes 85 units per minute

The layout of the machines on the factory floor are shown in Figure 19.2 below:

In this case the productive capacity of the line will be limited to 180 units per minute which is as much as the three B-type machines can cope with. There will be an eventual pile-up of semi-processed flares behind the B machines so long as the A-type machines are fully employed. What happens if the Production Manager introduces an additional B-type machine to overcome this bottleneck? There is now a bottleneck at the A stage of the processing. Both the B and C machines are under-utilised. In sorting out this problem the Production Manager will bear in mind the relative costs incurred in running the different machines. It will generally be expedient to ensure that the more expensive machines are fully utilised.

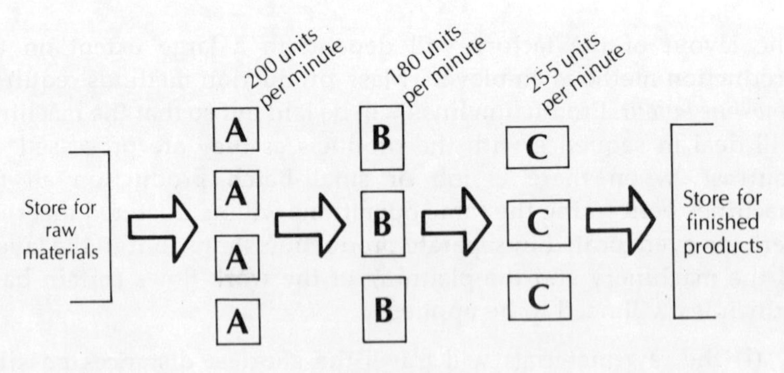

Figure 19.2

Inspection and quality control

With products made-up to a large extent of explosives and inflammable materials it is obviously essential to check the goods to ensure that they comply with minimum standards of quality – and safety. The earliest inspections might take place with regard to the inflow of raw materials. Some variation in quality is inevitable and tolerances (or margins of variation) will have to be fixed. If there are narrow tolerance levels the products will be of higher quality but they are also bound to be more expensive.

In the case of Kelwyn's products 100 per cent testing may be called for, but where less dangerous products are involved random sampling may be sufficient to retain control over the quality of the products. When goods are produced by mass-production methods the technique known as quality control is employed. Tests carried out over a period of time will establish the number and frequency of checks required to maintain the standards required. A quality-control manager may be given the responsibility for this function.

Case study – The New Product

The Chief Designer has completed his work on the new set-piece firework displays and the Production Manager of Kelwyn Fireworks, Brian Davies, has the task of putting the new product into production. The Sales Director, David Jessop, left for a short European tour last Friday and his recently appointed Personal Assistant, Julie Grant, found the following memorandum in her in-tray.

Kelwyn Fireworks plc
Memorandum

To Julie Grant
Personal Assistant

From David Jessop,
Sales Director
Friday

Set-piece Displays

I have a long list of potential customers lined up for the new set-pieces but they will lose interest if the delivery dates are too far ahead. I have asked Brian Davies to organise things as soon as possible, but he seems to be rather reluctant. Give him a few days and then send him a gentle but firm reminder. And try to find out why he's not as enthusiastic for the project as we are.

David Jessop.

Your tasks

1. Draft a brief reminder to the Production Manager (in the form of a memorandum) such as Julie Grant might have sent in accordance with the Sales Director's instructions (maximum 50 words).
2. Draft a memorandum such as Julie Grant might have delivered to her boss on his return, indicating possible explanations for the Production Manager's attitude to the new project (maximum 150 words).

CHAPTER 20

Economies of Scale

Large organisations have an inherent advantage compared to their smaller rivals in that they are able to achieve certain economies simply because of the large scale of their operations. It is a case of 'To him that hath shall be given'. The essence of the matter is that the overheads related to a larger output can be spread further. If this happens the cost per unit of production can be lowered, theoretically at least, for the benefit of the business proprietors (in the form of increased profits), the workers (in the form of increased wages), and the public (in the form of lower prices).

Another way of describing the phenomenon is to distinguish between fixed and variable costs. Costs of items such as building, plant and equipment are regarded as fixed, in the sense that the expenditure does not vary with differing levels of production. By contrast, other costs such as wages and purchases of raw materials vary with output – higher output being associated with more working hours and a greater consumption of raw materials. The result is that successive increases in the level of production are accompanied by falling average costs.

The economies are many and varied. A sample is given below:

(1) *Technological advantages*
More money can be spent on the most sophisticated machinery which will be fully utilised in the larger organisation. Similarly, specialists and top-line managers can be employed and fully extended. Any money spent on research or design can be spread over the large number of units produced, lessening the burden of these programmes.

(2) *Financial advantages*
The large organisation will be better known than the small one, and providing it enjoys a good reputation it will represent a more acceptable channel of investment for members of the public. The practical effect will be that the large organisation will be able to issue debentures at a comparatively low rate of interest, ask higher prices

for its shares and vie for competitive terms for loans from the banking fraternity.

(3) *Diminished risk*
A smaller organisation may have to limit its field of operations – according to the availability of capital. By contrast, its larger counterpart will be able to spread its risk by diversifying its operations – possibly to the point where risk disappears. In the case of the largest multinational corporations they may be involved in so many industries, in so many geographical areas, that when there is a decline in one sector there is an automatic expansion in another.

Of course a point is reached where the size of the business becomes so large that it becomes too unwieldy to manage, but this problem can be largely overcome by setting up a series of subsidiary companies which remain under the control of the holding company, but which are managed on a day-to-day basis by a separate managerial unit.

Here are some practical examples of the sort of economies which can be achieved:

(1) An aircraft corporation in the USA operates on a much larger scale than one of its British rivals. A new military aircraft is produced by both companies in response to a change in defence requirements. The prototype in each case costs about the same, let us say £400 million. Subsequent aircraft could be produced at, say £5 million each. Suppose the American company receives an order from the USAAF for 1000 of the new planes, while the British company receives an order from the RAF for 100 of its aircraft. If these are the only orders received by the respective aircraft-makers, what price would the American and British firms need to charge for their aircraft in order to break even? (Work it out individually – but compare results.)

(2) A firm in Northampton manufactures shoes. They produce some 20 000 pairs a week, and have recently begun to turn out a particularly attractive line in ladies' fashion shoes. In the course of one morning the Sales Manager deals with two customers, the first of whom agrees to buy 1000 pairs of the new shoes. It is a modest order and the price is fixed at the normal manufacturer's price. The second customer represents a large retail chain and offers to buy 5000 pairs of the new shoes every week for the next six months – if he can have them at a special price, 25 per cent lower than the normal price. The Sales Manager consults the Chief Executive and the price is agreed. What effect do you think this would have on the prices quoted in the respective stores which offer the shoes to the public?

(3) A clothing manufacturer in Rochester has concentrated his

production on denims, but sales are disappointing. He does some private market research and finds the main reason that his denims are not sought after is that a big international rival is advertising extensively on television, and young customers want to buy the denims with the well-publicised brand-name. He makes some inquiries and finds that the cost of advertising, if sustained, would put the retail price of his denims above those of his international rival. What do you think he should do?

Questions for the group to discuss

Since the larger business units have these inevitable advantages, will the smaller firms go out of business completely? Would that be a good or a bad thing to happen, from a consumer's point of view?

Case study – Small Cogs

Jonathan Kilby usually agrees with his girl friend Carol Marshall, but recently they were heard to be disagreeing quite strongly. The argument was about the sort of jobs they were going after. They are both students of North Wensleydale Technical College. They did very well in their recent examinations (in fact Carol obtained a distinction), but whereas he is determined to join the ranks of a certain internationally famous oil company, Carol is equally determined to find work in a smaller organisation. Apparently the disagreement flared up in the college canteen, and according to some of their class-mates the conversation went something like this:

Jon: Everyone knows a big company pays higher salaries. They can afford to, can't they?

Carol: And you're a very small cog in a very large wheel! I know someone who has been working in that sort of company for seven years. They didn't even know the name of a single director! It's all too impersonal for me!

Jon: It doesn't have to be like that, and anyway you're less likely to lose your job with a big international company! There are pension funds and sickness benefits – and better promotion prospects.

Carol: Why better promotion prospects?

Jon: Well, there are more jobs for top executives available in a big company – it's obvious.

Carol: And it's obvious that working for a smaller concern you would get more variety in your work – it would be more interesting.

Jon: Well, my uncle worked for a small furniture maker for twenty years. He thought he was going to be made works manager. He'd really earned it. And then the boss brought in his son – twenty years old – and my uncle had to start taking orders from him!

What do you think of their ideas? Which of them do you support? Do you think a large organisation would tend to be more impersonal than a small one? Why?

CHAPTER 21

Marketing

The marketing function is concerned with anticipating consumer demand for a product or service and then taking the necessary action to satisfy the needs which have been identified, the operations being conducted at a profit to the firm. The problem for any business is that the markets for goods and services are constantly changing. The advent of the contraceptive pill has led to a fall in the in birth-rate throughout the western world. All sorts of markets have been decimated as a result. Fewer prams and children's toys and books are now required. At the other end of the spectrum improved medical facilities have lengthened the lives of our people. The fall in death-rates augurs well for the providers of hearing-aids and comforts for the elderly. But it is not only demographic factors such as these which count. Spending power, or aggregate demand as the economists call it, represents another dimension to the market. If people have more money to spend the potential market has expanded. This could be the case where, for example, the Chancellor of the Exchequer reduces the amount of taxes payable. The USA is not only important as an export market for British businessmen because there are over 200 million inhabitants; the USA also happens to be one of the richest countries in the world.

Not so long ago the market for cigarettes seemed assured. More cigarettes were smoked each year. Then smoking tobacco in the form of cigarettes was associated with lung cancer and many other diseases. Prospects for further growth evaporated. Attitudes are ever-changing. Earrings are for females only. Until a famous pop star appears on television with a ring in his ear. Young men suddenly appear everywhere with rings in their ears.

Marketing is based on the hypothesis that all products have a life-cycle. They are introduced. With encouragement they begin to sell. With luck they begin to sell well. The sales reach a peak and may stabilise for a period, but eventually sales start to decline. Unless new products can be developed the business will fail. One way to overcome the problem of falling sales is to pursue a policy of diversification which, in marketing terms, involves introducing new products into existing markets or finding new markets for existing products.

The effect of introducing a new product

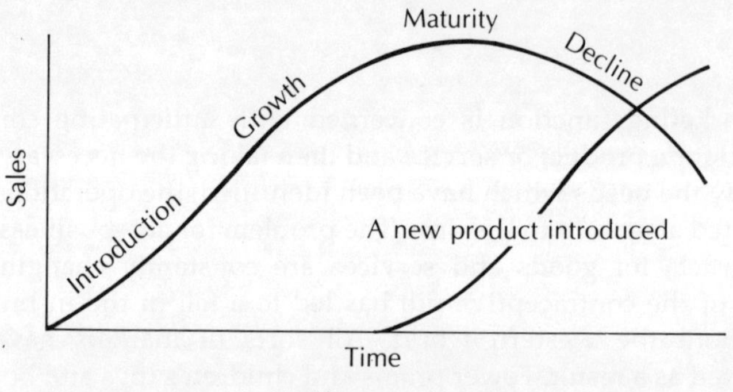

Figure 21.1

In Chapter 19 we read about Kelwyn's new set-piece fireworks. We might glimpse the nature of the product life-cycle through such an example. The people who buy the product for their wedding anniversaries, children's birthday parties, Guy Fawkes celebrations, etc., could be classified according to the stages in the cycle and to their attitudes when they buy the fireworks.

Stage	*Customer-type*	*Attitude*
Introduction	trend-setter	'I'll be the first one with this!'
Growth	followers	'We mustn't get left behind ...'
Maturity	traditionalists	'We always buy these (for our anniversaries).'
Decline	nostalgics	'We've always bought these (for the children's parties).'

Market research

The purpose of market research is to gain insights into the nature and fabric of the market for particular goods or services. The attempt to eliminate the guesswork in marketing can be based on any or all of the following techniques:

(i) *Desk research* – this involves an analysis of statistics which are already available within the organisation. This data could include information on past sales (by area and/or type of of customer), past expenditure on advertising, etc. But commonly it will be necessary to go beyond internal data in order to evaluate a market. External sources might include publications such as the *Monthly Digest of Statistics* and the latest Census of Population.

(ii) *Observation* – this entails watching customers as they make their selections in the market place.

(iii) *Experimentation* – involves testing customers' reactions by offering a similar product or service (perhaps even an identical one) in a small section of the market.

(iv) *Sample surveys* – aimed at discovering either facts or predilections (likes and dislikes). Fact-finding questions are asked such as 'What brand of coffee do you buy?' and 'How much coffee have you bought in the last seven days?' By contrast, 'Why didn't you buy Brand X?' is a question related to motivation.

When there is a national election, public opinion polls predict how much support each of the political parties can expect. Although only a comparatively small number of people's opinions are sought the predictions can be quite accurate. The same principle is utilised by market researchers to gauge the support which might be expected for the proposed goods or services. In a random sample each individual in a population has an equal chance of being selected for questioning while for a stratified sample the population is divided into appropriate segments before the random selections are made. So if it is known that 20 per cent of the total population under review are over the age of 60, then the sample is devised so that 20 per cent of the respondents are in this category.

The marketing mix

Once a market has been identified as a worthwhile target for the firm's goods or services the vital marketing plan can be developed. The plan will need to answer questions such as:

(a) What are the specifications for the product which is going to be sold?
(b) What price is it going to be offered at?

(c) How is it going to be sold? Through shops? By mail order?
(d) How is the launch going to be publicised?

In broad terms the plan can be seen as a sort of recipe. This is what is required if we are to produce the goods or services to satisfy the needs we have identified. Figure 21.2 indicates the basic variables/ingredients in the mix:

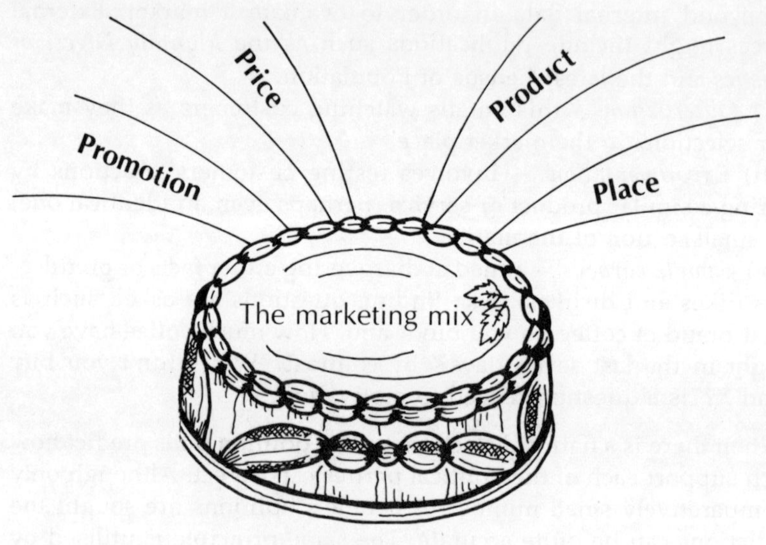

Figure 21.2

(a) *Product* – the better the quality the easier it is to sell – but the higher the costs of production the higher the price to be charged if a profit is going to be made.

(b) *Price* – almost anything can be sold if the price is low enough – but the project has to cover its costs and emerge as profitable – pricing policies also have to be related to those of competitors.

(c) *Place* – if outsiders (stores and shops, etc.) are going to be selling the product they will need to be suitably motivated – but incentives for them in the form of larger discounts mean lower revenues for the firm.

(d) *Promotion* – if the firm have something to sell it is vital they make the product known to those who are likely to buy it – but advertising is expensive and has to be cost-effective as do free competitions and attractive packaging.

Market share

The firm will be looking for substantial revenue from the sale of its products, but the problem has two dimensions. If sales increase from £2 million to £2.4 million during the course of a year the 20 per cent increase would seem to be a cause for self-congratulation as far as the marketing team is concerned. Yet during that period the market could have increased by much more than 20 per cent in which case the team should be asking themselves what is going wrong. Consider the situation represented by these figures:

Sales of Fireworks in the UK
(by total sales and shares of market)

	This year		Last year	
	£ million	%age of market	£ million	%age of market
X Ltd (market leader)	7.33	49	4.86	49
Y Ltd	3.95	26	2.09	21
Kelwyn Fireworks Plc	2.40	16	2.00	20
Other firms	1.32	9	1.05	10
Total sales for year	15.00	100	10.00	100

The adverse trend for Kelwyn Fireworks can be seen by reference to Figure 21.3. You are invited to draw in the shares of the market for the other companies.

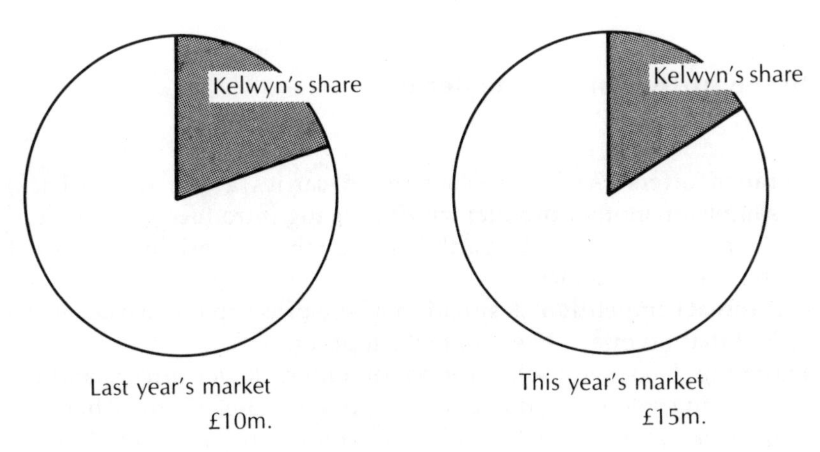

Figure 21.3

International marketing

Overseas markets have grown in line with higher standards of living in many parts of the world oft-times as a result of oil revenues. The world population explosion has also provided exporters with an extended market though the potential demand has to be backed by purchasing power before it can be converted to effective demand. This is particularly true with regard to many of the sophisticated western products.

Pros and cons of marketing overseas

Pros	*Cons*
(i) An opportunity to increase sales even though the domestic market is stagnant or shrinking.	(i) A lack of knowledge of the market may lead to over-dependence.
(ii) Possibility of charging different prices in the overseas market.	(ii) Products/services will probably need to be adapted for different tastes and climates, etc.
(iii) The chance to benefit from economies of scale achieved through higher levels of output/sales.	(iii) Costs of transport, insurance and documentation.
(iv) Possibility of obtaining government advice and financial backing.	(iv) Possible burden of tariffs and taxes.
	(v) Political and economic uncertainties in less-stable countries.
	(vi) Problems of obtaining financial settlement.
	(vii) Language and cultural barriers to be overcome.

Some further marketing terms

Branded offers: An established brand carries a free (piggy-back) sample of another product which is being introduced. The cost of the free samples will be partly offset by the increase in the sales of the existing product.

Cut-throat competition: A situation where prices in the market are so low that no one is likely to make a profit.

Dumping: Goods are sold overseas at a much lower price than they are being sold in the home country, possibly below cost where the overseas sales are not required to contribute to the recovery of overhead costs.

Ex-works price: The basic price of a product at the point of manufacture, excluding delivery and insurance.
Franchising: An entrepreneur sets up a business using the names and operating procedures of an existing business. Wimpy Bars and many self-service launderettes are operated under franchise agreements.
Lead time: The time-lag between receipt of an order and its completion. Minimised by the use of staff called progress chasers on the factory floor.
Mailing list: A classified list of names and addresses for use in mailing shots. Can either be purchased or built up from the firm's own records.
Market penetration: The extent to which the firm has succeeded in tapping the potential market.
Market segmentation: The total market is divided into sections according to varied features of the population. For example, old-age pensioners, graduates or one-parent families. Different marketing approaches may be adopted for each of the segments.
Merchandising: The selling effort is concentrated at the point of sale. The sales are made through eye-catching displays, special offers and especially attractive packaging, etc.
Penetration pricing: A lower pricing policy is pursued in order to make inroads into an existing market.
Sale or return: The retailer only pays for the goods that have been sold. The retailer is credited with the value of the goods returned to the supplier.

Case study – Male Scent

A ladies' magazine has recently conducted a survey among its readers and discovered that nine out of ten women are happy for their partners to use after-shave, but only one-third of them approve of men wearing perfume. (*Woman*, 6 August 1983.)

It seems a logical progression. First we are convinced that the smell of the human body is odious. We are encouraged to buy deodorants to kill the smell. Then we are convinced that even the huskiest of men should smell 'nice'. They are persuaded – perhaps with a degree of reluctance – to accept scented deodorants. And now a firm in the USA, in conjunction with a famous French *parfumeur*, is on the point of launching on to the world market a straight perfume for males. The ladies have their *Chanel No. 5*. The men will have their ...; well, we shall have to wait to see what it is going to be called.

Whether the idea is amusing or not, it is likely to be a profitable venture. There are four basic reasons for this:

(1) the ingredients are comparatively cheap.
(2) The American firm has virtually cornered the supplies of the less-common ingredients.
(3) In a sample of 143 women, 61 per cent said they found the scent 'rather pleasant', 32 per cent found it 'very pleasant indeed', and only 2 per cent thought it was 'rather unpleasant' or 'very unpleasant'.
(4) In a similar sample of younger males (aged 17 to 25), over one-half indicated that they would purchase the product if the price was reasonable.

There has been a considerable amount of research conducted by the American company, and these research costs will have to be recouped when the product is marketed. However, once these costs have been recovered, the costs of production are likely to be insignificant.

Your task

As a group you are asked to consider the following questions and answer them collectively:

(1) What name might the product be marketed under? Which of the names suggested do you favour?
(2) Do you think the scent will need to be marketed under different names in the different markets? The product is likely to be sold in Great Britain, the USA, France and West Germany.
(3) How would you suggest the necessary publicity campaign be mounted?
(4) Would you favour fixing the price low to aim at a mass market, or would you make the product exclusive and expensive?
(5) Do you think products like these are a waste of economic resources, or can they be justified? Could the same arguments be used for lipstick – or cocoa?

CHAPTER 22

Advertising

Here are two contrasting views on the role of advertising as it affects our daily lives. Which of the views do you prefer?

Against advertising

An enormous sum of money is spent every day on advertising. It is unproductive. If the money were not dissipated, the cost of the goods to the consumers could be substantially reduced. Work out how much is spent by television advertisers on 'commercial breaks' during any single evening and you will begin to appreciate the sums involved. And this is just one advertising medium! Somebody has to foot the bill, and that somebody is you – and I – through higher prices.

In normal circumstances the consumer is entitled to expect that healthy competition will keep down the prices of the goods he buys, but when a firm spends large sums on advertising it may be a device to restrict the entry of competitors into the market. The heavy expenditure a competitor would have to incur to gain a share of the market acts as an effective deterrent.

By their very nature advertisements are misleading. They play on our weaknesses, our susceptibilities, our egos and our vanities. They create a demand which would not otherwise exist. One London tobacconist and confectioner keeps his shop open in the evenings and watches television in between serving customers. Invariably he finds that within a few minutes of an advertisement appearing on the screen, people come in and ask for the particular line of chocolates or sweets advertised.

The dangers are indicated by some of the research which has been carried out on subliminal advertising. There is just one frame in a roll of movie film with, say, the word 'coffee' on it. This flashes on to the screen during a normal programme. It appears for such a small fraction of a second that it registers only in the viewer's subconscious. As a result some of the people subjected to the treatment decide to make themselves a cup of coffee – without having any idea as to why they want a coffee at that particular time. No wonder this invidious form of brain-washing has been banned! Yet there are more ways than one of skinning a cat, so they say. Have you ever wondered why some television advertisements are repeated over and over again during the course of the same evening? It may irritate, but it is certainly not accidental.

Would the world not be a better place without glaring posters fouling the landscape – without trivial jingles and film snippets distracting us during a serious television programme – without newspapers and magazines more than half-filled with specious advertisements? Is advertising not the art of persuading someone to buy something he does not really want? Is it not, at best, wasteful of economic resources, and at its worst unethical to the point of dishonesty?

(Note that under the Trade Descriptions Acts, 1968 and 1972, it is an offence for a trader to make untrue statements about his goods, services or prices.)

For advertising

Society in general and the consumer in particular benefit considerably – either directly or indirectly – as a result of advertising. The typical manufacturer has to assess constantly the nature and extent of the consumers' needs, and generate production accordingly. If he anticipates a greater need than there actually is, he can, through advertising, persuade the market to 'soak up' the surplus goods that have been produced. He can look on advertising as a sort of insurance policy – protecting him against his own too optimistic forecasts. If, as a result, he tends to overproduce rather than underproduce, who benefits? There are more goods than there would otherwise be – and there are more jobs. Advertising plays the role of an industrial lubricant.

Perhaps more important than the confidence it can give to the manufacturer is the stability that advertising helps to bring to the industrial scene. As demand for a product sags, it can be stimulated through advertising. This allows stocks to be stabilised, the workforce to be stabilised – and even prices to be stabilised. Without the possibility of advertising, work-forces would have to be laid off at the first sign of flagging sales. Alternatively, prices would have to be lowered – that would be acceptable to the consumer – but raised as sales picked up again. Running an industrial concern with advertising ruled out would be like driving a car without an accelerator.

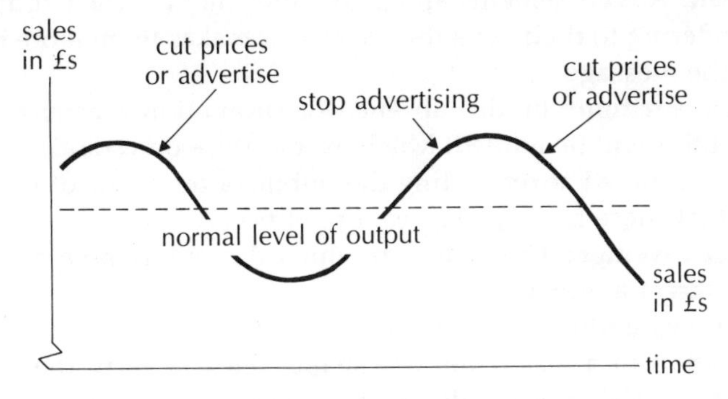

Figure 22.1

Commercial television is entirely dependent upon revenue from advertising, and national newspapers derive approximately half their revenue from advertising – either through classified advertisements or displays. Many newspapers and magazines would not be financially viable if advertising revenues were cut off.

Advertising can also be seen as a means of communication between those with goods or services to sell and those who might benefit from those goods or services. There are many forms of advertising, not least of which are window-displays, catalogues and employment agencies. Who says society would be better off without these devices?

Questions for the group to consider

(1) What restrictions, if any, would you impose on advertising?
(2) Do any of you have criticisms or grievances regarding specific advertisements or methods employed by advertisers?

Some advertising terms

Artwork: This refers to the pictorial or illustrative part of an advertisement.

Drip advertising campaign: A continuous programme of advertising over an extended period, say twelve months.

Dry-run: A rehearsal for a tv/video presentation where action, lines and cues, etc., are practised.

Ego bait: Advertisements aimed at flattering the target audience. By pandering to their egos the advertiser makes them more receptive to the message.

Market attrition: In the absence of promotional activities brand loyalties will be eroded. Much expenditure on established brands will be aimed at reminding the public of the name of the product so that these memory lapses do not occur.

Market coverage: The extent to which the programme has reached the target audience.

Media evaluation: A consideration of alternatives prior to the selection of a magazine, newspaper, etc., to carry the advertisement(s). The choice will be based on cost-effectiveness.

Target audience: The section of the population to whom the advertisement is intended to appeal. One of the groupings is socio-economic as shown below.

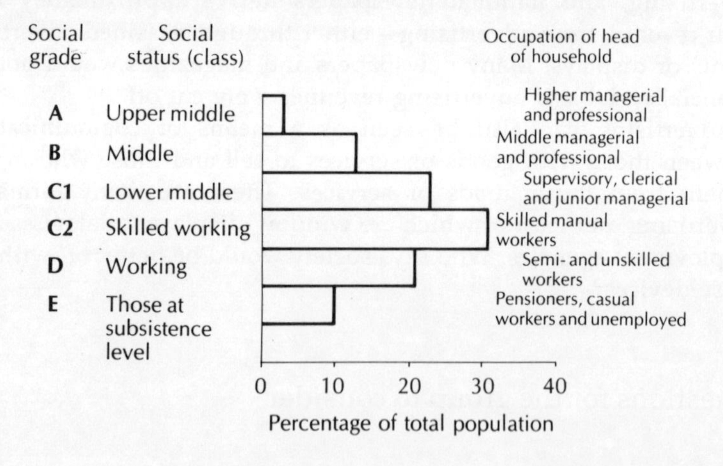

Figure 22.2

World brands: The advent of satellite and cable TV has opened up possibilities for international marketing companies to advertise throughout Europe and the world, if required, with a single commercial. This development is likely to be aided by a shared culture emerging from TV series and cinema films with world-wide appeal. Firms like Coca-Cola, McDonald's and Philip Morris (with Marlboro cigarettes) have already used this technique with success.

Case study – The Television Production

A certain company in North London produces low-priced furniture and it has now developed a new range of inexpensive kitchen equipment. The chief merit of the new line is that the table and four stools stack away in a very small space (130 cm. × 40 cm. × 30 cm.). Another feature is the range of colours. The units are produced in six different colours – including white. All the colours are very bright. The idea is that the units will fit into the smallest kitchen and pack away easily when not in use.

The company is now planning to go into large-scale production and is contemplating advertising on television in order to stimulate sufficient demand for the product. A Canadian advertising agency, Prince Pemberton Publicity, has proposed three films which might be used. Each would last between forty and forty-five seconds.

Film 1
An attractive housewife would be shown with her cheerful husband and two young children eating breakfast. Then there would be a shot of her – after the family had gone off to school and work – disassembling the unit and stacking it away. This would be done in front of an envious neighbour who would say things like 'But it's so easy to stack. It's so light. Could I get it in blue to match my decorations?'

The final shot would be of the housewife sitting on the compressed unit – singing a catchy advertising jingle.

Film 2
The second suggestion would involve the use of a well-known family of cartoon characters and the story of Goldilocks and the three bears. The film starts with Goldilocks (a real little girl) finding the house in the woods. She finds the porridge – and admires the table and chairs before she goes upstairs to bed.

Then the bears come in. They go to the porridge. Father Bear says what a clever fellow he was to suggest buying this fantastic kitchen unit. Mother Bear says how clever she is to be able to pack it away so quickly.

'You're not clever to do that,' says the Baby Bear, 'even a child – I mean even a baby bear can do it.'

Goldilocks, who has been looking through the key-hole, says she is going to tell her mummy and daddy about it when she gets home. They all join hands around the table and sing the jingle.

Film 3
In the third offering by the agency the new product would be demonstrated by one of the workers from the factory. Someone who was reasonably photogenic and clearly spoken would have to be chosen. Dressed in overalls he would give a straightforward and serious demonstration of the unit. Instead of the jingle at the finish there would be a shot of a flustered mother with her family in an overcrowded kitchen saying 'That's what we could do with.'

The advertising agency point out that it would be expensive to produce three films, so, rather than exceed the budgeted amount, just one of the ideas has to be selected.

Which of the three films do you think would make the most impact on potential customers? Why? And at what time of the day and with which sort of programme would the advertisement be most effective?

It has been agreed that the manufacturer's name, Schumaker Timber Products Ltd, is not suitable to include in the advertisement, but an attractive name is required for the product to be effectively marketed. The Marketing Manager favours the Packaway Unit, and the agency has offered two other alternatives:

(1) the Space Saver; or
(2) the Space Module.

Which of the names for the product do you prefer? Can you think of any other possible names for the product?

When you have chosen the best name for the product, can you work together on composing a two-line jingle which the agency would be able to set to music? The Marketing Manager has proposed

> You'll bless the day
> You bought your Packaway.

Can you do better?

Written work

Nanette Starkey, the furniture company's Marketing Manager has asked you, as her personal assistant, for your ideas. Draft her a brief memorandum of about 2/300 words.

CHAPTER 23

Distribution

So long as there is a high degree of specialisation in our society so that groups of us produce certain goods leaving others to satisfy our totality of wants, there is an inevitably complex pattern of distribution between manufacturers and consumers. Between the producers and the market-place there will be a collection of bankers and shopkeepers, carriers and wholesalers, insurance companies and advertisers. A study of distribution will include packaging, branding, store layout and changing patterns of consumption. However, here we shall concentrate on the retailing and wholesaling functions, leaving an examination of transport systems until the next chapter.

There are three basic channels of distribution:

1. Manufacturer to retailer to consumer

The definition of a retailer is someone who sells small quantities of goods at a time, the goods not being for resale. In other words the retailer, who will usually be a shopkeeper, is the last link in the distribution chain before the goods reach the consumer. When retailers are operating on a sufficiently large scale, however, they may be able to purchase goods directly from the manufacturers. Bulk buying will reduce their unit costs and this will allow them to charge lower prices to their customers. From the manufacturers' point of view the direct contact with their customers (the retailers) give them a better picture of the market and allow them to adjust their products and policies to the changing markets.

2. Manufacturer directly to consumer

Direct selling is another way of avoiding the sharing of profits with the wholesaler (middleman). In this case the manufacturer has direct contact with the consumers. Reactions to advertising programmes, or price and quality changes can be gauged first-hand. Manufacturers may acquire their own chains of shops. They will sell a variety of goods but will obviously press for the sale of their own brands. If the manufacturers do not own their own retail outlets they will depend on advertising through newspapers and magazines or (less frequently) door-to-door selling.

3. Manufacturer to wholesaler to retailer to consumer

The wholesaler becomes an intermediary in this, the traditional pattern of distribution. They obtain goods from many different manufacturers and sell them to a multitude of retail outlets in their catchment areas. The effect of mediation by the wholesaler is shown in the diagrams below:

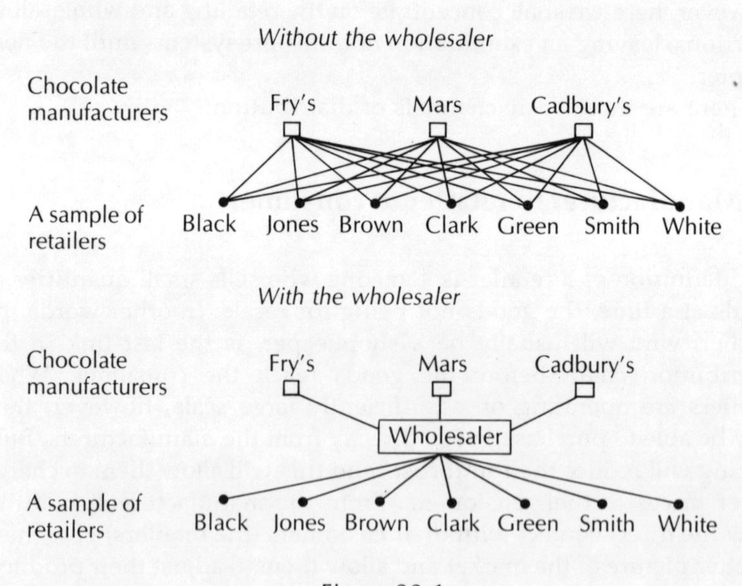

Figure 23.1

The wholesaler's functions

(a) To keep stocks, allowing the retailers to replenish at will and offering a choice and range of products.

(b) To arrange imports from abroad, dealing with documentation, currency problems, etc.

(c) To carry out certain specialised function such as

   (i) the blending of tea,
   (ii) the refining of sugar, and
   (iii) the grading of commodities such as wool and wheat.

(d) To give advice and information in relation to

   (i) new products and improvements in existing ones,
   (ii) changes in tastes and fashions, and
   (iii) complaints.

(e) To provide a delivery service where required, though in recent years cash-and-carry warehouses have been introduced which offer price reductions for retailers prepared to collect their own merchandise.

(f) To buy in bulk from producers and sell comparatively small quantities to retailers. This function is sometimes described as 'breaking bulk'.

The retailer's functions

(a) To keep small quantities of a wide variety of goods, thus giving the consumer as much choice as possible.

(b) To provide a convenient pick-up point for the customers, particularly where there is a parade (or cluster) of shops as in a typical high street.

(c) To offer information and advice to customers.

(d) To provide a feedback of consumer responses to the wholesalers and manufacturers.

Types of retail outlets

Type	*Definition*	*Features*
Department stores e.g. Harrods, Selfridges	A large shop set out in different departments, each specialising in a particular range, e.g. ladies' fashion, cosmetics, toys and games. Each department's performance separately assessed.	Personal service offered by assistants. Credit facilities. A wide range of amenities and services, e.g. restaurant and hairdressing salon. Size of store allows stock to be held in depth.

Type	*Definition*	*Features*
Multiple stores, e.g. Dorothy Perkins (lingerie), Hepworths (men's wear), Dolcis (shoes)	At least ten branches under central control. Selling a narrow range of merchandise. May be local or national. Shopfronts, internal layouts and displays are standardised.	Bulk purchasing and uniform pricing policies which can limit the range of discretions available to branch managers. Sell their own brands generally. Scale of operations will allow them to advertise on radio/television and/or in newspapers and magazines.
Variety chain stores, e.g. Boots, Woolworths, British Home Stores	Hybrid. Between the multiple and department store. Easily recognisable shopfronts. A wide variety of goods on offer. Internal layouts tend to be standardised. Customers left to select for themselves and encouraged to 'walk the floor'.	Customers know what to expect whether the store is in London or Newcastle. Bulk purchasing allows keener pricing. Quick turnover of stocks. Prime locations in shopping centres.
Supermarkets, e.g. Tesco, Sainsbury, International Stores	Large shops where customers are expected to serve themselves (self-service). Goods are paid for at check-outs. Full range of foodstuffs for family's weekly shopping. Layout of store designed to encourage 'impulse' buying. Often multiples.	Bulk purchasing allows keen pricing. Some items are often sold at a loss to encourage the public to come into the store (loss leaders). Customers can take their time over selection. Rather impersonal. Look for a high through-flow of customers. Danger of bottlenecks at check-outs at peak periods.
Hypermarkets	Extra large stores. Mass distribution at low competitive prices. Serves car-owning customers. Merchandise includes consumer durables. On town outskirts rather than city centres. Self-service.	Lower property outgoings plus bulk purchasing allows keen pricing. Free car parking usual. Cash-and-carry expected.
Discount stores, e.g. Comet, Supreme	Reduces the prices of all goods and does not rely on a loss-leader policy on selected items. Consumer durables such as television receivers and freezers.	Concentration on a limited range of products so as to maximise price reductions through bulk buying. Widespread press advertising.
The independents	Shops owned by small traders. The trader usually has just the one shop.	Limited capital. Small turnover. Owners need a variety of skills and resources, but can enjoy a personal relationship with their customers. Flexible opening hours. More flexible policies generally. Difficulty found in matching the prices of larger units able to buy in bulk.

Type	*Definition*	*Features*
Voluntary groups, e.g. V. G., Spar	Wholesalers combined with retailers to form a group. The independent retains control of his business while gaining some of the benefits of large-scale operations. Shops identified by group logos.	Group offer advice and finance to their members. Advertising for the group to benefit all the members' shops. Loss leaders can be introduced for the group. Wholesalers benefit from a 'captive market'.
Mail-order houses, e.g. Peter Craig, Burlington	Based on direct-mail and press advertising. Catalogues are often used by the larger firms. The Catalogue Houses specialise in footwear, clothing and household goods, and offer credit terms.	Shopping from home. Normally possible to return if dissatisfied. Warehouses can be sited out of towns. Cheaper rents and costs of administration.

A task for you

Working in twos or threes, complete the list above for the following types of outlet:

(i) markets (open or covered),
(ii) automatic vending machines,
(iii) mobile shops,
(iv) party selling,
(v) door-to-door selling.

Modern trends

Fashions and tastes are constantly changing, and producers of goods and providers of services have to adapt their policies accordingly. In the early part of the century London was lit by gaslight. Gas mantles (through which the flames burn) were in great demand. That market has now disappeared. In the 1930s rayon stockings were in vogue. Today they are unheard of. A couple of decades ago non-electric adding machines were to be found in most offices. They are already museum pieces.

One example of the sort of change which is occurring in the pattern of distribution – in this case with regard to men's wear – can be glimpsed from the following diagrams.

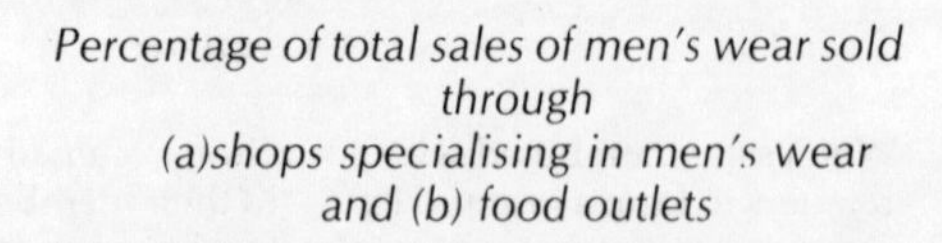

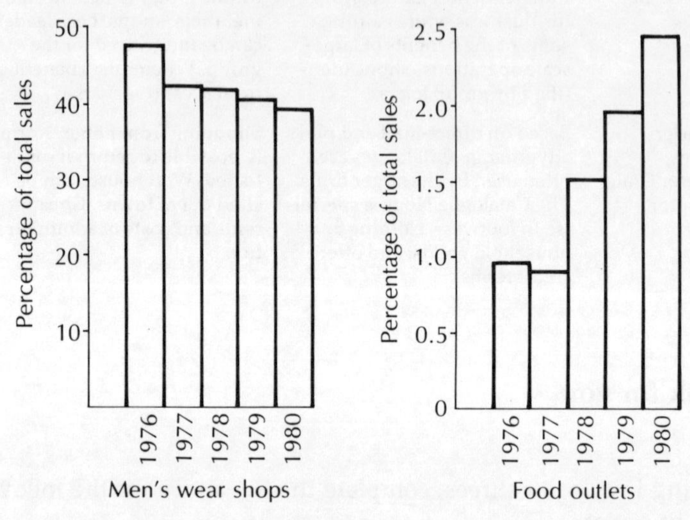

SOURCE: *The Menswear Report 1982;* London, Euromonitor Publications.

Figure 23.2

Another task

After a brief study of these bar charts, can you make six statements about the trends emerging? For example, sales of men's wear through food outlets tripled between 1977 and 1980.

It is not only the channels of distribution which are subject to change. Fashions can be expected to change as will the sizes of the different markets. A craze for jogging among middle-aged men is likely to bring with it an upsurge in demand for track-suits from those who have recently discarded them. While, as the *Menswear Report* points out, because of the drop in the birth-rate, men in the 15- to 25-year-old age-group who in 1980 formed 16.5 per cent of the male population will have dwindled to 13 per cent by the year 2001 according to present estimates. One can see the likely effects of this contraction on the sale of jeans, sportwear and T-shirts, among other things.

Unemployment is another factor to be brought into account. To the extent this affects younger people their spending power will be reduced. In the words of the report, 'the problems of targeting a market of consumers with increasing spending power will be an important consideration in planning retail marketing policies'.

It seems that in distribution generally, at a time when profit margins are being squeezed, entrepreneurs will increasingly sell merchandise which brings them a profit regardless of the traditional boundaries. So we find Tesco, the famed food supermarket, branching out into clothing and toys, and Boots, the famed chemists, branching out into children's clothing, pet foods and equipment, records, home computers and typewriters.

The advent of the microchip will obviously affect distribution in a variety of ways. Stock levels will be controlled more effectively and the through-flow of customers at check-outs will be speeded up through the use of price sensor devices. Commonplace already on the supermarket shelves are bar codes (see example below). These are used both at the point of sale and in warehouse and stockroom situations. Numeric data are represented by a series of bars of varying thickness and at varying distances apart.

An example of a bar code device as used in a food supermarket.

The bars are read by scanning the code with a light pen which transforms the data back into numeric form. Later ideas used by firms such as Debenhams and the John Lewis Partnership include invisible magnetically encoded stripes and data can be fed back immediately to a central stock-control point (at the distant head office). It is the cost of such systems rather than technical limitations which inhibit further development.

Dr G. T. Jones's explanation of what happens at Sainsbury's food stores gives a hint as to the direction technology is taking in the distribution industry:

> The data capture terminal, either mounted on a trolley or carried on a shoulder strap is taken round the store by an operator each evening after trading. Each stock line has an associated bar coded tag mounted on the shelf beside it. The operators note which lines are required for reordering and pass the Plessey light pen over the appropriate bar code. They then key in across the keyboard of the terminal how many cases of that line are required. The terminal records on its tape cassette all the necessary information.... On average each shop will place 1000

> orders per night. The data terminal is then linked to a transmitter and the information from the tape cassette is transmitted to Head Office.... The order information can then be processed by the computers, and picking lists transmitted to the distribution depots by 9.30 in the evening.... It has proved to be an enormous success and the Sainsbury management claims that it is the most significant innovation that has been made by Sainsbury's in its entire history....

Data Capture in the Retail Environment, Manchester, National Computer Centre Publications, 1977.

Some distribution terms

After-sales service: A repair and maintenance service provided by the retailer. For purchasers generally the choice is often between after-sales service or no after-sales service but a lower price for the goods.

Brands: A brand is a name under which a manufacturer sells goods. Many retailers are now selling goods using their own brands, e.g. Finefare, Waitrose, Co-op, etc. Marks & Spencer use the 'St Michael' brand for their merchandise.

Convenience foods: These are prepacked foodstuffs which require a minimum of preparation before they are eaten. They find favour particularly with working parents.

Impulse buying: Certain merchandise such as ice cream and cheaper jewellery are not usually planned purchases. They are purchased on the spur of the moment. Note the chocolates and sweets at the check-outs in supermarkets.

Leakage: Loss of merchandise through staff dishonesty (pilfering), thefts by the public (shoplifting) and stock deterioration.

Precinct: A specially designed shopping area for pedestrians, cars being excluded.

Recommended resale price: This is a guideline price stated by the manufacturer. Discounts and reductions offered by retailers are based on this price.

Slow-moving stock: Some stocks will not be sold easily. The problem might be an unrealistic price, poor display, unsatisfactory quality or seasonal demand.

Stocktaking: The periodic counting of goods on the shelves or in the stockroom for accounting purposes.

Trading stamps: Stamps are offered in accordance with the value of purchases and can be exchanged for cash or goods from the issuing company at a later date. Is seen as a sort of bonus for the purchaser and might thus stimulate sales.

Case study – Sunday Trading

This is a role-playing exercise and you are asked to play the part of members of the Union of Shop, Distributive and Allied Workers. At a recent meeting of your branch the membership were strongly against Sunday trading, but a discussion has been going on through the letter columns in the local paper. The editor has now offered to print two short articles putting forward the opposing views. What arguments do you think should be put forward by the union branch? What arguments do you think might be put forward by the other side? The branch secretary has particularly asked you to consider this point so that the opposition's 'guns' might be 'spiked' as far as possible in the union article.

When you have completed your discussion you are asked to individually draft a 200 – 300-word article such as might be submitted to the newspaper editor. Proof-read each other's articles before submitting them to your tutor for assessment. Use a typewriter where possible.

To add fuel to your discussion you might be interested in some of the views expressed in an article on Sunday trading in the magazine *Men's Wear*, 3 February 1983:

Andrew Noble – Managing Director of Debenhams Stores:

> The retail market will not expand simply because the opening hours of shops increases.... Wages will certainly rise, probably as much as 16 per cent, yet retailers will see no corresponding increase in their market shares.... Opening on Sundays will mean longer hours for our employees increasing the unattractiveness of retailing as an occupation. Either higher wages would be needed as compensation or standards of service would become lower....

Mr Ray Whitney – M.P. for Wycombe:

> Sunday trading would create jobs, increase demand, and would not cause prices to rise.... In the past 20 years, the amount of money spent in shops has dropped from 46 per cent to 36 per cent of people's incomes.... Retailers compete for people's time as well as their money....

CHAPTER 24

Transport

A fairly sophisticated transport system is essential in any industrialised economy. On the one hand, raw materials are taken to the factories for processing. The finished goods are carried to warehouses and shops and ultimately to the homes of the consumers. On the other hand, people are carried to and from their work-places and, increasingly in an age of micro-chips and robotic production lines, people can be expected to use additional leisure hours for holiday travel.

The role of transport in world trade can be gauged from a single example. Consider the chocolates which in various forms find favour with the majority of us. First, the Ghanaian and Nigerian farmers grow the cacao beans. The beans are sold and delivered to certain collecting points on the widest variety of ancient and modern forms of transport. Handcarts, lorries and railway wagons are utilised for the journey to the exit ports of Accra and Lagos. There they are loaded on to ocean-going ships bound for European ports such as Bristol and Rotterdam. After two or three weeks at sea the beans will be unloaded on to trains, lorries or Rhine barges and finally reach the chocolate factories. There the beans will be added to milk and sugar and the temptingly delicious chocolate will emerge. The manufactured chocolate will be sold to customers all over the world and some will even find its way back to the shops and stores of Ghana and Nigeria. The pattern of the return journey will be quite similar to the original one. Indeed, though distances and forms of transport may vary, a fairly predictable pattern emerges (see Figure 24.1).

Peak traffic

One of the problems encountered in transport systems concerns variations in demand which create overburdening at certain times and idle capacity at others. For example, buses and trains in London

A typical pattern of transport from several ports of origin to several destinations

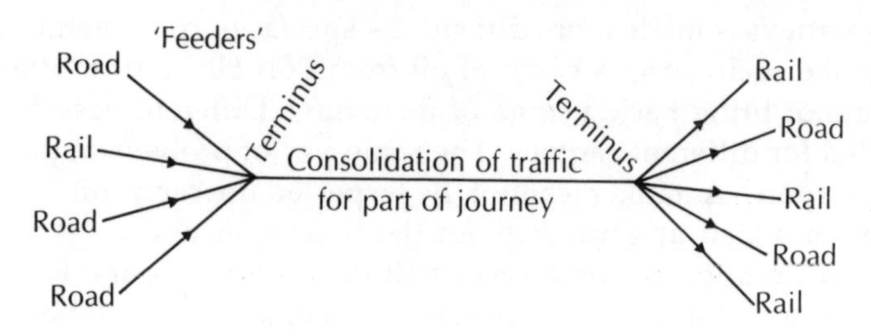

Figure 24.1

may be unable to cope with the massive flow of commuters travelling to and from work. Yet, during the rest of the day the vehicles may be running with very few passengers. Or transport requirements may be seasonal so that during the months of July and August there will be an excessive demand for coaches, while out of the peak holiday season coach operators will be obliged to lay up their vehicles and dismiss the drivers.

A number of remedies are available:

(i) Staggering the starting and finishing times of workers (flexible working hours).

(ii) Reducing fares in off-peak hours or seasons (perhaps lowering fares for senior citizens so long as they travel at appropriate times).

(iii) Operating night schedules where there is a pile-up of traffic.

(iv) In the case of goods, storage facilities could be provided at termini to stabilise traffic flows.

(v) Mechanical appliances such as cranes and fork-lifts might be employed at terminals so as to speed-up the turn-round of carrying units (vehicles).

Return loading

Janet may find it costs £3 to take a taxi from the station to her hotel. She feels that is very expensive.

'It only took ten minutes,' she says.

Yet, for the taxi driver the journey does not end at the hotel. Unless another fare can be found the trip back to the station is at the taxi operator's own expense.

This is a common problem in the transport industry. Vehicles need to return to the point of origin, unless they are 'tramps' moving from one point to another without a predictable pattern. Utilisation of return journeys is made more difficult by special-purpose vehicles so that a tanker delivering a cargo of oil from Port Harcourt to Buenos Aires cannot bring back a cargo of foodstuffs. Different vessels will be needed for different cargoes. The same sort of problem applies to road transport. A tanker cannot be expected to carry oil in one direction and load up with milk for the return journey.

A partial solution in some cases will be to offer favourable terms for 'back loads', but the basic problem remains and inevitably adds to the costs.

Containerisation

Loading and unloading goods is a time-consuming and therefore expensive element in the cost structure of the transport industry. One of the techniques devised to minimise this burden is containerisation. The containers vary in shape and size, but the most common forms are those classified by the International Standards Organisation (ISO). Containers are usually fully enclosed, with a length varying between 2 and 12 metres and both height and width of 2.4 metres. The standard containers are 6 and 12 metres. They are usually made of steel or aluminium and fully enclosed with a door opening out at one end. However, to deal with awkwardly shaped goods, some are open-topped with a fixed tarpaulin cover. Refrigerated versions are also available.

With standard units stacking becomes more efficient and less time is taken in handling and identifying consignments. Goods can also be switched from one type of vehicle to another more easily, say, from ship to train.

Containerisation reduces the cost of handling goods at transfer points and speeds up the turn-around of vehicles. The containers will give protection against the elements and should reduce losses resulting from pilferage and rough-handling.

Against the savings must be set the cost of the containers and the special lifting devices required.

Forms of transport compared (can you add to the list?)

Form	*Principal vehicles*	*Merits*	*Demerits*
1. Rail	Electric, diesel, or steam trains	(a) Can carry heavy/bulky freight or large numbers of passengers in a single haul	(a) Fixed tracks and terminals
		(b) Times of departure and arrival can be given (regular services)	(b) Tracks need to be maintained
		(c) High speeds possible	(c) Support transport normally required at terminals
2. Road	Buses, coaches, lorries, motor-cars and vans	(a) Door-to-door journeys	(a) Problems of traffic congestion in urban areas
		(b) Routes can be varied	(b) Limit to weight and bulk of freight
		(c) Operating units are smaller and less costly	(c) Road systems have to be maintained and are land-hungry
3. Sea	General cargo ships, container ships, tankers, dry bulk carriers	(a) The open sea has no fixed traffic lanes	(a) Voyages only possible between ports (deep-sea ports required for larger vessels)
		(b) Heavy and bulk cargoes can be carried	(b) High capital costs
		(c) Intercontinental trade possible	(c) The usage of specialist vessels, such as oil tankers, is restrictive.
4. Air	Airliners	(a) The fastest method of travel	(a) Not suitable for heavy/bulky freight
		(b) Can increase time available for tourists in their holiday resorts	(b) Terminals are fixed and limited in number
		(c) May be the only available method of transport for some commodities, e.g. perishables	(c) Limited services available

Modern trends

Transport is a function of prosperity so that world recession reduces the need for transport facilities in the same way that rising living standards create a greater demand for all forms of transport. With the advent of the microchip and robotic production lines we may find ourselves with more leisure time. Perhaps we can look forward to longer holidays and shorter working weeks. That would no doubt increase the demand for passenger transport of all kinds.

The revolution in information technology is also likely to make a substantial impact on transport. At one extreme, communication satellites will provide global operators with more extensive data, while at the other extreme people will find it possible to shop without leaving home, using the telephone coupled with video cassettes and/or piped television. As in other areas of business computers will increasingly allow us to organise the transport systems more efficiently and safely.

One less certain development relates to town centre traffic. For many years it has been government policy to encourage factories and offices to move away from town centres. In some cases the effect has been to create what might be described as urban wastelands and it can be argued that such relocation policies should be reversed. To the extent that this happens it will be necessary to provide the appropriate transport systems to enable the decaying town centres to be revitalised without being over-congested.

Some transport terms

Carrier: A person or firm carrying goods as a business.

Chartering: The hiring of a ship, train, aircraft, bus or motor coach for a certain period or for a particular journey/voyage.

Charter party: A contract between the person hiring the vehicle/vessel and the vehicle/vessel owner.

Ferry: A shuttle service, usually waterborne and crossing a river or channel.

Flight path: The planned track of an aircraft.

Freight: Another term for goods, particularly heavy or bulky goods.

Freightliner trains: These have low skeletal wagons to allow containers to be loaded and unloaded more quickly. Lorries can deliver the containers to the depot steadily during the course of a day and the longer trains which result reduce the unit costs of transport significantly.

Igloo: A lightweight container used for air freight. It has a tubular superstructure and a covering of fabric. It is shaped like an igloo.

Manifest: A list of passengers or freight on a ship or aircraft.

Pallet: A form of container. Has a wood or metal base which allows it to be handled easily by fork-lift trucks.

Roll-on–roll-off: Motor-vehicles drive on to a ferry vessel and drive off when they reach the opposite shore.

Stripping: Taking goods out of a container.

Tachograph: A device fitted to a vehicle which records on a disc the time and distance travelled during a journey. Drivers have described it as 'the spy in the cab'.

Assignment: Multiple Choice

Place a tick in the box following the response which most accurately completes the statement:

1. One of the most favoured versions of the Channel Tunnel between England and France is that which involves a rail link. If this plan was implemented the transport operators most likely to benefit would be

   A. a firm operating a hovercraft service between Calais and Dover. ☐
   B. an airline operating between Heathrow and Le Bourget. ☐
   C. coach tour operators. ☐

2. The owners of oil tankers would be pleased to hear that

   A. oil prices are rising. ☐
   B. a new method of producing nuclear energy safely and cheaply has been discovered. ☐
   C. oil prices are falling. ☐

3. A firm of road hauliers would expect their profits to rise as a result of

   A. a major modernisation programme by British Rail. ☐
   B. a new law being enacted which allows lorries to carry larger loads. ☐
   C. lower speed limits for heavy lorries on motorways. ☐

4. Passenger fares on the railways would be most likely to be reduced as a result of

   A. a decrease in the number of passengers using the railways. ☐
   B. an increase in the wages of railway workers. ☐
   C. the closure of unprofitable branch lines. ☐

5. Airline operators would be most likely to benefit from

   A. a rise in the general standard of living. ☐
   B. the building of a channel tunnel. ☐
   C. a world recession. ☐

For group discussion

How do you think the problem of traffic congestion generally and car parking in particular should be dealt with in our large cities? What do you think of the idea of banning private cars from our city centres?

Would you like to see unprofitable railway lines and bus services axed? Consider any problems you have locally with regard to public transport.

CHAPTER 25

The Office Function

In many ways we can compare the business organisation to the human body. The production department can be equated to the human hands by means of which we make things. By the same token the transport and distribution departments can be likened to the feet. The mouth is the means by which we sell ourselves to others and the brain is the place where we make our decisions and so is akin to management. And what role in this analogy is played by the office? The function of the office can be seen to be similar to the role of the nervous system in the human body. We touch something hot with our fingers and the signal is carried to our brain which instructs us to move our fingers from the excessive heat without delay. Our central nervous system is the means by which the brain is given information upon which it then acts sending out appropriate signals, again through the central nervous system, to the various parts of the body, so that the desired actions can be taken. That is much the same function as is carried out by those who are actively involved in one way or another in the admixture of offices found in a typical business organisation.

The same principles are applied whether we are writing letters, answering the telephone or making entries in the books of account. The same basic role is being played whether the staff in question are functioning in a sales office, a wages office or any other office in the organisation. The office generates paper or, increasingly in the age of the computer and the microchip, the memory store. But the purpose is always the same, to produce an information bank which can be used in the decision-making process, allowing the business to respond effectively to changing stimuli.

Information is vital if rational decisions are to be made. Some decisions will be of major importance. Should the head offices be transferred from London to Liverpool? Or should 20 per cent of the work-force be made redundant? Other decisions will be of minor importance. Should we send a reminder to one of our clients whose account is now overdue? Or should we upgrade Sally Jones or Ricky

Smith – or both? Whenever decisions like these have to be made, information (or facts) have to be available. The decision-making process requires that we consider the range of options and evaluate them. The evaluation entails a weighing-up of the pros and cons. And ideally the pros and cons will be geared to facts. The function of the office is to provide the grist for the decision-making mill.

Offices, wherever they exist in the organisation, provide the following services:

(i) A communications network by means of which contact may be made with other members of the work-team, customers and external advisers.

(ii) A processing operation by means of which data are collected and collated. Information is converted into a designated form acceptable to management.

(iii) A storage and retrieval system whereby information is retained and made available as and when required.

(iv) Protection for the organisation's cash and other assets. The records maintained in the offices provide the check-lists for stock-taking and physical inspections of assets. In large organisations particularly it would be easy for assets to 'disappear' in the absence of detailed records.

Telephoning

A firm can spend endless amounts on advertising with the purpose of acquiring new customers. Then along comes a member of staff who deals with the customers insensitively on the telephone and customers are quickly lost. All staff should understand that without customers there can be no work and no pay. The customers are the lifeblood of any business. They should not be kept waiting, especially if they are making a long-distance call. If they cannot be dealt with expeditiously they should be telephoned back. Messages should be noted – and followed up where necessary. For the person on the other end of the telephone the call is giving them an 'image' of the firm. They will judge its overall efficiency and worthiness according to what they hear.

A telephone message-pad may be useful for recording incoming messages when the appropriate staff cannot be contacted immediately. The messages can then be passed on to them for attention as soon as possible. A simple example is shown opposite:

Incoming Telephone Message

For: Mr James Rider, Sales Manager
Received by: Sue Peters *Date*: 19/1 *Time*: 11.25

Message: Mrs Gordoni has not yet received the catalogue she was promised last week. She can be contacted at 01 564921 until 4 p.m.

Of course it is dangerous to assume that just because the message is now nestling on Mr Rider's desk that it will be attended to and some sort of check will need to be made that the complaint is being dealt with.

Filing

The purpose of a filing system is to retain copies of correspondence and other information so that it can be referred to as and when required. Consider the case of an executive who receives a letter from a client.

> 'Further to your letter of the 13th. I would like you to sell the securities referred to without delay. The market seems set to fall at any moment....'

Which letter is the client referring to? What *precisely* did we suggest? What if we have difficulty in tracing the letter and the market falls before we can take the steps we have ourselves suggested?

Pity, too, Miss Lewis who takes a telephone call from a client who says:

> 'Ah yes, Miss Lewis, this is Mr Sprague from International Wires. I have your letter in front of me with regard to the new contract which is being negotiated. We are ready to close the deal but we're not too happy about the changes to clause 2 you're suggesting....'
>
> 'I'm sorry Mr Sprague I don't seem to be able to find a copy of the letter I sent you. I've got a vague idea it was something to do with....'

It is only when you have been put into an embarrassing position like this that you can really begin to appreciate the need for an efficient filing system. There must be an unambiguous classification whether it is geographical, alphabetical, numerical, by subject or any combination of these. Where there is a danger of files (or letters) being removed, a tracer system must be incorporated so that the missing items can be speedily located.

While filing duties are often delegated to junior staff an efficient filing system and competent filing clerks are vital to a well-run office. Without them the life of the office executive would be intolerable.

Types and classifications

Among the data to be stored will be incoming letters, copies of outgoing letters and a variety of internal memoranda. Before determining the system of filing to be employed certain basic questions need to be answered.

1. How long will it be necessary to retain the records for both legal and administrative reasons? Under the Limitation Act, 1980, a legal action cannot be brought after the expiration of six years from the date on which the cause of the action accrued. Bearing in mind that copies of correspondence may be required as supporting evidence in the event of a dispute over a contract, for example, this legal requirement will often be a governing factor.

2. How important are the records? In designing a filing system it is always necessary to relate the costs of keeping the records to the benefits to be gained. The system should be planned to cope with normal requirements rather than the remote or exceptional situation.

3. How accessible does the information need to be? The system should allow the user to retrieve information with certainty and without unacceptable delay. It often means that users and files need to be fairly close to each other, but as filing systems become increasingly computer-based this requirement becomes less important. It will be increasingly feasible to put into store, retrieve and reproduce a wide variety of data through the media of distant computer terminals. The material to be filed might usefully be divided between that requiring speedy and continual reference and that required 'in case of need'. The active files will need to be constantly updated and immediately retrievable, while the archival storage may be dealt with 'off-peak' and as inexpensively as possible.

A decision as to the method of classification will be called for even where the material is to be microfilmed or fed into the memory store of a computer. The following basic options are available:

(a) *Alphabetical*

No matter whether the system is technologically advanced or based on traditional methods, records will normally be sorted and stored in some sort of alphabetical order. The layout for a traditional filing cabinet might be as shown in Figure 25.1.

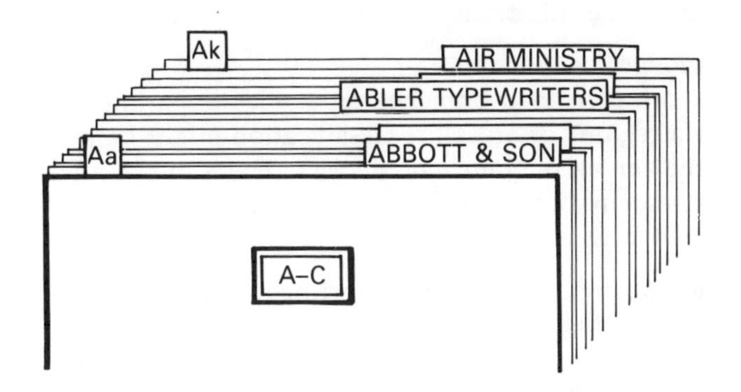

Figure 25.1

Certain rules need to be established with regard to names such as McDonald and Macdougal. Which comes first? And where does Mack fit in? The golden rule must be consistency, but it is also useful to refer to the telephone directory and see how the problem is coped with there.

(b) *Numerical*

There may be an advantage in allocating numbers to the files where correspondents are numerous. Insurance companies, for example, use the policy numbers as the point of referencc. An alphabetical index will also normally be required so that customers and numbers can be related where numbers are not known.

(c) *Alpha-numeric*

This is a hybrid system whereby the first letter of the correspondent's name prefixes a number which is allocated in sequence. So a file relating to correspondence with John Crosby might be given a reference C 334. Thereafter the customer will be asked to quote this reference in future communications. It explains the item found as part of the heading on many letters:

When replying please quote | C 334 |

(d) *Subject*

In this system all records relating to a particular subject are brought together. Thus, a building society might bring together files relating to its general business under the broad headings of

(i) Depositors,
(ii) Borrowers,
(iii) Mortgage applications, and
(iv) Bad debts.

The order for filing will be alphabetical (or alpha-numeric) within these subject classifications.

(e) *Geographical*
Where a company has branches or a sales department is broken down into regions or areas the classification might be geographical with a file for each branch or district. The sub-classification will normally remain alphabetical.

(f) *Chronological*
In this case documents are filed according to their date of origin. This type of sequencing is not usually used in isolation, but within each file or folder correspondence is usually placed in chronological order no matter which type of classification is employed.

Centralised *v.* decentralised filing systems

Is it better for all files to be kept in one place or should each department have its own set of records to maintain independently?

Pros and Cons of a Centralised System

	Pros		*Cons*
1.	System can be sited in the best place from point of view of senior management	1.	Delays may be unavoidable for outlying units.
2.	Economies of equipment and space can be achieved.	2.	There is likely to be a lack of flexibility and special needs of outlying units may be neglected.
3.	Specialised filing staff can be employed. Tighter control can be exercised.	3.	Central filing staff may lack contact with and knowledge of department activities.
4.	As data storage becomes increasingly computerised centralisation will be necessary in any case.	4.	Filing as a whole-time activity may be tedious for the staff concerned.

Reprographics

Photocopying devices have become standard equipment for even the smallest offices so that single copies of documents (or as many as required) can be reproduced speedily and easily. More sophisticated (and expensive) machines can produce hundreds (or even thousands) of copies quite rapidly and many have the facility for enlarging or reducing the size of the copies reproduced and producing multi-colour work where required.

Word processors are essentially hybrids combining the functions of typewriters and computers. Standard letters, price lists, circulars, etc., can be prepared and stored in the computer memory until required. Copies can then be printed out in volume with modifications in ones or batches as required.

Letter-writing

Whatever has to be written in a letter the tone should always be courteous. No matter what has been said or written by the customer/ client, rudeness can never be justified. By the same token curtness should be avoided no matter how overworked you might be. The aim should always be to act as a professional administrator.

Incoming mail should be dealt with promptly. Delays do not reflect favourably on the organisation or the individuals concerned. There has to be a system of priorities with the more important customers receiving attention first. However, there is no merit in maintaining a backlog of unanswered mail. With an appropriate effort the backlog could be eliminated and then reverting to a normal work-load there would be no need for a return of the backlog. Of course there will be peaks of work from time to time which create difficulties.

In replying to a letter or writing in response to a telephone call you should always make sure you have covered all the points at issue. If it is going to take time to look into some of the questions raised it would be polite to briefly acknowledge receipt of the message and explain the reason for the delay. A diary note a few days hence would help to make sure that any promises made are kept.

If a letter is to be well-received it has to be signed personally. The stereotyped letter which has obviously been produced for mass circulation is impersonal and does not inspire confidence. Nor does a procuratory signature when an assistant is authorised to sign in the absence of the executive.

p.p. John Doe

Of course such an arrangement is sometimes necessary, but it is better for the letter to be formally signed by the assistant explaining briefly the executive's absence.

Internal communication/correspondence

While many of the niceties can be dispensed with when the telephone calls and written memoranda are to colleagues in the same organisation it is as well to remember that the people you are dealing with are sensitive human beings and that you are far more likely to get their co-operation if you treat them with respect.

The role of the secretary/personal assistant

From a practical point of view the roles of secretaries/personal assistants are largely determined by the executives to whom they are responsible, but they will invariably be a vital part of the management team. They will not only have their own substantial areas of responsibility, but will also assist generally in the co-ordination of the work of the executive and the department they both serve. Secretarial work is likely to cover an infinite variety of tasks, which is why secretarial training needs to be so broad and wide-ranging, but a typical job description would include tasks such as:

(a) *Diary keeping* – the whereabouts of the executive should be known – it may be necessary to give diplomatic reminders of planned events/ meetings etc. – meetings will be arranged, noted in the diary and mentioned to the executive – adequate breaks should be left between appointments to allow the executive to tidy up details from the first and prepare for the second.

(b) *Arranging meetings* – with clients and/or other executives – providing files and general information as required – dealing with associated correspondence – preparing agendas – writing minutes – meeting clients and socialising as necessary – presenting an appropriate image (particularly to outsiders) – ensuring that plans approved are implemented according to the wishes of the executive.

(c) *Letter-writing and telephoning* – sorting incoming mail according to priorities – dealing with routine correspondence – preparing letters for executive's signature – providing files and other information to enable replies to be formulated – ensuring that letters are replied to – helping executive to make telephone contacts (by dialling numbers, getting through to appropriate extensions, etc.) – making routine calls on behalf of executive – acting as a diplomatic 'buffer' between the executive and 'less welcome' callers.

(d) *Generally acting as an aide* – taking an interest in the executive's work and work-load – reducing the burdens where possible – rescuing the executive from interviews which are lasting too long – acting as an extension of the executive's eyes and ears.

Secretarial skills

The scope of the job might also be gleaned from an examination of the sorts of skills called for. There can be few jobs in industry and commerce which call for a wider range of skills (see Figure 25.2).

Secretarial skills

Ability to project a pleasant personality whilst acting in a thoroughly professional manner. A smart appearance is a vital part of this projection. Many important clients gain their first impression of the organisation through the secretary.

Ability to communicate effectively with a diversity of people by telephone, face to face and by correspondence (in foreign languages if required). The ability to distinguish between essence and trivia as when taking minutes of meetings.

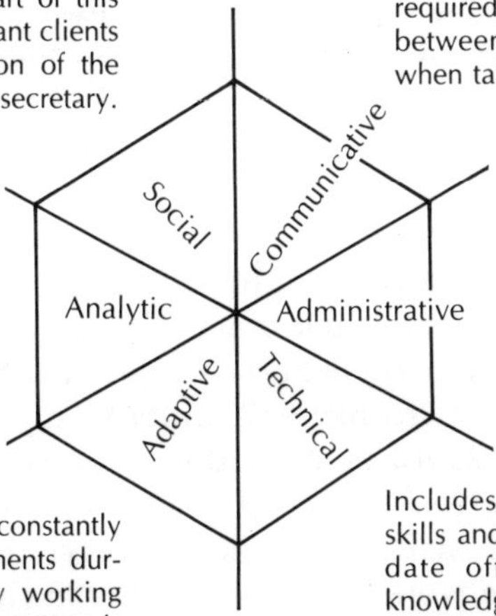

An ability to read and understand a computer print-out or a set of accounts. Also the ability to conduct research into letter files and/or archives to find out what has happened in the past, virtually playing the role of detective.

Social

Communicative

Analytic

Administrative

Adaptive

Technical

An ability to appreciate the nature of the problems faced by business managers so that contributions can be made to the managerial process as and when required, particularly with respect to the functions of planning and co-ordination.

A capacity to adapt to constantly changing work requirements during the course of every working day. The work of a secretary is extremely varied. The secretary also needs to be aware of technological advances so that skills can be up-dated.

Includes shorthand and typing skills and the ability to use up-to-date office equipment. Basic knowledge of the business environment called for (law, politics and economics) together with an appreciation of business accounts and computer uses.

Figure 25.2

From the executive's point of view

While the secretary/personal assistant is obviously in a subordinate position the role is a crucial one for the executive or manager. A mediocre executive can be converted into a high-flyer with the support of a first-class aide. And even an outstanding executive can be improved with the right sort of backing. The roles should be mutually supportive. We are dealing here with another form of teamwork. The executive should never forget that the aide too has an ego. It is motivating for the aide to be told as much as possible about what is going on. The communication should be two-way.

Modern trends in the office

Dr Allan Cane, writing in the Chartered Building Societies Institute's *Journal* in November 1982, forecast the development of the paperless office:

> Each executive will have on his or her desk one or more television-like screens and a keyboard or other device to communicate with the computers which control all the electronic devices in the office. These would include electronic files to replace conventional filing cabinets, intelligent facsimile and copying machines, a variety of printers able to print anything from letter-quality characters to four colour diagrams and a telephone system with a host of facilities from an answering service to video-conferencing (face-to-face conferences between executives separated by distance using television pictures sent over the telephone wires).

He also points out, however, that there is some consumer resistance to these developments and that office managers are not rushing to ditch their electric typewriters and conventional filing-cabinets.

The advent of the microchip will undoubtedly affect the office in much the same way as it has affected the factory. Fewer people will be required to do a given volume of work. New skills will need to be developed by office staff who will also need to be increasingly adaptable. The office worker of the future is likely to be seated at a multi-function workstation having access to a great variety of other users and a data bank of almost infinite information. If such information is to be utilised effectively at the personal level it requires an office staff with the broadest possible base of business training.

A lot of people will be affected by these developments. More than one worker in every three works in an office, and large numbers of these are women. Women account for about 75 per cent of all clerical staff and 98 per cent of secretarial staff. So while the introduction of robotic production lines affects mainly men the electronic office will become a major influence on the career prospects of women. Not that the role of the office will necessarily be diminished. In this chapter we have been looking at some of the different departments and functions in a business. The multi-function work-station would no doubt be able to exercise control over purchasing, sales, market research, production runs, accounting and all other procedures. In other words the advent of the microchip might well serve to centralise the decision-making powers and the general office may become even more the very hub of the business (see Figure 25.3).

Case study – Secretarial Duties

Polly Trehearne recently joined the staff of Travers & Bercholz, stockbrokers in the City of London. She was assigned as Personal Secretary to Lawrence Travers, one of the senior partner's sons. Her young boss, in his mid-twenties, had only been working for the firm three months himself.

It was on the Monday of her second week, and Lawrence was in the middle of dictating some letters when he straightened up suddenly:

'It's just as well I looked at my diary', he said, 'I see I'm due to play golf with Harry Pritchard this afternoon. I'd better have an early lunch.'

A few minutes later he left.

Polly was busy at her typewriter when the internal telephone rang.

'I've got a Mr Sundberg from Dayton, Ohio, for Mr Travers. He's waiting at reception', said the girl on the switchboard.

'Mr Travers is at lunch', said Polly.

Polly looked at Lawrence's diary anxiously. Sure enough. There it was. Mark Sundberg – 12.30 – with a big star against the entry. And it was easy to see how the mistake had occurred. Her boss had turned over two pages of his diary. It was next week he was supposed to be playing golf with Pritchard!

Polly tried to keep a cool head. She hurried to Sophie in the next office, and explained her predicament.

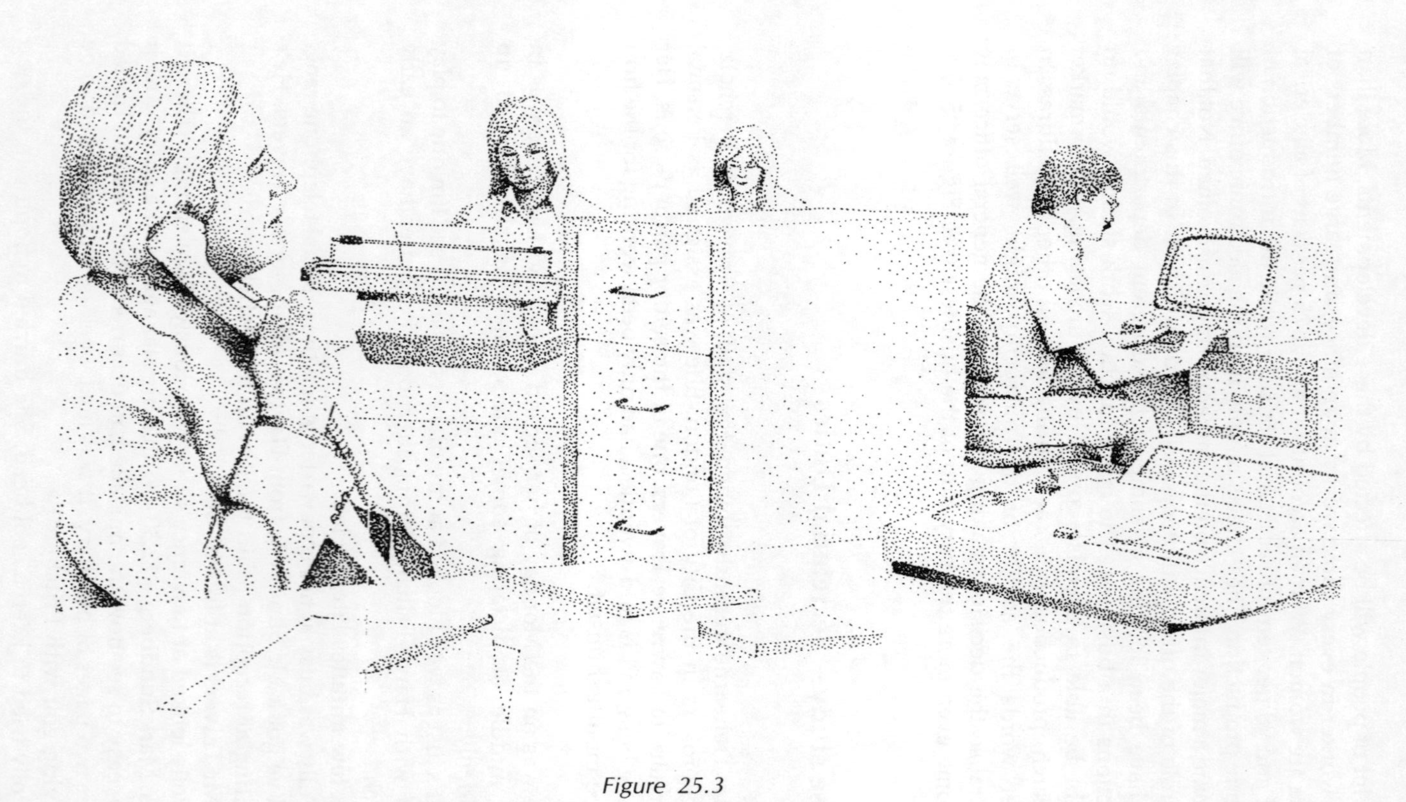

Figure 25.3
(From *Arts and Business Education Catalogue*, Macmillan, 1983)

'Oh yes', said Sophie, 'Mr Sundberg is an important American client. He flies over every so often to discuss his portfolio with one or other of the partners. But neither of them is in at the moment.'

With mounting concern Polly established that there was no one around with knowledge of the Sundberg stock-lists. In fact the files were confidential to the partners. Polly had to deal with the problem herself.

Questions for the group

(1) How do you think Polly should have dealt with this problem?
(2) Do you think Polly was in any way responsible for the mistake?
(3) How do you think problems like this could be avoided in the future?
(4) What are your views on executives who play golf in working hours?
(5) What rules do you think Lawrence Travers should have made about signing and sending out the letters he had dictated?

CHAPTER 26

The Accounting Function

Sue is the Personal Assistant to the Marketing Manager. They have just finished entertaining a small party of business executives from a Japanese company. At the end of the proceedings Sue was asked to call a taxi and escort them to the airport.

'Claim back the taxi fare and any other expenses you've incurred,' said her boss. She did just that. But oh what a fuss! Her boss had to sign a chit and when the cashier refunded her the expenses she had to sign a receipt.

'Anyone would think they were doing me a favour,' she said rather irritatedly.

People who study the world of business may sometimes conclude that too much emphasis is placed on the financial aspects. Yet that is what business is all about. In the private sector at least people are in business to make money. And accountants are employed to help in the achievement of this objective. In the simplest terms the accounts on which their role is centred are designed to answer the following questions:

(i) How much is owed to and by the business?
(ii) How much profit has been made?
(iii) What taxes are due to be paid?
(iv) How do the liabilities and assets compare?
(v) When decisions are to be made how can the options be evaluated?

Let us consider some examples in relation to the various functions we have been examining in this section of the book.

How much is owed?

How much do we owe to particular creditors for items we have bought but not yet paid for? For example, some new machinery was bought for use on the production lines. How much did it cost? How much have we paid so far and how much of the account is still outstanding? By referring to the ledgers we can find the answers to these questions.

Quanta Industrial Machinery Ltd

198–		£	198–		£
31 Mar	Cheque	1500.00	5 Jan	Machinery	15 860.00
30 June	Cheque	5250.00			

What does the account tell us?

Then there are the various customers who have bought goods on credit from our salemen. We have to place limits on the amount of goods they can buy from us without paying for them immediately. In the case of Alan Briggs our Credit Manager has put a limit of £1000 on his account. One of the salemen is now inquiring whether he can arrange for the delivery of another £500.00 worth of goods to him. What do you think?

Alan Briggs

198–		£	198–		£
15 Jan	Goods sold	625.00	21 Feb	Cheque	100.00
28 Feb	Goods sold	920.00	17 Mar	Cheque	525.00

Suppose that Mr Briggs telephones the Credit Manager and asks what the problem is. How do you think the Credit Manager would answer him? Note the importance of the data bank represented by the accounting system in dealing with situations like this.

How much profit?

Some people regard profit as a dirty word, yet it tells us whether scarce economic resources are being utilised effectively or wasted. Every activity involves the employment of capital, labour and land. These can be viewed as economic inputs. As a result of skilled entrepreneurial activity the resultant outputs can be expected to exceed the inputs. Outputs − Inputs = Profit. If all the businesses in the country were running at a loss we would not be able to provide our people with free education, a national health service or national defence. It is the surplus (or profit) created by our businesses which gives us our comparatively high standard of living.

For the individual firm it is necessary to note what revenue has been received and what expenses have been incurred in a given period. The calculations are usually shown in the form of a trading and profit and loss account. The example shown below relates to the business of a retailer, Gareth Williams, who runs a small sportswear shop in Cardiff. Where manufacturing is involved the accounts become a little more complicated but the principles are the same.

Trading and Profit and Loss Account
for year ending 30 June 198—

Dr			Cr
	£		£
Purchases	15 000	Sales	38 000
add Opening stock	1 500		
	16 500		
less Closing stock	2 500		
Cost of goods sold	14 000		
Gross profit for year	24 000		
	£38 000		£38 000
Wages	15 000	Gross profit	24 000
Rent	3 000		
Depreciation of assets	1 000		
General expenses	1 000		
Net Profit	4 000		
	£24 000		£24 000

Profit can also be visualised as the difference between the value of the net assets at the start and the end of the year after allowing for additional capital introduced and for capital withdrawn by the proprietor(s). The two concepts are reconcilable within the accounting system.

What taxes are due?

A substantial portion of all company profits is paid over to the U.K. government in the form of Corporation Tax while the government's slice of profits from sole traders and partners takes the form of income tax assessed on the individuals. Value-added tax has to be added to virtually all sales and this has to be accounted for to the tax authorities, subject to a deduction of the VAT which has been charged to the firm on its purchases.

When wages are paid over to employees it is necessary to deduct income-tax according to their tax codes. This is called the Pay-As-You-Earn system. This tax also has to be accounted for to the tax authorities and is another reason why accurate wages records need to be kept.

How do the liabilities and assets compare?

Through the accounts we can learn whether our business is expanding or contracting and perhaps just as important whether we can meet our commitments. Businesses operate largely on a credit basis. Goods are purchased on, say, three months' credit so that before the purchaser has to settle the account the goods can be sold and the proceeds banked. In these circumstances it is essential that a business does not lose the confidence of its suppliers. If credit terms were to be withdrawn it would put the business at a considerable disadvantage.

Another aspect of the same problem is that any unpaid creditor may sue the firm for payment of an outstanding debt. If the firm is unable to resort to sufficient liquid assets (i.e. assets which are readily convertible into cash) the whole body of creditors is likely to seek payment of outstanding accounts and the firm will be forced into bankruptcy (liquidation in the case of a company). The role of the accountants in the business is to ensure that such a situation never develops. They are concerned with the management of cash-flows and with the maintenance of a healthy working capital which is defined as the difference between current assets and current liabilities.

There is a balance-sheet produced to show the value of the assets and liabilities in the business as on the last day of the trading period covered by the trading and profit and loss accounts. In the case of our friend Gareth Williams's sportwear shop the balance might take the following form:

Balance Sheet as at 30 June 198—

	£		£	£
Capital	10 000	*Fixed Assets*		
Add net profit for year	4 000	Fixtures & Fittings	4 000	
	14 000	*Less* depreciation	1 000	
				3 000
Less drawings for year	6 500			
	£7 500	*Current assets*		
		Cash in hand	300	
Current liabilities				
		Cash at bank	3 200	
Creditors	1 500			
		Stock in hand	2 500	
				6 000
	£9 000			£9 000

Some questions for you to consider

On this evidence what weaknesses, if any, do you see in the business? How much working capital is there? Why do you think there are no debtors listed? Where do you think debtors would appear on the balance-sheet if there were any?

There is another value in recording the assets acquired by the business in that it tells you what assets are owned. What materials and equipment have to be accounted for? Through the accounting system it is possible to keep track of the various items in the business. Without this detailed record many assets in the larger enterprise would undoubtedly disappear. The accountants help to keep both fraud and pilfering at bay.

Decision-making

Much of the data used in the decision-making process emerges from the accounting system. The cost accountants calculate how much it costs to produce particular goods (or services). We know then how much we need to charge our customers if we are to cover our costs. It is a critical exercise because if we underprice our products we may find ourselves in a situation where the more we sell the bigger the loss we make. Conversely if we overprice our products we might price ourselves out of the market.

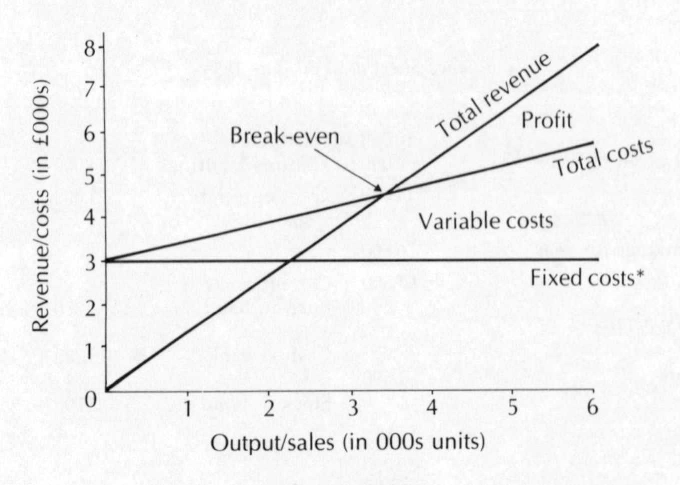

Figure 26.1

Contemplated projects need to be validated. Break-even analysis can be undertaken on the lines indicated in Figure 26.1 indicating the level of production and sales required in a given period before any profit begins to appear.

Some questions for you to consider

(1) How many units would we need to produce and sell before we broke even?
(2) What would be the effect if we only produced and sold 2000 units?
(3) How much profit would we make if we produced and sold 5000 units?
(4) What would be the effect if the variable costs increased by 20 per cent?

Ratio analysis

A basic technique employed by accountants is to compare one statistic with another. For example, the net profit is compared to the capital employed in the business (so-called Return on Capital Employed). The result is compared either with previous results in the same business or with similar results in other businesses. So there are warning signals when the return on capital falls from 12 per cent to 8 per cent from one year to another, or when we note from statistics provided by the Centre for Interfirm Comparisons (run by the British Institute of Management) that other firms in a similar business are getting a return of 15 per cent per annum. The effect of the ratio analysis conducted by the accounting division over a wide range of activities is to enable problem areas to be identified so that appropriate remedial policies can be devised. This is essentially the contribution made by the accounting function to the decision-making process.

Case study – The Glass Aviary

When Harry Firth was made redundant by the Lancashire glass-works after he had served for over twenty years it seemed as if the bottom had dropped out of his world. However, he took a chance and used his redundancy pay to set up a business at his favourite seaside resort. He bought a small gift shop close to the beach and working at his bunsen burner in the view of passers-by he makes a variety of delicate and very attractive birds from all over the world. The particular merit of his ornaments is their authenticity. Harry has always been interested in wildlife, but now he is able to combine his knowledge of ornithology with his skill in glass-making. While he works on the ornaments in the shop window his wife and daughter attend to the customers in the main shop. Of course the retail trade is seasonal, but he has landed a few contracts to provide local department stores with some of his more ornate creations.

He has just completed his second year in the business and the accounts for the two years are shown below. They are presented in vertical form as contrasted with those of Gareth Williams, but the accounting principles involved are precisely the same. You are asked to study the accounts and then play the role of personal assistant to Harry's accountant, John Ford, who has just produced the accounts from information supplied by Harry. John has asked you to draft a letter to Harry for his signature, enclosing a copy of the accounts for his approval. He wants you to set out any problems you see as emerging from an examination of the accounts.

Harry Firth trading as The Glass Aviary

Trading and Profit and Loss Account for year ending 31 December

	First year		Second year	
	£	£	£	£
Sales		78 288		88 215
Less Cost of sales				
Purchases	51 455		54 251	
Opening stock for year			12 337	
			66 588	
Closing stock at end of year	12 337	39 118	18 897	47 691
Gross profit for year		39 170		40 524
Wages	15 268		19 878	
Depreciation on fixtures and equipment	750		750	
Other outgoings	2 653	18 671	1 109	21 737
Net profit for year		£20 499		£18 787

Balance Sheet as at 31 December

	First year £	£	Second year £	£
Fixed assets				
Freehold shop		35 000		35 000
Fixtures and Fittings	3 000		3 000	
Less Provision for depreciation	750	2 250	1 500	1 500
		£37 250		£36 500
Current assets				
Stock at end of year	12 337		18 897	
Debtors	125		6 350	
Cash in hand and at bank	265		1 325	
	£12 727		£26 572	
Current liabilities				
Creditors	3 926	8 801	18 325	8 247
		£46 051		£44 747
Represented by				
Capital		40 000		46 051
Add Net profit for year		20 499		18 787
		60 499		64 838
Less Drawings		14 448		20 091
		£46 051		£44 747

CHAPTER 27

The Functions of Management

Every business organisation has objectives. They are expressed in terms of profit and revenue forecasts, financial budgets and so on. Marketing plans have to be integrated with production plans and manpower planning has to be co-ordinated with them both. They have to be mutually supportive and they also have to be under constant review so that they can be adapted to reflect the changing market and advancing technology. A broad framework of company objectives for, say, the next five years is essential in the larger organisation. This overall plan is usually described as the corporate plan. Such a plan offers the following advantages:

(i) It gives the executives in the organisation a sense of purpose. They know what is expected of them and what they will have to do to enhance their career prospects.

(ii) It puts the parochialism of functions and divisions into perspective. In the same way that the members of a department should be functioning as a team the departments should work together for the benefit of the whole business entity.

(iii) It provides criteria (or yardsticks) by which short-term and/or comparatively trivial options can be judged.

Within the framework of the corporate plan managers will be given targets and will in turn set targets for their own work-teams. Consider some examples. The Sales Director at Kelwyn Fireworks has been set a target of £2 million sales of the new set-piece fireworks over the next twelve months. How is he hoping to achieve this target? Of course through his subordinates. In fact, after discussion with them he has set them the following individual targets:

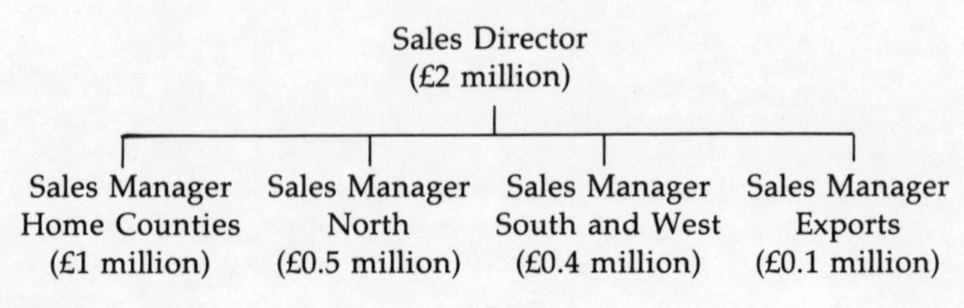

You will no doubt be able to offer possible explanations for the break-down of the target in this way. You should also bear in mind that each of the area sales managers will now need to sub-allocate their targets to the various members of their own sales teams.

The same principles will be applied to the allocation of the capital expenditure incorporated in the master budget. £250 000 might have been allocated to the Production Manager for the purchase of new machinery during the year. How will it be allocated among the different production lines? The outcome might be as indicated here:

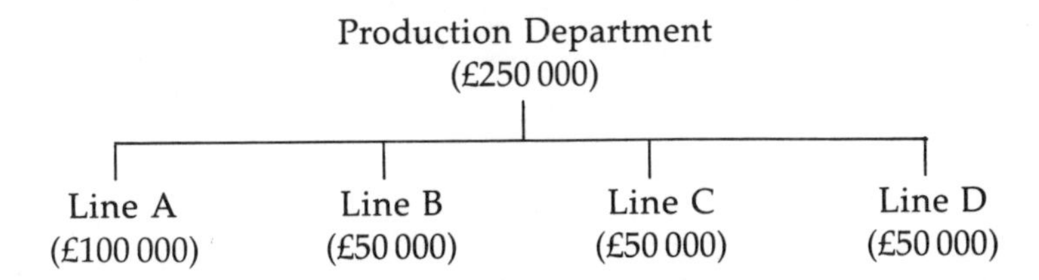

While many of the targets will be expressed in financial terms managers are obviously involved in controlling their work-teams and so behavioural standards will also have to be set. Whether the objectives are physical, financial or behavioural, however, certain basic and inherent problems are likely to be encountered. If there is too much flexibility and non-adherence to the targets is treated lightly the device will fail to stretch performance in the way intended. If, on the other hand, the application is too rigid discretions will evaporate and something such as budgetary compliance will become a sort of straitjacket. Decisions will be made which adhere to the budget rather than maximise profits or minimise costs. Similarly, sales targets which turn out to be too demanding could end up as demoralising with sales staff selling less rather than more as a result of the too-optimistic target. It may be equally damaging if sales targets are too easily attained because the sales force may then tend to 'rest on their laurels' once the monthly sales level has been reached. An example of the problem arising in a behavioural area is where an office manager insists that no one is allowed to leave the office until the stroke of five. Discipline may necessitate such a rule but it may also bring with it a counter-response from staff who stop working at five o'clock precisely no matter what they are in the course of doing. There is a fine dividing-line between control and motivation. If a manager exercises too much control over staff, motivation is likely to suffer, but too little control will bring the same result. It is this need to balance opposing factors which makes management a more difficult art than is generally appreciated.

The functions of management now begin to emerge and might be displayed in Figure 27.1 in the form of interlocking gears. Thus:

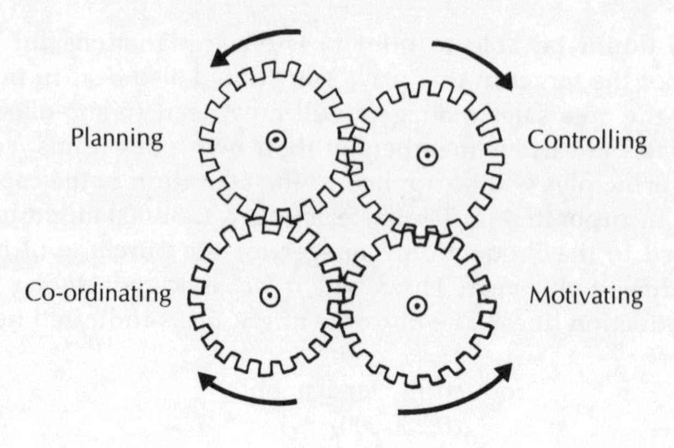

Figure 27.1

Planning

Picture the manager who comes into his office every morning and says, 'What problems have we got to contend with today?' The day's work becomes a battle to deal with a pile of paperwork before the time runs out. The format is repeated day after day. The technique is known as 'management by crisis' and has little to commend it. By contrast planning involves the anticipation of problems. If problems are foreseen, remedial action can be taken so that crises do not take place. The situation could be compared to driving a motor-car. The bad driver concentrates his attention on the leading edge of his bonnet – and runs into a herd of cows. The good driver looks as far ahead as he can – sees the herd long before he comes to it – and finds an alternative route so that the hazard can be avoided completely. Good management is all about anticipation.

The sorts of questions which need to be asked are:

(1) What are the significant opportunities available to us? Which of them should we be exploiting? What plans do we need to develop to exploit them?
(2) What returns are we getting on our assets? How does it compare with our competitors? What should our returns be in five years' time? What do we have to do to optimise our returns during the next five years?
(3) What threats do we face now and in the future? What can we do to avoid them or mitigate the consequences?

Controlling

Having had targets, objectives and standards set for them by those to whom they are responsible in the organisational hierarchy and having set appropriate sub-goals for the members of their own work-team so that the main goal can be attained, managers will exercise control by means of the following devices:

(a) Monitoring progress towards the selected goals.
(b) Identifying deviations in performance as they occur.
(c) Rectifying the deviations by applying appropriate remedies, or changing the targets where this is permissible and has become necessary.

An example might be given from the behavioural side. Suppose an Office Manager had been asked to reduce absenteeism in his department during the current year from 10 per cent (an average of one day's absence for every nine at work) to 8½ per cent (a ratio of 1:11). He has presently reduced absenteeism to about 9 per cent and assumes this to be the result of an admixture of job rotation and job enrichment (see page 61) which was introduced under the guidance of the Personnel Manager. But the Office Manager is still short of the target set for him and has to consider the further options available to him. He examines the attendance records of his staff to find out those with the worst records. He interviews them to find out their explanations and, in general, makes his displeasure known. All members of staff will now be aware of his interest in their absences and this should bring down the absentee rate closer to the end-of-year target.

Co-ordinating

If the whole organisation is seen as a composition of work-teams whether we are looking at the Board of Directors or the typing pool, the team leaders (or managers) have the responsibility for ensuring that the members of their groups are directing their efforts in line with the groups' objectives. Those familiar with physics will be aware of the theory known as the parallelogram of forces. It could well be used to explain the co-ordinating role of managers in any business situation. The point to note is that the business (and every department or work-group in the business) will reach its target more

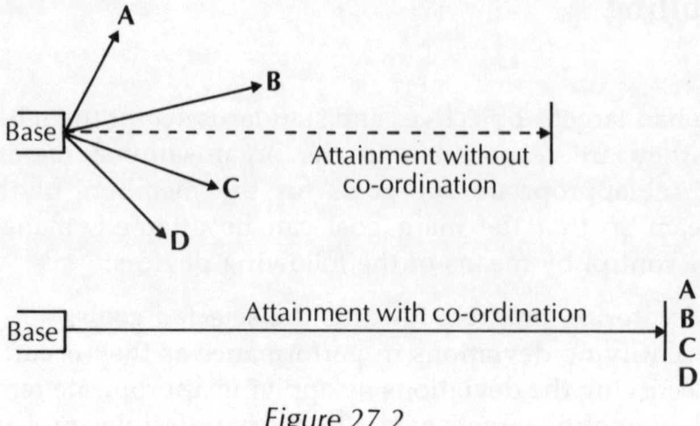

Figure 27.2

easily and effectively if everyone is pulling in the same direction (see Figure 27.2).

An example of a situation where members of a team are pulling in different directions is where one salesperson is taking a hard line with customers and refusing to give refunds on goods returned, while the person selling in the next 'patch' is allowing customers refunds whenever they are dissatisfied with their purchases. This sort of inconsistency is damaging to the firm's interests. At a higher level in the hierarchy it could be that the design team for a firm's products are producing goods which are not made to last while the sales team are building up an image of dependability and durability for the firm's products.

Motivating

The rudiments of industrial psychology were explained in Chapter 5 and every manager needs to understand something about psychology whether the knowledge is acquired from college courses and textbooks or 'the university of life'. We learn also from sociology that people are persuaded to comply with social norms through the application of a system of rewards and punishments. If they behave acceptably they are rewarded with approbation. If they behave unacceptably they are punished by ostracism and ridicule. In this way the majority of people in society, preferring rewards to punishments, follow the conventional patterns of behaviour.

For managers the language is slightly different but the principles are the same. They are advised to use what is called the 'carrot-and-stick approach'. The controlling mechanism is summarised in the table below:

	Carrots		*Sticks*
1.	Promotion (including the promise of promotion).	1.	Verbal reprimands (private or public – the latter being the more punitive).
2.	Pay increases (or the promise of them).	2.	dismissal or the threat of dismissal – but after compliance with legal formalities.
3.	Increased responsibility	3.	Transfer to more onerous/less pleasant duties.
4.	Improved status.	4.	Strict enforcement of rules (timing of breaks, punctuality, etc.)
5.	Praise (private or public).	5.	Withdrawal of sympathy and support.

Management styles

Four different styles of management are generally identified:

(a) *The autocratic or 'tells' style* – the leader/manager/supervisor takes the decisions without recourse to the work-team, issues instructions, and expects them to be carried out without question. While this style of leadership does not lead itself to highly motivated work-groups it is unavoidable when decisions have to be made quickly or where managers are themselves subjected to this style by those above them in the hierarchy.

(b) *The persuasive or 'sells' style* – here the manager appreciates that the team have to be motivated if their performance is to be optimised. So time is spent explaining the problems and 'selling' them the ideas deemed necessary to overcome them.

(c) *The consultative style* – whereby the manager confers with the group *before* making decisions and takes account of their views and attitudes when reaching a decision. While this type of leadership has much to commend it, the value of the discussions may be negligible if the manager's discretions are strictly limited.

(d) *The democratic or 'joins' style* – here the manager jettisons authority and becomes an equal member of the group to discuss a problem. Decisions are reached by consensus or agreement. Laudable, but not generally suitable for situations requiring positive action.

The broader view

In a political democracy the people are ultimately sovereign and any form of organisation which is to survive must prove that it is beneficial to society. Arising from this reality is the philosophy which suggests that the function of businesses is to serve the society which harbours them. They are obligated to avoid polluting the enviroment or harming their hosts in any way.

This notion does not necessarily conflict with that of profit maximisation. A distinction has to be drawn between short-term and long-term maximization of profit. If long-run profit maximisation is the goal rather than what might be called 'the fast buck', the firm will need to concern itself with public relations and matters such as business ethics, integrity and social responsibility.

Case study – The Single Seater

Play the role of the Board of Directors of a large engineering company. The principal item on the agenda for this meeting concerns a new single-seater four-wheel motor-vehicle which has been designed and developed by the company's Special Project Division. It is the first time the Division has been involved in this sort of venture. Until now it has concentrated on the production of components for the car industry. The prototype vehicle produced has just finished its trials and the following features are noted:

(i) The vehicle uses a specially processed form of paraffin as fuel. The cost per gallon is about half the cost of the lowest-grade petrol.

(ii) The fuel consumption is 200 miles per gallon at a cruising speed of 30 miles per hour. The maximum speed is 40 miles per hour, but it takes ninety seconds to reach this speed from a standing start.

(iii) The new fuel is very inflammable, but the fuel tank has been reinforced and all the materials used in the construction of the chassis have been specially fireproofed with a new type of liquid asbestos.

(iv) The body shape is basically similar to a conventional car, though on a smaller scale of course. The shell is made of a single cast of fibre-glass with a single door for entry.

(v) The overall length is 2.5 metres and the width is 1.2 metres.

(vi) There are no gears – one pedal governs the speed – the other is the brake.

(vii) If 10 000 vehicles could be produced and sold every year, it is estimated that the price could be as low as one-quarter of the cost of the smallest family saloon presently on the market.

(Note that a well-known West German car firm has shown an interest in the invention.)

Questions to be answered

(1) What are your views? On the evidence you have, how do you rate the potential of the new invention? How would you market it?
(2) Which features do you think would be most attractive to the public generally? Which features would be least attractive? If just one improvement could be effected, what would it be?
(3) How would you publicise the invention? At what time would you start an advertising campaign? Which media would you use? Speculate on the sort of advertisement which might be appropriate.
(4) Do you see any long-term problems arising for the company? Why?

A written report

When you have completed your discussions you are asked to play the role of Personal Assistant to the company's Sales Manager, Michael Weston. He has asked you to draft a 400–500 report setting out the problems which are going to face him during the remaining stages of the single-seater project. As he explains it to you he knows the sorts of problems which confront him, but he would like your ideas too, just in case there is something he has not spotted.

CHAPTER 28

Further Case Studies on Business Organisation

A. *The Jumbo Jet*

A mixed party of 625 Americans are flying in to Heathrow next month. They are coming on a 'Grand Tour' of Europe, under the auspices of Trans-Atlantic Tours Inc. They are spending six days in Britain, five days in France and Belgium, five days in Germany and Austria, and five days in Switzerland and Italy – twenty-one days in all, including travelling time.

According to the part of the brochure devoted to Britain, the tourists have been invited to

> See the famous old country where it all started ....
> Have a drink of beer in a real English pub ....
> See how the Royal Family live ... look in on the English Queen ....
> Don't forget to take your ciné-camera on this trip .... your buddies will never believe you.

There are pictures of the Queen, Buckingham Palace, a Beefeater, and an external view of a village pub with a thatched roof.

The only details about the composition of the party are contained in the notes which have been forwarded by the tour operators. They read:

> The majority of the party are motor-workers and their families, but there is also a sizeable group of retired folk, most of whom come from the Boston area. In our experience the males generally outnumber the females on this sort of trip – maybe 3 to 2. Interests are expected to be wide and varied. One 'young' lady of eighty hopes it will be possible to visit Edinburgh, where her mother was born.

Your task

As a group you have been given the responsibility for planning the six-day tour of Britain. You are expected to exchange ideas on the subject in the first part of the exercise and then to complete the itinerary form together (see Table 28.1).

Additional information

(1) Thirty luxury coaches are to be made available to the party immediately on their arrival at Heathrow.

(2) No hotels have been booked at this stage, but the organisers have numerous contacts in different parts of the country and accommodation in any major town can easily be arranged.

(3) There will be six American guides accompanying the party. A contingent of nineteen British guides will be attached to the party on arrival in London. The whole operation will be under the control of the US Tour Manager, Nancy McGiven, who will precede the party by twenty-four hours at each 'port of call'.

(4) Detailed plans are not required beyond those set out in the accompanying form, but general ideas and criticisms can be offered during the discussion.

Table 28.1 Itinerary form

		Main visits
Day 1	a.m.	Arrival at Heathrow (estimated 1000 hours)
	p.m.	
Day 2	a.m.	
	p.m.	
Day 3	a.m.	
	p.m.	
Day 4	a.m.	
	p.m.	
Day 5	a.m.	
	p.m.	
Day 6	a.m.	
	p.m.	Depart from Heathrow at approx. 1700 hours

B. *The Stately Home*

Lord Angerford lives in Bletchworth House, which is situated to the north-east of London, some two and a half hours driving time from central London. It is not one of the more famous stately homes, but the house is recognised as an excellent example of Georgian architecture, and it is situated in attractively undulating woods and pastures.

The Angerford family have always had a wide variety of interests, and this is reflected in the scope of their possessions. The house contains one of the finest collections of antique French furniture in the world, thanks to the refuge given to a number of aristocrats fleeing from the French Revolution. Some of the rooms in the house were given the names of the more illustrious guests and continue to be referred to by those names today. The present Lord Angerford has a passion for old firearms and has a unique collection of duelling pistols and sporting guns from all over the world. His father was more concerned with horse-racing, and this accounts for the fine stables on the estate – and the presence of some fine thoroughbred stallions.

A rather surprising feature of the estate is a very old single-track railway line which has been kept in working order. This is explained by the fact that the earlier generation of Angerfords were railway enthusiasts and pioneers. This stretch of track is all that remains of a branch line built specially for the benefit of Lord Angerford's great-great-grandfather. It enabled a special train to take him from Bletchworth House to the railway's headquarters in London whenever there were important meetings. The track stops at the boundaries of the Bletchworth estate, and there is no rolling stock in evidence. However, a group of steam-train enthusiasts recently proposed to purchase a late Victorian steam-engine with two carriages from the same period if Lord Angerford was to agree to hire them his track at an appropriate fee. These items are apparently in perfect condition thanks to the devotion of the members of the society in question.

As a result of the rising costs of upkeep of the house and the estate, together with the large sums claimed by the state in the form of death duties (the duties payable total over £1¼ million and arose on the death of Lord Angerford's father two years ago). Lord Angerford is looking into the possibility of commercialising the Bletchworth estate. Among the ideas already proposed are:

(1) Use the estate as a tourist attraction – especially for Americans.
(2) Develop a railway museum.
(3) Produce a leisure centre where a variety of sports and other facilities are offered to the widest possible range of ages.

What do you think of these ideas? Do you have any other ideas on how the estate might be exploited commercially?

The accompanying map (Figure 28.1) indicates the main features of the estate.

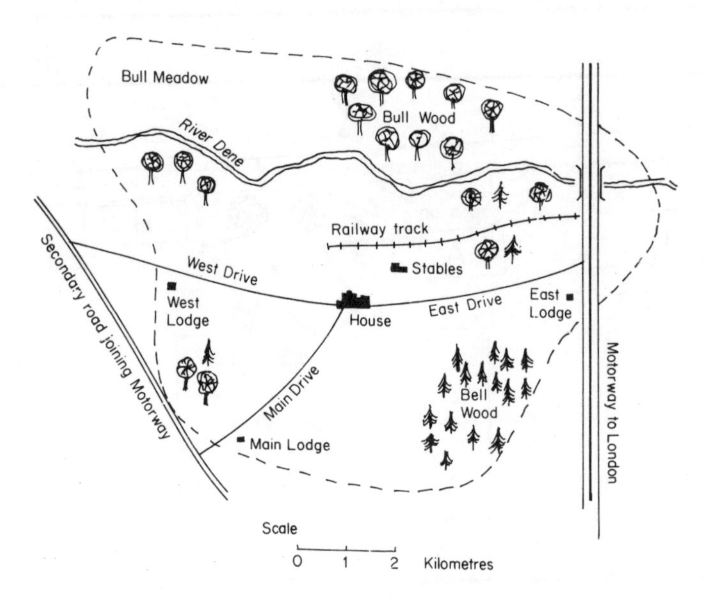

Figure 28.1 The Bletchworth estate

C. *The Holiday Camp*

The plan shown as Figure 28.2 is of a new holiday camp being built on the Isle of Wight by Laroche Enterprises Ltd. The main attraction is the lovely scenery and equable climate, but the proprietors intend to make the camp attractive in its own right.

A = Reception area with offices and store-rooms above.
B = Restaurant with ballroom above..
C = Theatre/cinema
D = Brick-built block of 84 one-room flatlets on three floors each with toilet and shower-room *en suite*.
E = 130 single-room timber chalets sited back to back each with wash-basin and toilet.
F = Communal laundry and bathrooms.
G = Staff quarters – 30 timber chalets each with their own kitchen, toilet and shower.
H = Camp supermarket – also open for passing trade.

Bernard Laroche, who is the Chairman of the developing company, is having lunch with Vincent Morrison, his Chief Executive. During the meal Bernard is told the details of the building programme on the Rochford site, and is obviously pleased when he hears that the camp

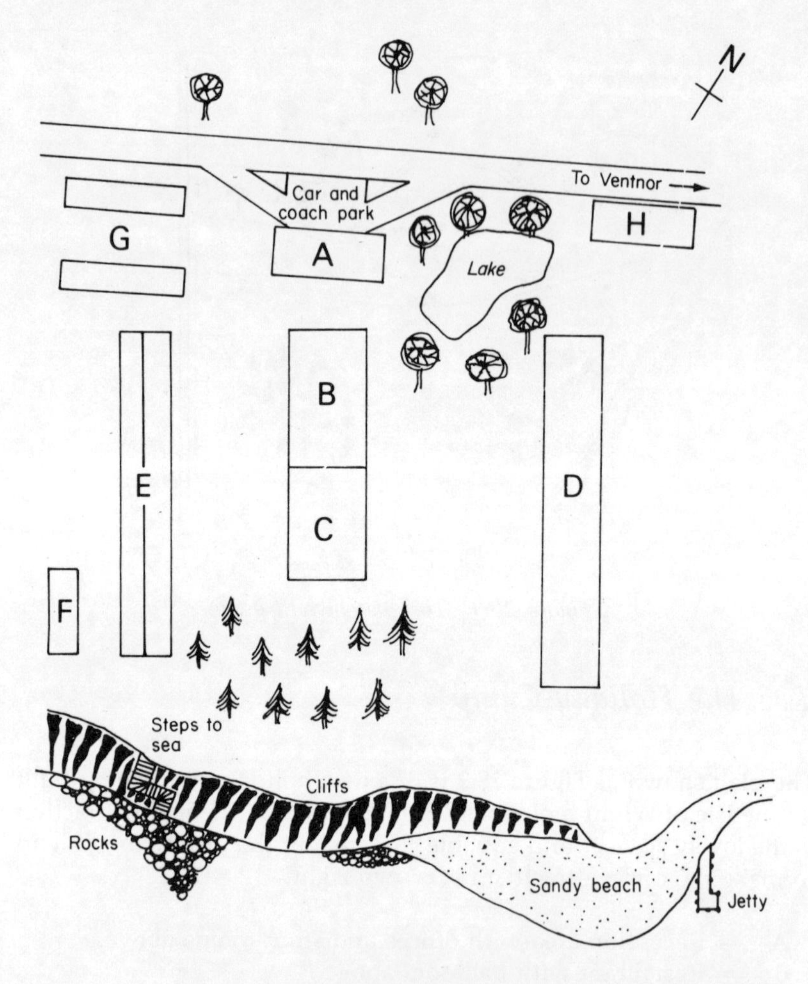

Figure 28.2 A plan of Rochford holiday camp on the Isle of Wight

should be operating within the next six months. However, he surprises his companion when he begins to indicate the sort of market he has in mind.

'You know, Vincent,' he says, 'I've been discussing things with some of the other directors, and we are toying with the idea of making this a holiday camp for Senior Citizens. The Isle of Wight is tailor-made for them. And older retired people aren't tied to school holidays – or even the summer months.'

Vincent's raised eyebrows indicate that this is a new line of thought for him. But the Chairman asks him to think about the idea and let him have a report as soon as possible.

In the privacy of his hotel room Vincent Morrison looks at the plans again, together with a few additional notes he has made about the development. The additional features are as follows:

(1) There are lifts in the flatlet block.
(2) Covered walks are planned from the flatlet block to the restaurant.
(3) Central heating is to be installed in all buildings other than the chalets.
(4) The restaurant is to be partitioned so as to allow two different classes of service to be offered.
(5) The maximum number of guests who could be catered for are (i) in chalets 260, and (ii) in flatlets 336, making a total of 596.
(6) The natural lake supports a small population of rare ducks. It was planned to convert this into a heated swimming-pool of a similar shape.

Your task

Play the role of the new Personal Assistant to Vincent Morrison, the Chief Executive of Laroche Enterprises Ltd, who has asked for a formal report expressing your views on the development of the new

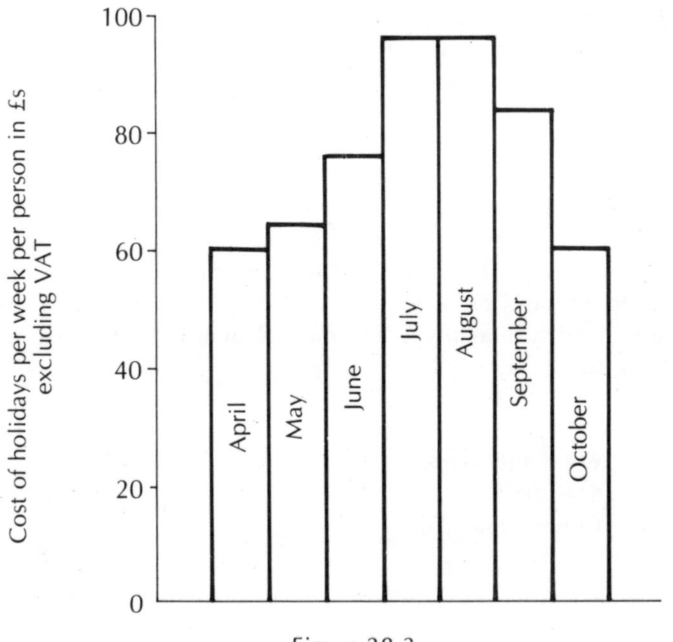

Figure 28.3

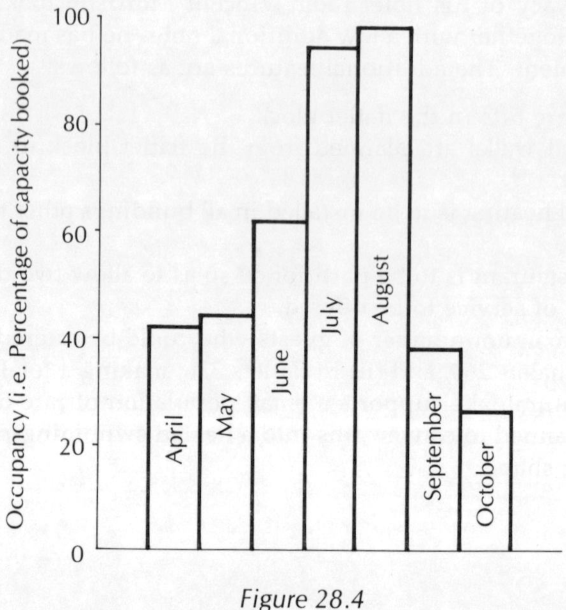

Figure 28.4

site which has been set a profit target of £250 000 a year by the Chairman. Laroche own five other holiday camps all of which are a similar size and capacity. They are in North Wales, Ayrshire, Norfolk, Kent and Dorset. Figure 28.3 shows the tariff structure used at these camps. They have also undertaken some research on the rate of occupancy of berths at the various camps and the results are shown in Figure 28.4.

Your chief has particularly asked (a) for your ideas on how the camp might be staffed economically and effectively and (b) how you feel the camp should be promoted. The present arrangements are that the camps are advertised extensively in three popular Sunday newspapers during January and February. Prospective campers send for a brochure and book directly with the London Head Office.

The expenditure at the Weymouth (Dorset) site for last year was typical of the holiday villages in the Laroche group.

	£
Food and drink	237 000
Staff pay	225 000
Other expenses	74 000
Total costs of running the site	£536 000

PART 4

ON THE THEME OF MONEY

CHAPTER 29

Sources of Business Finance

Money is at the heart of business. Money is needed to pay wages, to acquire materials to make up into manufactured goods and to reward those who attempt to anticipate the needs of society and stand to lose if they fail to do so. Money is the lubricating agent which allows the diverse elements in the economic system to interact effectively. If a business runs short of money in the private sector it will be wound up (if a company) or closed down (if the proprietor is bankrupted). People will lose their jobs and the flow of goods and/or services it has been providing will dry up. Money, then, is the life-blood of business and executives of all types will find much of their time and energy devoted to coping with problems of a financial nature.

Finance may be called for at any of the following times:

(i) When a business is being first set up.
(ii) When expansion is planned.
(iii) When a shortage of working capital has developed.

Ploughed-back profits

The pockets of the business owners are likely to be a prime source of funds. Apart from their initial outlays further contributions will take place when surpluses from trading are retained in the business. Profits made by a sole trader or by partners are withdrawn from the business through the medium of Drawings Accounts, while company profits are distributed to shareholders in the form of dividends. Funds which are not taken out of the business can be used for expanding the operations or rectifying adverse cash-flows which threaten the liquidity of the undertaking.

Inter-company loans

When a company is part of a group it may be able to utilise surplus funds generated by other companies in the group. Inter-company loans will normally be arranged at favourable rates of interest and will not need to be backed by securities.

Trade credit

When goods are purchased from suppliers it is not usual to pay for them for some time. During the time the accounts are unpaid the effect is that the trade creditors are financing the firm's operations. Cash discounts are often offered to encourage bills to be paid within a set time, say, twenty-one days. Of course, the same situation applies in reverse. When we sell goods or services we often have to wait for payment and in this case we are, in effect, providing funds for our customers' operations. If, however, it is desired to convert debtors' balances into cash without delay it is possible to resort to a practice known as 'factoring' (or invoice discounting). Specialist companies can be approached with a view to their purchasing the book debts at a discount. They will collect the debts and keep any accounting records required.

Another way in which trade creditors can be used to provide funds for the business is through the medium of the *bill of exchange*. This is much like a cheque except that the sum mentioned is payable at a future date, say, in three months' time. The person who receives such a bill can normally take it to his bankers and ask them to discount it. The effect will then be that the payee's banker is financing the transaction. So, for the price of the banker's discount, the buyer is given three months' credit and the supplier is paid at once.

Industrial hire-purchase is another source of short-term finance with repayments spread over a period of, say, two years.

Bank overdrafts and loans

The commercial banks are the traditional short-term lenders. Before they lend money to one of their customers they will usually want answers to the following questions:

(i) For what purpose is the loan required?
(ii) How much is required and for how long?
(iii) How will the loan be repaid?
(iv) What security is available to cover the loan? For example, if property deeds are deposited with them the bank will acquire rights to the property if the loan is not repaid.

The bank will often ask for someone to guarantee the loan. In the case of a company it may be the directors who are required to sign a form of guarantee so that if the loan is not repaid the bank will be able to claim any shortfall from the directors (called the guarantors). When the bank are evaluating the application for a loan they will expect the borrower to bear a substantial element of any risks involved. It would obviously be dangerous from their point of view if the failure of the project for which the funds were required resulted in the loss of the bank's funds only.

The distinction between a loan and an overdraft? When a loan is granted a loan account is opened in the name of the borrower. The appropriate amount is debited to the loan account and credited to the customer's current (cheque) account. Interest is charged on any amount outstanding on the loan account regardless of any credit balance on the current account. By contrast, when the bank agree that the customer's current account may be overdrawn, after putting up any security that may be required, the customer simply draws cheques until the debit limit has been reached. The advantage from the borrower's point of view is that interest is only paid on the debit balance on the current account and this is likely to be much lower than the balance on the loan account. However, the bank is only likely to offer overdraft facilities where these are required for very short-term borrowing. Obviously too, from the bank's point of view, what represents a saving of interest to the customer represents a loss of interest to them, so they are reluctant to grant overdraft facilities except where the borrowing is very short-term.

Ordinary stocks

The first thing to note is that the terms 'stocks' and 'shares' tend to be used interchangeably when related to the capital of limited companies. Ordinary Stocks (or shares) are commonly described as 'equities' which is an indication that they are entitled to what is left of the assets and profits after the prior claims have been met. The stock is broken down into units of, say, £1 each, which is then referred to as the nominal value. This is what the original shareholders pay for the shares when the company is set up. Ordinary Stock units normally carry votes. Non-voting Ordinary Stock is usually designated as 'A' stock. Details of voting rights will be found in the terms of issue or in the Memorandum and Articles of Association. The voting rights are important because whoever owns a majority of the voting shares is able to control appointments to the Board of Directors. The dividends on Ordinary Shares will be related to the profits of the company so that when substantial profits are made the Ordinary shareholders can expect good dividends. If, on the other hand, the company fails to make any profit the Ordinary shareholders will receive no dividends.

Preference stocks

Dividend rates on Preference Stocks are fixed at the time of issue and when payment is due to the stockholder this is calculated by using the rate in conjunction with the nominal value of the stock. Thus, a person who contributes capital to the company through the purchase of 8 per cent Preference Stock units of £1 each will receive an annual dividend of 8p for every unit held. The Preference Dividend has to be paid out of profits and there are no dividends without profits, but the Preference Dividend is payable before any profits are allocated to Ordinary shareholders. If the Preference Stock is described as non-cumulative it means that when a dividend is not paid one year it is lost permanently to a stockholder. Otherwise the stock will be regarded as cumulative and this means that unpaid preference dividends from previous years have to paid before the Ordinary shareholders can claim a dividend for themselves.

Again it is necessary to refer to the terms of issue or the Memorandum and Articles of Association to learn the rights of the preference stockholders in the event of a winding-up of the company.

An example of how dividends are calculated

Gentry Jeans Ltd have issued the following stocks which now represent their capital structure:

Ordinary Stock (units of £1 each)	100 000
10% Preference Stock (units of £1 each)	20 000

Last year the company made a profit fo £28 000 one-half of which the directors decided to 'plough back into the business' by transferring it to Reserve rather than distributing it as dividend to the shareholders. How much dividend did the Ordinary and Preference shareholders receive?

	£
Profit available for distribution	= 14 000
Preference Dividend (10% on £20 000)	= 2 000
Remainder for Ordinary Dividend	£12 000

Ordinary Dividend will be

$$\frac{12\,000}{100\,000} \times 100 = 12\% \text{ or 12p per unit.}$$

All dividends will be paid over less tax at the standard rate.

Debenture stocks

A company may also acquire funds through the issue of Debentures. The Debentures are similarly issued in units (usually of £1) and are transferable, but, whereas the holders of Ordinary and Preference Stocks are members of the company, Debenture holders are outsiders. The debentures entitle the holders to a fixed rate of interest on their loans, the rate being fixed at the time of issue. How is the rate of interest selected? The company would prefer the rate to be as low as possible, but unless they make the debentures sufficiently attractive the investors will not buy them.

The interest is payable on the Debentures whether or not a profit is made by the company and the rights of Debenture holders in the event of non-payment will be set out in a trust deed. This document will also name the trustees who are to act for the Debenture holders (usually an insurance company or a bank).

The loan may be secured by charges on the assets of the company, particularly freehold property and in this case the securities will be described as 'mortgage debentures'. Well-known companies may not need to offer such a degree of assurance to investors and they will be able to issue unsecured debenture/loan stocks.

EXAMPLE: Deborah Finney owns £1000 11½ per cent unsecured loan stock in Gentry Jeans Ltd. The company pays interest to the debenture holders half-yearly. How much would Deborah receive for each payment?

$$\frac{11\frac{1}{2}}{100} \times £1000 \times \frac{1}{2} = £57.50 \text{ (less tax)}$$

Methods of issue

When a company seeking funds decides to invite members of the public to purchase their securities a variety of methods are available. The choice between them will depend to a considerable extent on the reputation of the company and the size of the proposed issue.

(a) *Direct issue to the public*
The company will take expert advice (from an issuing house) before deciding which type of security it should offer to the public and at what price and terms. This is probably the most expensive method of issuing new securities for the following reasons:

(i) There is a legal requirement for a very detailed prospectus to be published in the national press.
(ii) A large number of applications could result in a great deal of administrative work. If there is an over-subscription surplus cash will need to be controlled carefully and returned to the subscribers.
(iii) Underwriters will need to be used to take up any stock which the public do not want. The commission may be up to 10 per cent of the issue price. Underwriters will be necessary because a minimum subscription has to be set out in the prospectus and if this amount were not to be received by the company all subscriptions would have to be returned.

(b) *Offer for sale*
An issuing house may be prepared to buy a large block of shares from the company with a view to selling them to the public later at an enhanced price. The advantage to the company is that the public may not be prepared to buy shares or debentures in an 'unknown' company, but they will gain confidence when they are offered the same shares by a reputable issuing house. It will be assumed that an appropriate amount of vetting has taken place.

(c) *A placing or introduction*
A company may find that a small number of clients can be found to purchase large blocks of securities. Insurance companies and invest-

ment trusts may be interested in companies with long-term growth prospects. Once a company's shares have been granted a quotation they are going to be easier to sell because the investors will be able to convert them into cash without difficulty. Apart from vetting the company before granting a quotation the Stock Exchange Council will want a sufficient number of the securities made available so that a proper market in the shares may be established.

(d) *A rights issue*
This is a popular way of raising moderate amounts of money. In this case from the existing shareholders. In a typical case the company will offer, say, one new ordinary share for every four ordinary shares already held. The price at which they are offered is usually very favourable so that shares worth £1.25 according to the value of the company's assets might be offered by way of rights issue to the shareholders at 75p per share. The low price is justifiable in that only the existing equity owners stand to benefit.

EXAMPLE: Gentry Jeans Ltd wish to raise a sum of £50 000 by means of a rights issue. The equity of the company is valued at £200 000 so the existing ordinary shares are likely to be worth about £2 each. The company offer the existing shareholders 1 new share at £1.50 each for every 3 shares they are already holding. This will bring in to the company

$$\frac{100\,000}{3} \times £1.50 = £50\,000$$

Finance for the smaller companies

Only the larger companies can hope for a quotation on the Stock Exchange, but smaller companies can seek support from a number of specialist institutions which have been developed to help them. For example, if a company needs permanent funds of between £5000 and about £2 million, perhaps to introduce a new production line or to move to new premises, it can approach the Industrial and Commercial Finance Corporation with its proposals. This corporation was set up by the banks, but a rival concern, Equity for Industry, is run by a group of insurance companies.

Capital gearing

The relationship between the equities and the fixed-interest borrowings (preference and debenture stocks and bank loans) is described as the 'capital gearing'. When the proportion of fixed-interest securities is much above 50 per cent of the total capital we say the company has a 'highly geared capital structure'. We say the capital structure is low-geared if the proportion of fixed-interest borrowings is below about 25 per cent of the total.

Yields and prices

What price will an investor pay for the company's securities? To answer that question we need to ask another question. What sort of yield can the investor obtain on investments in similar companies? If, for example, an ordinary stock unit of £1 in a similar company is paying dividends of 20 per cent per annum and costs £2 to purchase the yield from the investment will be 10 per cent per annum. If we assume that an investor is looking for a return of 10 per cent per annum on his investment how much will he be prepared to pay for our ordinary stock if we are paying dividends of 15 per cent per annum. The formula required is

$$\frac{\text{actual return}}{\text{expected return}} \times \text{nominal value} = \frac{15}{10} \times £1 = £1.50$$

Case study – Capital Structures

Three companies are operating in the same industry and are broadly similar in every way except as to how their original capital was provided. Their respective capital structures are as shown in Table 29.1.

Your first task

Working in sub-groups of three or four (so-called 'buzz' groups), complete Table 29.2, thereby showing the rate of dividend which

Table 29.1

Alpha Ltd

	£	£
Ordinary Stock (£1 units)	200 000	
10% Preference Stock	800 000	
(£1 units)	———	1 000 000

Beta Ltd

	£	£
Ordinary Stock (£1 units)	500 000	
8% Preference Stock (£1 units)	500 000	
	———	1 000 000

Gamma Ltd

	£
Ordinary Stock (£1 units)	1 000 000

would be payable by each of these companies within a given range of distributable profits. (Assume that all distributable profits are distributed.)

Table 29.2

Level of distributable profit	Ordinary dividend rates		
	Alpha Ltd	Beta Ltd	Gamma Ltd
£80 000	0%	8%	8%
£100 000			
£120 000			
£140 000			
£160 000			
£180 000			

Which sub-group is able to submit a complete and correct table to the tutor first?

Your second task

Working the same sub-groups again, prepare a fresh table showing the prices that could be expected for Ordinary Shares in the three companies at the different profit levels, based on an expected yield of (i) 8 per cent per annum, and (ii) 14 per cent per annum. Then, after comparing the two tables, each sub-group should submit to the tutor four brief statements indicating the effects of capital gearing on ordinary dividends and prices.

CHAPTER 30

The London Stock Exchange

From the earliest beginnings of the London Stock Exchange in the late seventeenth century there have been two separate strands in the dealings. On the one hand are the dealings in the stocks issued by the government and on the other hand are the dealings in the securities of the larger limited companies (now mostly 'public limited companies'). In this duality the exchange no doubt reflects the make-up of our mixed economy.

The valuable role it plays in the economy might be summarised under the following headings:

(a) By providing a market which brings together buyers and sellers of existing securities it facilitates borrowing by both the government and the larger companies.

(b) Through the Stock Exchange *Daily List* it advertises the current prices of the quoted securities.

(c) It protects the investing public against fraud by the extensive vetting undertaken before a quotation is granted to a company.

(d) The general movement of prices as reflected in the *Financial Times* Index of Ordinary Share prices is a barometer reflecting the opinion of experts generally on the country's economic prospects. Stock Exchange prices are extremely sensitive. There is little that can happen in the world which does not have some effect on share prices. International tension, changes of government in distant countries, political scandals, industrial conflict – all have their effect on share prices.

Membership

The London Stock Exchange is governed by a Council elected by ballot of its members. The members can choose to be either brokers or jobbers. These dual roles are a unique feature of the London Stock

Exchange. Brokers are agents acting as intermediaries between their clients and the jobber. They buy and sell stocks and shares on the instructions of their clients and are paid a commission according to a published scale, ranging from ¾ per cent to 1½ per cent for typical transactions. Larger deals will attract lower commissions than this. One of the useful services provided by a broker for his client is a report offering specific investment advice. Jobbers are principals and buy and sell stocks and shares on their own account. They deal only with brokers and other jobbers, never with the public.

A typical transaction

Jennifer Rowe has £2000 she wishes to invest. She already owns a selection of stocks and shares (called a portfolio) and in her particular circumstances her broker has advised her to invest the £2000 in the purchase of ordinary shares in H. P. Bulmer, the cider-makers. In considering the advice to give his client the broker will no doubt have in mind, among other things, the advisability of spreading the risk (diversifying) so that there is a wide range of investments in Jennifer's portfolio. Jennifer asks him to buy the Bulmer shares as he has suggested. The broker, or his clerk, then goes to the Stock Exchange and approaches one of the jobbers dealing with breweries and distilleries securities.

'Bulmers Ordinary?' he queries.

At this stage the jobber does not know whether the broker is interested in buying or selling for his client.

'297 to 302p', replies the jobber, the lower price being the price at which he is prepared to buy, the higher price being that at which he is prepared to sell.

The broker then goes to two other jobbers who quote prices of 295 to 300p and 293 to 298p respectively. Why do the jobbers quote different prices for the same security? If they are holding too many Bulmers shares they will quote lower prices to reduce their stock, and if they are short of stock they will raise their prices to discourage buyers and encourage sellers.

Jennifer's broker will go to the third jobber and tell him he is buying 647 of the 25p Ordinary Shares at 298p each. This was the best bargain for his client because the other brokers were offering the shares at 300p and 302p. Each of them will make a note of the transaction in their respective dealing books and that completes the bargain. The motto of the Stock Exchange is 'My word is my bond'.

A form will be prepared to transfer the Bulmer shares to Jennifer

Rowe. It will be signed by her and by the person or persons selling the shares which she is buying. This form of transfer will be lodged with the Registrar of Bulmers and he will arrange for details of Jennifer's holding together with her name and address to be noted in the Register of Shareholders. When the company make their next distribution of profit Jennifer will receive a cheque representing the appropriate dividend.

You may be surprised that a share with a nominal value of 25p should be changing hands at 298p, but the company has prospered greatly over the years and the price of its shares will continue to rise as long as the growth continues. The company does not benefit directly from the high price paid for their shares but if they wish to raise funds in the future from a new issue of ordinary shares they will be able to quote a price close to the market value.

Types of securities traded

Figure 30.1 shows the breakdown of securities by group classification and market value. The market value for this purpose is the total value of the issued securities and is calculated by multiplying the total stock units by their market price. Thus, if a company has issued one million ordinary shares and the quotation on the Stock Exchange is £2 the market can be said to have valued the equity of the company at £2 million.

Gilts

One of the ways in which the British government raises funds for the various projects with which it is involved is to issue fixed-interest stocks in much the same way as a company does. The stocks are known as gilt-edged or gilts on the Stock Exchange because the British government is unlikely to default either when redemption is due or in the payment of interest in the meantime. The prices are quoted for £100 of stock.

Let us consider one of these stocks, 6¾ per cent Treasury Loan 1995/98. Suppose our friend, Jennifer Rowe decides to invest £1000 in this security. Her broker finds the best price quoted by the jobbers is 71 – 73, so he buys £1320 of the stock at 73, which amounts to

$$£1320 \times \frac{73}{100} = £963.60$$

The costs of the transaction will bring the total expenditure to £1000. This stock pays interest half-yearly on 1 May and 1 November so on these dates Jennifer will receive an interest warrant from the Bank of England for

$$£1320 \times \frac{6.75}{100} \times \frac{1}{2} = £44.55 \text{ (less tax)}$$

What is signified by the dates included in the description of the stock? These indicate the dates between which the government has agreed to repay the stockholders. So, if Jennifer holds the stocks until 1995 and the government decide to repay on that date rather than the later date Jennifer will then receive £1320. A capital gain of £320. But if the government have a choice of date like this which will they choose? It all depends on the level of interest rates when the redemption dates arrive. If the government could repay the 6¾ per cent loan and issue a similar one at a lower rate of interest they would do so. However, if interest rates are higher than 6¾ per cent when repayment is due the government will repay the loan at the last possible moment to avoid higher interest charges.

Some government stocks have a single redemption date in which case the government has no choice. An example is 13¼ per cent Exchequer Loan 1996. A few stocks have no redemption dates. These are described as undated. The interest rates are so low that the government is unlikely to redeem them in the foreseeable future. An example is 3½ per cent War Loan.

Takeovers

Companies can and do buy shares in other companies. It is the means by which subsidiaries are acquired and complex groups of companies are developed. As we saw in Chapter 29, acquiring a majority of voting shares gives one the power to appoint directors and thereby control the policies of the company which has been taken over. Take-overs and amalgamations may be engineered with any of the following objectives:

(a) To acquire the shares of the other company at a bargain price.
(b) To enjoy economies of scale as a result of the enlarged operations.
(c) To eliminate competition by acquiring the business of the competitor.

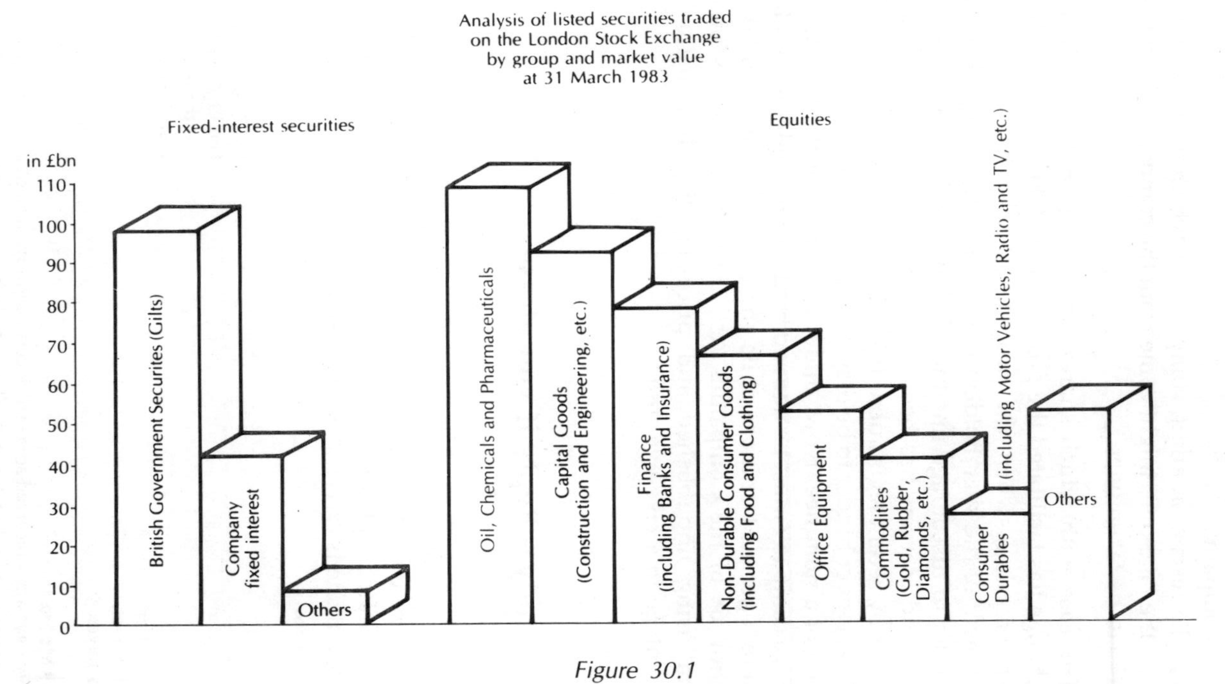

Figure 30.1

SOURCE: *The Stock Exchange Fact Book, 1983*

(d) To secure future supplies of raw materials, etc., at a reasonable price.
(e) To ensure markets for the goods or services of the parent company.
(f) To rescue an ailing company, in which case the impetus for the take-over might come from the company which is seeking to be taken over.

The ease with which shares can be acquired through the Stock Exchange has facilitated the process of the take-over bid. There have been occasions when the procedures have been abused to the detriment of the shareholders in the company being taken over and in order to discourage unethical behaviour the City Code on Take-overs and Mergers has been formulated. This has been backed up further by recent legislation. It has been customary for the intention of a take-over bidder to be disguised by the purchase of shares in the name of a nominee. Now, under Section 26 of the Companies Act, 1976, a company must be notified by the shareholder within five days where 5 per cent or more of its shares have been acquired, and by Section 68 of the Companies Act, 1980, an 'insider' is prohibited from using unpublished and price-sensitive information to his advantage in a take-over bid.

Case study – Reply if you please

Play the role of assistant to Alan Martin, a chartered accountant, who has received the following letter from one of his clients. He has asked you to draft a reply for his signature. Mrs Perkins's husband died last year, but she is carrying on their small tobacconist and confectionery business.

The Tuck Shop,
The Esplanade,
Cresthaven.
Yesterday's date

Mr A. Martin, F.C.A.,
High Street,
Cresthaven.

Dear Mr Martin,
A few days ago I received some stock certificates from Cadbury Schweppes which had been transferred into my name. They had belonged to Tom. I must admit I have no idea what they are worth and whether I should keep them. Tom always looked after that sort of thing. I would appreciate it if you could tell me, very simply, something about these stocks. All I know at the moment is that cheques come from the company every now and again.

There is one certificate for 500 Ordinary Stock units of 25p each. Tom bought these a long time ago and paid much more than 25p for them. The other certificate is for £500 8¼ per cent Unsecured Loan Stock 1994/2004. I don't like that word unsecured, and do I have to wait all that time before I get my money back? I've seen the ordinary shares quoted in the newspapers but the prices don't make sense.

I hope you can help me.

Yours sincerely

CHAPTER 31

The Banking System

The purpose of a banking system is to utilise the surplus funds available in the economy which would otherwise be sterile and unproductive. There are two distinct phases in the process. First, the surplus funds have to be collected and this requires banks which inspire the confidence of the public generally and a culture which includes the habit of banking. Then, the surplus funds which have been collected have to be utilised effectively. This is a natural division because there are two distinct groups of people involved. First, there are those who have surplus funds, and this includes the vast majority of us at some time or other. Then, there are those who require funds. Of course we could all do with additional funds, but the banking system needs to filter the applications so that only those who can organise successful projects have funds made available to them. The situation can be explained through Figure 31.1.

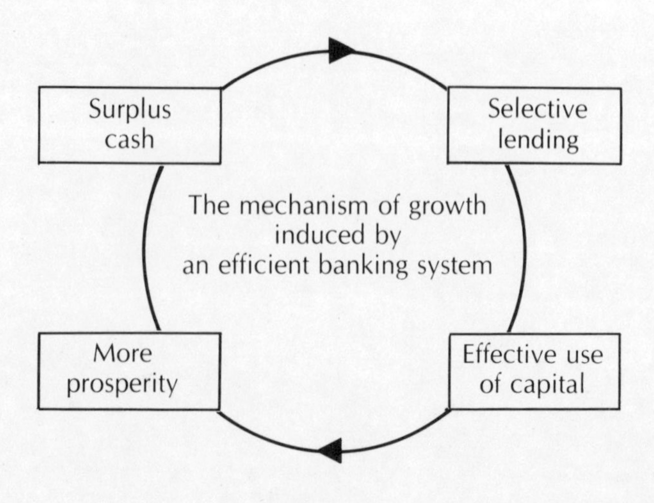

Figure 31.1

The commercial banks

The 'High Street' banks perform a number of vital functions for the community. For the public at large they provide a safe deposit for money and savings. It is not necessary to carry large sums around on one's person. The danger of loss through robbery or burglary is considerably reduced – if not eliminated completely. For those who want an easy method of paying their bills there is the cheque account. The banks do not credit interest to these accounts and if the balance falls below a certain level they will charge a commission according to the number of entries on the account. Most account-holders are also given credit cards which allow them to purchase goods and services immediately while paying for them later. The card can also be used to draw cash from any of the bank's branches up to the specified limit. And if you run into short-term financial dificulties or would like the bank to help you purchase a more expensive item than you can presently afford, the bank may give you overdraft or loan facilities.

Should you prefer to receive interest on your account rather than have the use of a cheque book, you can open a deposit account – which, however, may require notice before money is withdrawn.

The banks accumulate funds from depositors and these surpluses are then available to lend to businessmen (and others) who can use them safely and profitably. There is a marked tendency for banks in Britain to provide short-term rather than long-term loans though the pattern is changing. By contrast German banks are often prepared to finance companies by buying stocks and shares in them. Of course, this gives the German banker a greater say in how the company is run. In Britain the prime concern is to keep assets sufficiently liquid. Everyone with a cheque account expects to withdraw their funds from the bank whenever they wish, and the bank is therefore concerned to ensure that their obligations can be met.

In the 'old days' many a bank became insolvent through a so-called 'run on the bank'. It only needed a rumour to circulate that Banker A could not meet his commitments and all his depositors would clamour for repayment. Given time, perhaps Banker A would have been able to collect in all the money he was owed. Then he would have been able to pay out all he owed to the depositors. But confidence is crucial to the business of banking, and once the public has lost faith in a banker his business is at an end. This situation is hardly likely to arise today with our Big Four Banks (Barclays, National Westminster, the Midland and Lloyds). For one thing they are such large and powerful institutions that their solvency is hardly likely to be questioned, and for another thing they are so vital to our national economy no government is likely to stand by and let them face major difficulties unaided. The stakes are too high!

The economic functions of the banking system in the UK in which the commercial banks are the linch-pins might be summarised as follows. Their objectives are:

(i) To encourage saving by providing a safe haven for cash surpluses.
(ii) To provide expertise in deciding which projects are financially sound, so that the surpluses available are transferred to those who can use them effectively.
(iii) To stimulate trade by providing an easy method of payment in the form of the cheque or the credit card.
(iv) To provide funds to the government through the purchase of short-dated securities, essentially with less than five years to maturity.
(v) To help to determine interest rates in conjunction with the government and the Bank of England.
(vi) To buy and sell foreign currencies for their customers and generally conduct the market in foreign currencies.

The most profitable investments for the banks are the loans and overdrafts granted to their customers. But these are the least liquid assets other than their premises. The most liquid assets such as short-dated bills of exchange will be the lowest yielding. So the banks have the task of striking a balance between profitability and liquidity.

The Bank of England

If the government intends to exert its influence on the economy it must control the banking system and it does this largely through the Bank of England. The Bank of England is the government's bank as well as the bankers' bank. As the central bank it carries out the following operations:

(a) It is the note-issuing authority in England and Wales.
(b) It serves as Registrar for all the government's stocks.
(c) It maintains the gold and foreign exchange reserves in its Exchange Equalisation Account – used for settling international debts.

(d) It pursues the monetary policy as directed by the government:

(i) issuing directives requiring the banks to take particular courses of action;
(ii) calling for special deposits from the banks which have the effect of reducing the volume of funds available for lending;
(iii) influencing the interest rates to be charged by the banks;
(iv) conducting open market operations which involve selling government securities so as to reduce the money in circulation or buying government securities to increase the supply of money (through the Government Broker); and
(v) prescribing a minimum reserve asset ratio (liquid assets to liabilities) for the banks.

(e) It acts as the centre for the cheque-clearing system through which inter-bank payments are made, thereby settling the differences arising from the cheques presented by the customers of the various banks.

Payments by cheque

Jane Stanton sees an electric typewriter advertised in a daily newspaper. At £100 including costs of delivery it seems too good a bargain to miss. She sends off her cheque to the company named in the advertisement and waits for her typewriter to arrive. The path travelled by the cheque is shown in Figure 31.2.

The parallel lines across the face of Jane's cheque mean that it cannot be cashed over the counter at her bank, but must be passed through an account. This is a protection against theft because the cheque is then traceable.

Payment by standing order

A customer may have regular payments to make, say for insurance premiums, and in this case a single instruction can be given to the bank for repeat payments. The order might take the form shown on page 215.

The bank will then debit John White's account as instructed and credit the insurance company's account at the Midland Bank.

The basic mechanism of the cheque clearing system

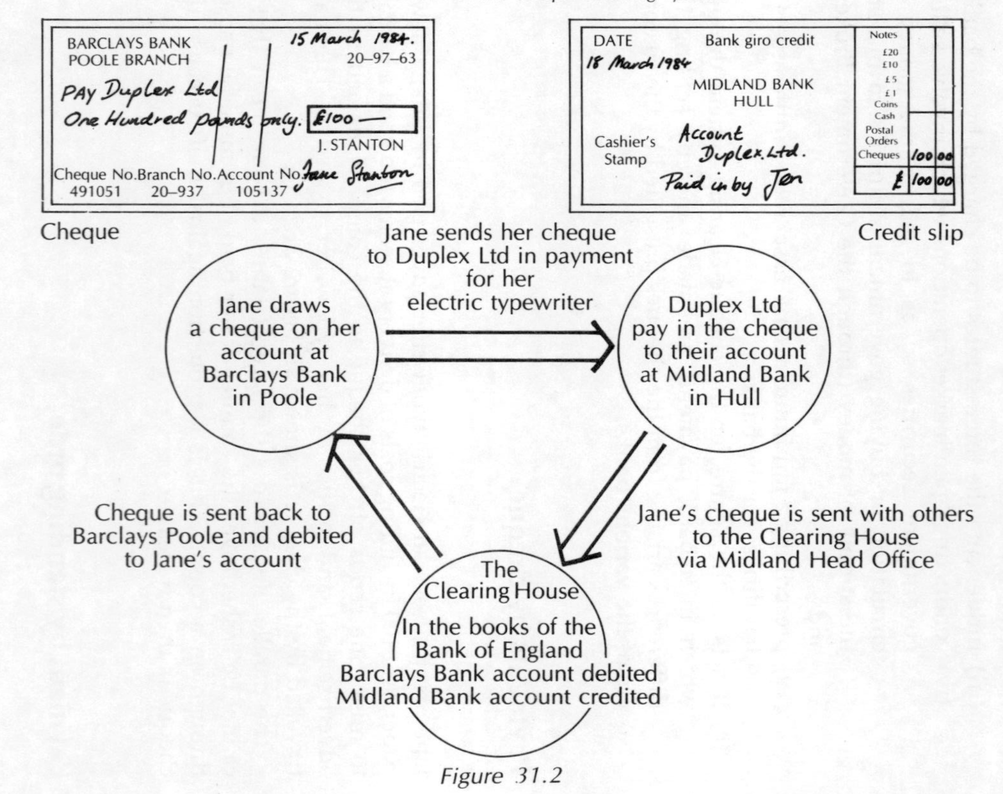
BARCLAYS BANK
POOLE BRANCH
15 March 1984.
20–97–63
PAY Duplex Ltd
One Hundred pounds only.
£100 —
J. STANTON
Cheque No. Branch No. Account No.
491051 20–937 105137
Jane Stanton
Cheque
DATE
18 March 1984
Bank giro credit
MIDLAND BANK
HULL
Cashier's Stamp
Account
Duplex Ltd.
Paid in by Jen
Notes
£20
£10
£5
£1
Coins
Cash
Postal Orders
Cheques 100 00
£ 100 00
Credit slip
Jane sends her cheque to Duplex Ltd in payment for her electric typewriter
Jane draws a cheque on her account at Barclays Bank in Poole
Duplex Ltd pay in the cheque to their account at Midland Bank in Hull
Jane's cheque is sent with others to the Clearing House via Midland Head Office
Cheque is sent back to Barclays Poole and debited to Jane's account
The Clearing House
In the books of the Bank of England
Barclays Bank account debited
Midland Bank account credited

Figure 31.2

To The Manager,
Barclays Bank plc, Date
Winton Branch.

Please pay to Midland Bank plc, Threadneedle Street on account of Protector Insurance Company Limited, quoting policy number A/106/1259, the sum of £95 on the 1st April next and the same amount on the same date each year until further notice.

signed

John White

John White

Payment by direct debit

This form of payment is different in two respects from the standing order. First, the amounts transferred may be varied, and second, it is the recipient of the money who initiates payment. This puts the customer agreeing to have his account debited in this fashion in a rather dangerous position. For this reason the banks will only accept direct debits from approved organisations and they insist that the customer is notified in advance of any changes in the amount and date of payment.

Payment by giro credit (or credit transfer)

On page 214 we see an example of a credit slip used to pay in a cheque for £100 to the account of Duplex Ltd at the Hull branch of the Midland Bank. If the cheque had been paid in at another branch of Midland, or perhaps by Jane Stanton at her branch of Barclays at

Poole, the payment would have been described as a giro credit (or credit transfer). Through the clearing system the cheque would have been charged to Barclays on behalf of their customer, Jane, while Midland would have been credited on behalf of their customers, Duplex Ltd.

Overseas payments

Banks offer a variety of services to their customers engaged in overseas trade. Subsidiaries and agencies in various countries throughout the world have access to invaluable information regarding the standing of individuals and organisations as well as useful data about trading conditions generally in overseas markets. They are also able to facilitate the settlement of accounts. A direct transfer of funds is possible through the computer systems of the major European and American banks subscribing to SWIFT (The Society for Worldwide Interbank Financial Telecommunication).

Where an exporter wishes to retain control of the documents of title to the goods until the moment of payment or the acceptance of a bill of exchange a documentary letter of credit is usually employed. It works like this:

Stage 1 – Chilmac Ltd in Nottingham receive an order for 100 refrigerators at a price of £360 each from Joshua Ereobu in Lagos, Nigeria. Chilmac's bank checks with its agents in Lagos that Joshua Ereobu is reliable and able to pay the purchase price (£36 000).
Stage 2 – Joshua's bank in Lagos gives the UK bank a Documentary Credit for £36 000 in favour of Chilmac.
Stage 3 – Chilmac issues an invoice, insures the tractors and draws a Bill of Exchange on Joshua for the sum in question. Chilmac deliver the refrigerators to the shippers who give them a Bill of Lading in return. This becomes the document of title to the refrigerators while they are in transit.
Stage 4 – Chilmac hand over all the documents to their bank and if these conform to the Documentary Credit Chilmac will be paid. The UK bank sends the documents by airmail to the Nigerian bank and claims the purchase money. Joshua's account is debited with the amount due.
Stage 5 – The refrigerators arrive at Lagos and the shipper releases them to Joshua in exchange for the Bill of Lading.

The volume of international trade would obviously be much reduced if it were not for the facilities provided by the world banking community.

The creation of credit

Every bank loan creates a deposit. Take the case of the East Anglian farmer who borrows £18 000 from his bankers to buy a new combine harvester. He pays for the machine with a cheque drawn on Midland Bank, Norwich. The supplier pays in the cheque to his account at Lloyds Bank, Peterborough. Although Midland have granted their customer a loan the £18 000 remains in the banking system. All that has happened is that £18 000 has been transferred from Midland's account at the Bank of England to Lloyds account there. Since the banks generally lend about two-thirds of their total deposits Lloyds would be able to increase their loans by about £12 000 without reducing their reserve asset ratio. When they grant this loan the process will be repeated. This time the banks in receipt of the £12 000 of cheques will be able to give £8000 of loans to their customers. And so on. This is called the 'credit-creation multiplier effect.'

The government's monetary policy, operated by the Treasury and the Bank of England, will seek to control this power of the banks to create credit and hence influence the volume of money in circulation and the rate of inflation.

Modern trends

Banks are likely to face serious problems at a time of recession. Falling sales and losses experienced by their business customers often lead to bad debts for the bankers as loans fail to be repaid. In order to avoid heavy losses banks are obliged to 'call in' their loans and this spells disaster for their customers. The problem is compounded because banking is becoming increasingly international. Britain's membership of the European Economic Community (the Common Market) has been one explanation for this. Another factor has been the growth of international consortia (groups of banks combining resources to finance oil exploration, etc.). International debts might be expected to prove harder to collect than domestic ones. However, the internationalisation of banking is two-way. On the one hand British banks are expanding their operations overseas and on the other hand a number of foreign banks are beginning to look covetously at the British market.

There is also more competition between the various banking institutions at home. At one time the dividing-line between banks and building societies was clearly drawn. The role of the building society was to attract savings and to lend the funds collected to people who wanted to buy their own houses. The societies secure the loans by a mortgage, holding the deeds of the property until the loan has been repaid. The banks were not interested in this market because the loans are long-term (for as long as twenty-five years), but recently we have seen banks prepared to lend money for house-buying. The building societies have responded by offering limited cheque facilities to their customers. There is strong competition between the commercial banks for 'down-market' customers who still do not have bank accounts, but a strong challenge for this section of the market is also coming from institutions such as the National Giro Bank and the Trustee Savings Banks.

Organisational changes are also in hand among the Big Four. In an effort to trim costs a system is being pioneered in which a town-centre branch is the hub for a group of 'money shops'. The central branch offers a full range of banking services while the outlying branches offer a reduced range, becoming essentially points for receiving credits and paying out cash.

Advancing technology also affects banking as much as other industries. Credit cards have been followed by cash-dispensing units which allow customers to collect cash from the bank even when it is closed. The talk now is of 'plastic' money. It may well be possible in the not-too-distant future to shop at the supermarket for your provisions, pass the basket through a sensoring device which will tot up the cost of your purchases, and finally feed your credit card into the device so that your bank account may be charged accordingly. Fewer staff will be needed at the supermarket exits and fewer cashiers will be needed by the banks.

Your assignment – your own business

You are required to work in small groups between three and five where possible for this assignment. Your bank manager has agreed to give you a £20 000 loan to set up your own business providing you can satisfy him as to the soundness of the project. There are no restrictions as to the type of business which may be considered.

Thought and discussion will be necessary before you decide the sort of business to set up. The location, the competition, the risks generally will need to be examined. Some research will be called for. When you have talked over your plans the small groups are invited to present their proposals to the rest of the group, giving as much detail as possible. When giving the presentation your tutor might wish you to play specific roles such as the accountant, the sales manager, the general manager, etc., enabling you to cover the various aspects of the project.

Written work

Finally, each group is required to draft an appropriate letter to the bank manager setting out the basic details of the proposals.

CHAPTER 32

Exchange Rates

The individual has to spend within the limits of his income. True he can borrow money, so that for a limited period he can spend more than he earns, but in the long run his consumption is determined by his income. In the same way that an individual receives money and spends it, so does the state. Indeed, the state is subject to very similar constraints. Whereas the individual is likely to get his loans or overdrafts from the neighbourhood bank, the state will get its loans from the International Monetary Fund. In each case the loan is likely to be temporary and repayment will eventually be required.

Great Britain's receipts come from the following:

(i) Goods exported to the rest of the world. Largely these consist of manufactured goods such as motor-cars and machinery.
(ii) Expenditure by foreign tourists and other visitors. When people from overseas visit Britain they spend large sums on hotel accommodation, entertainment, travel and presents.
(iii) Services rendered to the world for such things as shipping, insurance and banking facilities. These items form the large part of what are known as our 'invisible exports'. They are called 'invisible' because, unlike the goods exported, you cannot see them.
(iv) Money sent to Britain by Britons living and working overseas – for the accounts of their relations and dependants.

In addition to these receipts there are those resulting from past investment overseas. Britons who have invested in overseas enterprises receive interest or dividends from their stocks and shares. The government also receives interest on various loans it has made.

All these operations require the *purchase* of sterling in exchange for some foreign currency, or put another way these operations create a demand for sterling, and the value of sterling tends to rise as against other currencies.

Conversely, Great Britain's outgoings are the result of the following:

(i) Goods imported from the rest of the world. In Britain's case it is mainly food and raw materials which are imported. We used to import a great deal of oil, but that situation has changed with the advent of North Sea oil.
(ii) Expenditure by British tourists overseas. Those of you who have had holidays abroad will appreciate how necessary it is to buy foreign currency at some time before or during the trip.
(iii) Transfers from people residing in Britain to their relations and dependants overseas.
(iv) Interest and dividend payments.

These operations require the *sale* of sterling in exchange for foreign currencies. They create a demand for foreign currencies and tend to lower the value of sterling against them.

The government's record of these monetary transactions with the rest of the world is known as 'the balance of payments'. The monthly figures are closely watched to see how well the economy is functioning.

There are also payments and receipts on capital account which occur when loans are made or repaid, or when stocks and shares are bought or sold overseas. This generates further purchases, or sales of sterling, as the case might be.

On the one hand there is a build-up of demand for a particular currency (say, sterling) and on the other hand there is a build-up of supplies of that currency. The demand and supply are equated through the price mechanism. Thus an increase in the demand for a currency raises its value in terms of other currencies, while a decrease in the demand will lower its value.

At one time 5 US dollars ($) were equal to £1, but at the time of writing the value of the £ has fallen so that £1 is now worth about $1.50.

Sometimes rises and falls in the exchange rates are resisted by the governments concerned – in an attempt to stabilise the prices of the currencies (i.e. exchange rates).

The Exchange Equalisation Fund

The Bank of England, acting on behalf of the Treasury, holds large sums of foreign currencies as well as sterling balances. At times the Bank of England prefers to buy further stocks of sterling rather than see the value of sterling fall; or conversely the Bank sells sterling when sterling is in short supply and the price is beginning to rise unduly. In this way, with other central banks pursuing a similar policy, the exchange rates can be reasonably stabilised to everyone's advantage. But long-term pressures cannot be resisted, and if a country is unable to balance its accounts, its currency will be devalued. This will have the effect of making imports dearer and exports cheaper to the customers, and will bring the situation towards an equilibrium.

Forward foreign exchange

When a firm is involved in international trade it will have to be decided whether payment is to be made in sterling or in the foreign currency. This will be part of the negotiations between the two parties. The danger is that the rate of exchange will change between the date of the contract and the date of the payment. Consider, for example, the case of the London department store which agreed to purchase $75 000 worth of dresses from a New York dress manufacturer, for delivery in three months' time. At the time the transaction was agreed the rate of exchange was $1.50 to the £. But by the time the dresses are delivered and payment is required sterling has fallen in value and the rate of exchange is $1.25. The dresses which were going to cost them £50 000 are now going to cost them £60 000 (i.e. £75 000/1.25). It is going to be difficult to make any sort of profit on this particular purchase now.

To overcome this problem the department store could enter into a forward foreign-exchange contract with its bank, by means of which the bank agrees to provide the dollars at a rate of exchange agreed now. Obviously such a forward rate will generally be less favourable than the so-called spot rate. The discount charged by the bank can be viewed as a sort of insurance by the importer (or exporter), while the bank will cover its position by matching deals as far as possible.

Case study – Grand Prix

As a racing driver young Stuart Fenwick was becoming quite famous. He had won a number of minor events and had been well placed in some of the Grand Prix. Then he was involved in a serious crash in the Indianapolis 500. His injuries were serious and his career in motor racing – certainly as a driver – was finished. However, his father owned a big garage in North London and Stuart turned his attention to designing. He produced a prototype which did very well in trials, but it needed much more spent on it before it could be raced.

While he had been racing abroad much of his prize money had been paid into overseas bank accounts. Stuart had been hoping to utilise these on future trips, but in view of the cash crisis he decided to instruct the overseas bankers to remit the outstanding amounts to his account in London. The amounts transferred – before being converted into sterling – were as follows:

from	Japan	46 478 yen
	Italy	130 000 lire
	Sweden	3687 kronor
	Germany	1800 deutschmarks
	Spain	74 807 pesetas
	United States	46 723.74 dollars
	Austria	48 743 schillings

When the sums had been transferred Stuart found that his account had been credited with a total of £33 357.23, which was less than he expected, but the difference was accounted for by the costs of the various remittances.

The exchange rates which were effective when the funds were transferred to London were as follows:

	Exchange rates (quoted to £ sterling)
Austria	28.75 schillings
Germany	3.95 deutschmarks
Italy	2300 lire
Japan	370 yen
Spain	225 pesetas
Sweden	11 kronor
United States	1.50 dollars

Your first task

Working in groups of two or three, calculate the amount that was deducted as costs by the remitting banks – in total. Compare your calculations. Pocket calculators would ease your task.

Questions for the group to consider together

(1) If you were planning to go to Spain for your holiday next summer, would you be pleased or dismayed to hear that the Spanish government had devalued the peseta by 15 per cent?
(2) What would you advise Stuart to do if there were persistent rumours that the German Mark was about to be devalued and he was about to transfer the balance in his account in West Germany to his London bank?
(3) Why do businessmen generally prefer stable exchange rates?
(4) If the value of the £ falls so that the exchange rate moves from $1.50 to $1.40 to the £, what would be the effect on the following situations?

 (i) A company which makes whisky and exports large quantities of it to the USA.
 (ii) An investor who holds a lot of American securities in his portfolio.
 (iii) A firm of tour operators operating from London who organise tours of Britain and Europe for American holiday-makers.
 (iv) An American collector who is bidding for a Rembrandt painting at a London auction.
 (v) An American executive who is working for a US bank in London and being paid a salary of $40 000 per annum.
 (vi) A British pop group who have arranged a tour of the United States.

A project for the group

Find out as much as you can about the various foreign currencies in use. Draw up a comprehensive list together with the current exchange rates where possible. The currencies and rates could be displayed on a map of the world if available. Graphs could also be used to plot a sample of exchange rates over a period of time.

CHAPTER 33

Insurance

The college was having a Rag Week. One of the activities planned was an outdoor one-day funfair: a marvellous idea, but it would cost a lot to hire the field and equipment the Rag Committee had in mind. Undeterred the Committee reckoned they would get great fat receipts which would more than cover the costs. They told their plans to one of their lecturers, expecting him to congratulate them on their business acumen, but he frowned.

'What happens if it pours with rain all day?' he asked, 'you'll still have to pay the hiring fees.'

The Committee were about to depart crestfallen when he called them back.

'Of course', he said, 'You could take out an insurance against it raining on the day of the funfair.'

That puzzled them, so he had to explain.

'The insurance company will ask the local meteorological office for records of rainfall over, say, the last ten years. If your funfair is on 2 July, they will ask how many times it has rained more than 0.2 inches on 2 July over the last ten years. If that has happened only once in the ten years, then those are the odds against it happening this year. One chance in 10 – or 10 per cent. How much cover is required? The cost of hiring the field and equipment is £200 you tell me, so that is how much cover you require. The insurance company will expect you to pay a premium. In the example I've given you the premium would be, say, £20. That is 10 per cent of the cover you want. They would also charge something extra for administration costs, and after all they are in the insurance business to make money. The premium they charge you will be about £30 in the example I've given you.'

All insurance cover is based on calculable risk. If the risk cannot be calculated, the insurance company cannot do business. They are professional risk-takers but not gamblers. Because they deal in large numbers of risks, the element of risk is removed.

Let us take another example. John Kershaw is 35 and in good health. What chance is there that he will die during this coming twelve months? No one knows, but the insurance company can study the mortality tables for last year. If 1 per cent of men in John Kershaw's age group died last year, the company can reckon that this statistic will be repeated this year, and charge a premium accordingly – £1(plus administration expenses and profit) per £100 of insurance cover.

There are certain other basic principles which will help you to understand the machinations of insurance.

Indemnity

The insurance company will indemnify (or cover) you against loss. But it will not allow you to make a profit on the transaction. If John Kershaw's house burns down and it was deemed worth £20 000, that is how much the insurance company will pay out to him even though the property was insured for £30 000. You will note that the ground on which the property stands was not destroyed by the fire. If it were possible to make a profit out of this sort of transaction, there would be more arsonists around!

Utmost good faith

The parties to an insurance contract are expected to disclose any relevant facts, so that if John Kershaw used his garage as a petrol store and failed to disclose this to the insurance company when the policy was taken out, it would be able to avoid paying out the insurance monies in the event of a fire. The insurance company must know what risks they are covering.

Insurable interest

If someone takes out an insurance policy, they must have an insurable interest in whatever is being insured. A husband can insure against the death of his wife, but not against the death of a public figure. One requires little imagination to work out what would happen if, for example, one could insure against the assassination of a politician.

In some ways the problems of banks and insurance companies are similar. They are certainly both concerned with the question of *liquidity*. The banks need to gear their assets to meet the instantaneous demands of their depositors, while the insurance companies have to be prepared to meet the claims of their policy-holders, whether the claim relates to property damaged by fire, claims by people injured in road accidents, ships lost at sea, or death. Both banks and insurance companies would be unable to carry on their businesses if the public lost confidence in their ability to meet their commitments. And both institutions will include a preponderance of government securities in their investment portfolios. The banks will tend to hold the very short-dated gilts, while insurance companies will choose a wider range of gilts and even invest in selected fixed-interest industrial stocks (debentures and preference) and in equities with a potential for long-term growth.

The cash which flows into the coffers of the insurance companies comes from two basic sources:

(i) the policy-holders pay premiums for the cover they receive; and
(ii) the stocks which are held in reserve generate interest and dividends.

The outflows of cash take three basic forms:

(i) payments to meet the claims of the policy-holders;
(ii) administration costs (including salaries paid to employees); and
(iii) distribution of profits to shareholders (except where the firms are 'mutual', i.e. non-profit-making).

British insurance firms have a world-wide reputation thanks to their integrity and the traditional speed with which they settle claims. Much of their business is conducted with overseas clients and so long as the premiums they receive from these clients exceed the claims made by them, the insurance business represents a valuable invisible export.

The main types of insurance cover

Type of insurance	*Risks covered*	*Special features*
Marine and Aviation (a specialty of Lloyds of London)	Loss or damage to (a) cargo (b) vessel. Responsibility for insurance determined by conditions of sale: *cif* (Cost, insurance and freight) Seller insures for benefit of buyer to port of destination.	Cover can be for individual shipments or for shipments over a period of time or up to a certain value. A *general average* clause is applied when a part of the cargo is jettisoned to save the rest of the cargo

Type of insurance	*Risks covered*	*Special features*
	c & f (Cost and freight) Buyers responsibility from time goods are put on board.	and/or the ship. A constructive loss occurs when the cost of recovery would exceed the value of the goods recovered.
Goods in transit	When goods are lost in transit a claim might be made against the carrier, but if the carrier is able to avoid the liability the owner (or person responsible for the goods) will have to depend on any insurance cover which has been arranged.	Open cover is usually effected when substantial volumes of goods are transported over a period. In this way the protection is automatic within the limits agreed.
Fire	Damage to buildings and contents. Normally includes damage by lightning and flood.	Additional premiums are required to cover against loss of earnings during rebuilding.
Theft	For business premises; usually limited to pilfering, but a fidelity guarantee will cover losses through dishonesty of staff.	For private accommodation; includes losses through burglary.
Motor	(i) Road Traffic Acts require all drivers to be insured against claims arising through death or injury. (ii) Third party cover relates to claims for damage to other people's property. (iii) A comprehensive policy extends cover in (i) and (ii) to damage to insured's own car.	A no-claim bonus may be offered to drivers who have not made a claim under the policy during a given period.
Employer's liability	Claims arising through injury to or death of employees during the course of work.	A legal requirement for all employers, as a means of ensuring that they have the funds to meet any claims.
Third-party	Claims by other people for acts or omissions causing death or injury.	An example would be where someone walks through a plate-glass door and claims that it was inadequately marked.
Export (a speciality of the Exports Credit Guarantee Department)	Losses resulting from the insolvency of the importers or their failure to pay for the goods.	It is always necessary for the exporter to bear part of the risk. The ECGD is a government service aimed at encouraging exports.

Type of insurance	*Risks covered*	*Special features*
Life assurance	The sum assured becomes payable on the death of the person whose life is insured. In the case of an endowment policy is coupled with the payment of a specified sum at the expiration of a fixed period.	A useful device for insuring against loss of earnings resulting from the untimely death of a key member of staff. Profit-sharing policies entitle the holders to a share in the profits made by the company. In the case of the so-called mutual offices the whole of the profit made is distributed in this fashion.
Industrial life assurance	Involves the smaller policies in respect of which premiums are payable at intervals of less than two months and are received by means of collectors who visit houses for this purpose.	The sums involved are small and this tends to make the business uneconomic. But some people who would not otherwise be reached are able to benefit.
Pension schemes	While the state pension scheme introduced in 1978 provides both a basic flat-rate pension and an earnings-related pension, many employers operate their own schemes to provide additional pensions. The management of many of these pension funds is entrusted to life offices (with their special expertise in long-term investments).	Pension schemes may be non-contributory so that the employer pays the entire cost or they may be contributory, in which case employees pay a set percentage of their salary into the fund.

What other types of insurance can you add to this list?

The insurance market

As in any market, there is a demand side and a supply side. The demand side is represented by those who seek insurance cover. They become policy-holders once the contract has been executed. The supply side is represented by the various institutions which are prepared to offer cover. When cover is provided these are known as the insurers. The companies vary widely in size and the classes of business which they undertake. The Insurance Companies Act, 1974, sets out the requirements enabling a company to undertake insurance business. The principal aim is to ensure that those who offer cover are able to meet claims when they are made.

Lloyd's

Lloyd's is an insurance market which covers almost all types of risk and about three-quarters of all premium income is generated overseas. As well as marine insurance the underwriting syndicates offer cover for the largest jet airliners and high-risk projects such as the towing of rigs to off-shore oilfields.

The syndicates vary from a few to 700 or more members and where the insurance is for a large amount a substantial number of syndicates may share the risks in agreed proportions. Each member of the syndicate is, in turn, individually liable for the proportion of the risk accepted on his behalf.

Insurance intermediaries

Those who are looking for insurance cover and those who are prepared to provide it are often put into touch with each other through *insurance brokers*. In law the brokers are agents of their principals, the policy-holders, although they usually collect premiums and give help when claims are made.

In many parts of the country the link between insurers and policy-holders remains the *part-time agent*. Among the ranks of these will be estate agents, solicitors and accountants, whose contacts with the public are of such a nature as to make insurance business a natural extension to their professional services.

Case study 1

Scene 1 – 1 March

Emil and Simon work in the same office. The both have similar jobs and run similar cars. At lunch the conversation turns to motor insurance.

'How much does your insurance cost?' asks Emil.

'I'm insured with Alpha. I know it's a bit dearer than some, but I feel safer with a well-known company. I pay £180 a year, but I get a 40 per cent no-claims bonus', replies Simon.

Emil responds: 'Do you know I've got an absolute gem of a policy. It's with a firm called Zeta. I've never heard of them before. They are covering me with a fully comprehensive policy for £80. A friend of mine in Birmingham told me about them.'

Scene 2 – 31 March
Emil and Simon are having lunch together again. Emil is talking.

'The police say it wasn't my fault. But I've hit a snag with the insurance company. I sent in my claim and I've had a letter back saying their affairs have been put into the hands of a Receiver. It looks as if they'll only be able to meet part of the claim – and it will take months and months to settle.'

What are your views on this situation?

Case study 2

The Board of Directors of Romulus Food Stores Ltd have become risk-conscious after a serious fire at one of their branches. They operate a chain of food supermarkets in the London area.

They have drawn up a list of the risks they run and want to know to what extent and in what manner they can combat each of these risks. Working together, you are asked to complete the following table:

Risks	*Remedies*
(1) Pilfering by both staff and customers	
(2) Fire damage to premises	
(3) Buildings being out of use during rebuilding after fire	
(4) Falling sales	
(5) Death of key members of staff	
(6) Bad debts	
(7) Till errors	
(8) Bad publicity (contaminated food)	
(9) Cut prices offered by competitors	
(10) Labour turnover	

CHAPTER 34

Government and Business

In a mixed economy such as we have in Britain the government is expected to modify the workings of the free market economy. In a free market economy the allocation of resources is determined by the price mechanism activated by the laws of demand and supply. How do the laws of demand and supply operate? They can be glimpsed through the workings of a typical supermarket. You might notice that the price of apples tends to go up by a few pence a lb. towards the week-end. Why? Because more people are shopping on Fridays and Saturdays and when demand for any commodity increases the price goes up. Looking at the opposite situation you will find the price of apples comes down in the autumn. Why? Because all over the country apple trees are bearing fruit and when the supply of a commodity increases the price will come down. If apples are expensive it means either that they are in great demand or short supply. If the price for apples is exceptionally high more resources are likely to be switched to apple-growing. Of course it is not only to apples that the laws of demand and supply relate. Why do lawyers get paid more than machine-minders, and why do diamonds cost more than plastic beads?

Some would argue that the government should interfere less in the economy and allow the market forces to operate more effectively. Others would argue that more government intervention is called for to negate waste and social inequality.

A major function of government in a caring society is to cater for the needs of those who are unable to care for themselves or who need sustenance and support. Indeed in a democracy no government could expect to stay in power unless they were able to provide for a majority of their electorate an acceptable life-style. The ultimate power lies with the voters. So the modern democratic government plays a sort of Robin Hood role taking from those it deems in need. One of the problems it faces in this operation is the need on the one hand to keep those who are earning high incomes and making big profits sufficiently motivated to keep up the good work, while at the same time coping with the endless numbers of deserving cases which abound in any society. These generally laudable activities impinge on business because the government 'robs the rich' by raising a variety of taxes on profits and selected goods and services. They may offer aid to ailing firms and/or subsidise those which are prepared to operate in economic black-spots. An overall picture of the way in which the government redistributes income can be gleaned from Figure 34.1 below.

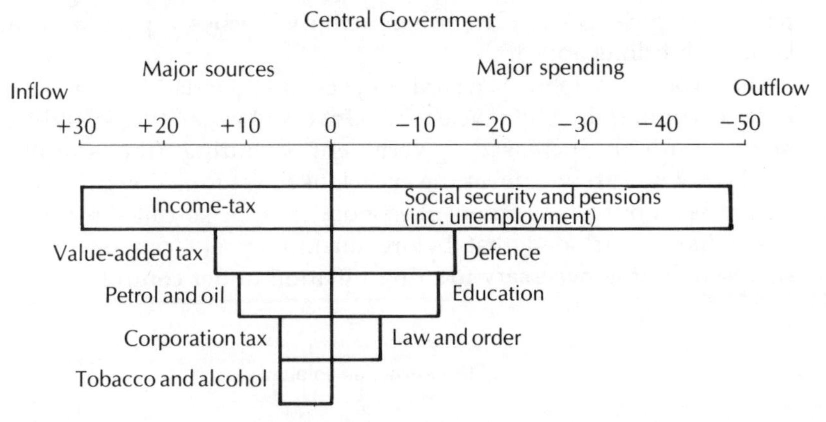

Sources: Central Statistical Office, *Financial Statistics,* June 1983; Board of Inland Revenue and HM Customs and Excise/Sunday Telegraph, 17 June 1983.

Figure 34.1

Businesses are affected by the redistribution of incomes in three different ways:

1. They have to bear the burden of some of the taxes which are imposed.
2. The levying of taxes discourages savings and reduces the flow of investment to support their projects.
3. The redistribution of income changes the consumers' spending patterns.

The trade cycle

Since the start of the Industrial Revolution in the middle of the eighteenth century fluctuations in business have developed a cyclical pattern. There is a surge of confidence as prospects for growth and expansion seem endless. Then the rate of growth and the confidence in future growth begin to decline. Orders for capital goods (plant and machinery, etc.) fall. There is unemployment in the heavy industries.

This reduces the demand for other goods and services and the boom gives way to recession. People begin to lose their jobs and because they have less money to spend fewer goods are bought and this leads to more unemployment. The situation worsens and the economy becomes the victim of a depression. Eventually businesses are forced to replenish their plant and machinery and the process starts to be reversed. Confidence picks up and jobs are created as order books begin to fill. Things look good for the future and the recovery gathers pace. The cycle is complete when activity reaches a peak and the boom conditions appear.

The economist John Maynard Keynes propounded certain measures to counter the trade cycle which involved generating spending-power through increased government spending (the so-called budgetary deficit) whenever the cycle looked set for a downturn (see Figure 34.2). But a new school of economists – the so-called monetarists – have concluded that before unemployment can be tackled successfully it is necessary to bring inflation under control.

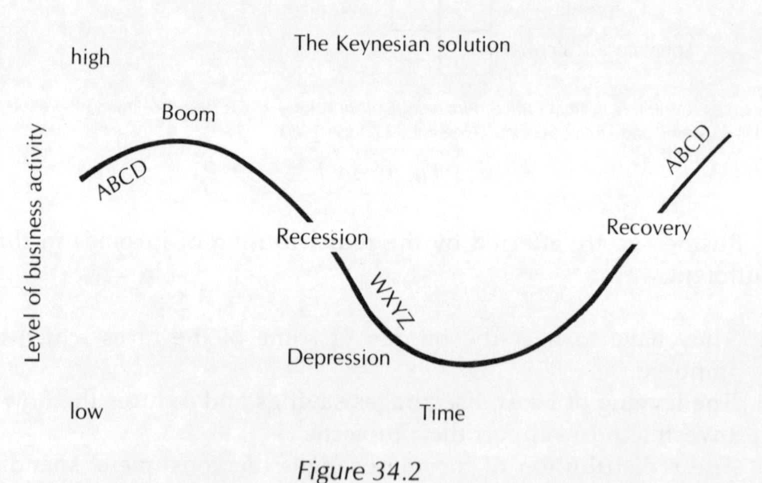

Figure 34.2

Remedial action

A = Budgetary surplus (more taxation and/or less government spending)	W = Budgetary deficit (less taxation and/or more government spending)
B = Open-market operations (Government broker sells securities)	X = Open-market operations (Government broker buys securities)

C = Bank of England calls for Special Deposits

D = Raise interest rates to discourage new projects

Y = Bank of England releases Special Deposits

Z = Lower interest rates to encourage new projects

Remedies for long-term unemployment

A new dimension to the unemployment problem has emerged in that many jobs are now disappearing as a result of the microchip revolution. Fewer people are required to achieve the same level of output, thanks to innovations such as robotic production lines and word processors. Yet this type of unemployment creates an opportunity as well as a threat. It could allow the members of our society to enjoy more leisure without a fall in their standard of living, but in order for this to happen certain ideas would have to be implemented such as:

(a) The introduction of work-sharing schemes with, for example, work divided up between morning and afternoon shifts or Monday to Wednesday shifts and Friday to Saturday shifts;

(b) the lowering of the age of retirement;

(c) the extension of the period of education either by raising the school-leaving age or allowing more people at work to broaden their visions or improve their skills by attending colleges or universities 'later in life';

(d) the introduction of shorter working weeks; and

(e) the giving of more/longer holidays.

For group discussion

What do you see as the weaknesses in these proposals? What ideas do you have for reducing the level of unemployment in our society?

The problems of inflation for businesses

The entrepreneur is constantly having to estimate costs and revenues in order to make decisions. If the costs and revenues are uncertain over a period of time the situation may become perilous. If costs rise faster than expected, profits will disappear and the business will fail. Yet if costs rise slower than predicted many customers will have been lost because too high prices were quoted. It is the uncertainty which creates the havoc especially for those who require time to manufacture goods.

Firms benefit from inflation in one sense. It is a help to them when they find that although they have produced goods inefficiently (i.e. at a high price compared to others) they will still manage to survive and make a profit as the price climbs to cover even the most exorbitant costs. This is particularly true when the rates of inflation are very high and when measures are applied successfully to curb inflation these marginal producers will be forced out of business.

Spiralling wage costs are particularly damaging where there is labour-intensive production. There is difficulty in fixing prices ahead. The tendency to over-compensate generally adds fuel to the fire by forcing up prices even higher. Any reduction in the rewards for the risk-taking entrepreneurs could lead to fewer projects being undertaken and therefore fewer employment opportunities.

Rising costs of raw materials will change production cost structures and necessitate an added tie-up of capital in stocks. Cash-flow difficulties could develop.

Where firms sell overseas they will find rising costs lose them their competitive edge in overseas markets. Market shares will tend to fall.

The final problem is likely to be faced by all businesses whenever there is inflation – even mild inflation. A firm will run its accounting system on the basis of historical cost. When a machine needs to be replaced after, say, ten years, the cost of replacement will far exceed the original cost. Thus with the same financial investment in the business there will be a decrease in the volume of the physical assets employed. An appreciation of this problem has led to the development of a more sophisticated accounting system for use in the larger companies.

Remedies for inflation

The main attack on rates of inflation which are considered too high is likely to be made through the supply of money. The measures might be a combination of:

(i) Cuts in government spending.
(ii) A budgetary surplus, with the Chancellor of the Exchequer collecting additional taxes but not spending them.

(iii) Sales of securities by the Government Broker.
(iv) A call by the Bank of England for special deposits from the commercial banks.
(v) A rise in interest rates to discourage new less-promising projects.

An incomes policy is a further option available. This would restrict increases in wages and dividends and avoid the development of a wages spiral.

Inflation involves the relation between the volume of goods and the volume of money in the economy and while attention is usually focused on the money side of the equation any measures which increase productivity can be viewed as anti-inflationary. Conversely any of the monetary measures mentioned above are ineffective to the extent that they result in fewer goods being produced.

Government objectives

In summary the logical economic objectives for any government would be:

(a) The allocation of resources in such a way as to ensure the highest possible national income in the long term.
(b) The redistribution of income so as to give support to the needy – without destroying the motivation required on the part of the providers.
(c) The stabilisation of the economy in terms of prices and employment so that steady economic growth can be sustained.
(d) The procurement of a healthy overseas trading position.

Your first assignment

In the first list overleaf there are six different business organisations. In the second list there are various actions which might be taken by the government. You are asked to consider the likely effects on each of the organisations.

The business organisations

1. A company which manufactures body-scanners for hospitals throughout the world.
2. A company organising coach tours to the Continent.
3. A firm of publishers concentrating on educational books.
4. A commercial bank.
5. A motor insurance company.
6. A London department store.

Government actions

A. The age of retirement is lowered by three years with old-age pensions becoming payable at that time.
B. Tax on petrol is increased by 2p per litre.
C. The school-leaving age is raised by one year.
D. The British and French governments agree to jointly finance the building of a cross-Channel tunnel.
E. Sterling is devalued in relation to the world's major currencies.
F. Income tax is increased by 5p in the £.
G. Expenditure on education and the health services is substantially increased.
H. The Bank of England calls for Special Deposits from the commercial banks.

An optional second assignment

Here are two quotations from the past, raising issues which remain with us at the present time. Write an essay expressing your views on one of these topics.

> 'So long as all the increased wealth which modern progress brings goes but to build up great fortunes, to increase luxury and make sharper the contrast between the House of Have and the House of Want, progress is not real and cannot be permanent.'

(From *Progress and Poverty* by the American reformer Henry George (1839–97))

> That grounded maxim
> So rife and celebrated in the mouths
> Of wisest men; that to the public good
> Private respects must yield.

(From *Samson Agonistes* by John Milton (1608–74))

CHAPTER 35

The European Economic Community

> The Community shall have as its task, by establishing a common market and progressively approximating the economic policies of Member States, to promote throughout the Community a harmonious development of economic activities, a continuous balanced expansion, an increase in stability, an accelerated raising of the standard of living, and closer relations between the states belonging to it (Article 2 of the Treaty of Rome, 1957).

The European Economic Community (EEC) was formed when the representatives of France, West Germany, Italy, Belgium, the Netherlands and Luxembourg signed the Treaty of Rome. Tariff barriers were progressively lowered between the member states until a large free-trade area was created. There followed a significant rise in the level of trade between the countries – which produced a correlated rise in the standard of living. The Community was subsequently enlarged to include Britain and other countries.

Apart from the aim of allowing the free passage of capital, people and goods between the member states, there is a Common Agricultural Policy which bolsters farm incomes within the Community. This is achieved by raising protective tariffs between the EEC and the outside world, and by support purchases on the internal market. The latter technique explains the 'beef mountains' and the 'butter mountains' which have occurred. The Common Agricultural Policy is highly favoured by those member states which have strong agricultural interests, but high prices for European farmers also mean high prices for European consumers.

The administrative headquarters of the EEC is in Brussels. A political unity is eventually envisaged, but this notion is not universally accepted. If the unification of Europe proceeds, it will be necessary to harmonise the laws of the member states as well as their economies. One area where laws diverge is in the field of industrial relations. For example, in West Germany workers function as members of the Board of Directors. There are two tiers of Directors. The Management Board is responsible for the day-to-day administration of the organisation – under the scrutiny of the Supervisory Board composed of 50 per cent worker representation. (Under the terms of the new codetermination, or *Mitbestimmung*, law that came into effect on 1 July 1977, the 650–odd West German companies employing 2000 or more workers must set up, within two years, arrangements for the selection of half of the members of their supervisory boards by their employees.) Other EEC countries have similar laws – but there is nothing to compare with these ideas in Britain.

In Britain some firms have works councils but they are not obligatory as they are in other EEC countries. Elected representatives from various sections of the firm meet periodically with management to discuss matters of mutual concern. Workers can indicate their problem areas and grievances, and take explanations from management back to their work-mates. Discussions on pay are usually excluded from such meetings. This is considered more appropriate for direct negotiations.

The matters discussed by the members of the works council may be comparatively trivial – if you consider holidays and car-parking facilities as trivial – but it is one way in which workers may become involved in the decision-making process. It gives the most lowly workers – or their representatives – direct access to management. It is an acknowledgement that workers have a right to participate in the making of certain decisions which will affect them. It will be interesting to see whether over the years further power devolves on the works councils so that they become involved in the making of more important business decisions.

The classical economic argument for free trade is that when tariff barriers are removed, it allows firms to compete against each other without artificial support or protection. The most efficient expand and move into the enlarged market, while the less efficient, unprotected by the tariff barriers which previously kept out the cheaper goods, go out of business. Each area within the Community will specialise in producing those goods, or providing those services, in which it has a comparative advantage. The same arguments apply to the world as a whole, and if tariff barriers could be lowered – or better still removed completely – there would be increased output and prosperity.

However, even the staunchest advocates of free trade will generally admit that there is an argument in favour of protecting infant industries in countries which are in the throes of industrial development.

One of the inevitable developments resulting from the creation of the free-trade area in Europe is that the size of business units will become larger. The economic adage is that the size of the market determines the scale of production within it. The largest business organisations in the world are undoubtedly American, and this is not simply because the USA is a rich country. Undoubtedly the fact that there is a large trading area without tariff barriers between the constituent states has meant that American firms have benefited from a large domestic market. Operating on a large scale, they have been able to enjoy a variety of economies which only large-scale operations allow.

Questions for the group to consider

What are your views on the EEC? Do you favour economic and political unity for Europe? What are the likely effects on the British economy?

Case study – Strubank Chinaware

You are asked to play the roles of the members of the Works Council of Strubank Chinaware Ltd, makers of the famous Strubank range of high-quality dinner and tea sets. There are 2387 workers in the firm, including 320 administrative and sales staff.

There are three items on the Agenda for the current meeting and you are asked to deal with them:

(1) *The new works canteen.* The company has begun to operate a new canteen which cost £30 000 to build and equip. Complaints have been received from a number of workers who feel the prices for the meals are too high. Management has stated the view that the service should be self-financing, but non-profit-making. The charges are fixed to cover the cost of the meals plus a 5 per cent per annum interest charge on the construction costs of the canteen.

There have also been complaints about the lack of variety on the menu. There is different food available each day but there are only two alternatives offered for the main course. The canteen manageress has put forward the suggestion that there should be a Canteen Committee set up.

(2) *The new car park.* The company suffers from seriously inadequate parking space. A recent survey conducted by the works council

has shown that 860 workers would bring their cars to work if they had the opportunity to do so. A new and enlarged car park has been constructed which is capable of taking 320 cars. 100 of the available spaces have been provisionally allocated to the sales and administrative staff, and a further thirty spaces will be kept free for visitors to the works. Management has invited suggestions as to how the remaining spaces might be allocated, since a 'free for all' might lead to chaos.

(3) *Music while you work.* The management is contemplating introducing some form of 'music while you work' programme to the shop floor. They are looking for some ideas from the work-force.

Note that the working day is split into the following periods:

0830 – 1030
1045 – 1245
1300 – 1500
1515 – 1730

Final task for the group

Each member of the group should prepare a brief report setting out the outcome of the discussions. When the reports are available they should be compared to see whether there are any differences in the interpretation of the proceedings.

PART 5

CROSS-MODULAR CASE STUDIES

CHAPTER 36

Boardroom Problems

The Directors of Redknapp Kits Ltd are having their weekly Board meeting at the company's Head Office in Bristol. The company concentrates its resources on manufacturing plastic modelling kits under three brand-names:

(i) the First Step Kits, which are ultra simple and for young children;
(ii) the Modello Kits, which are the standard versions; and
(iii) the Exacto Kits, which were introduced last year and are designed for the serious modeller.

There are nine Directors on the board, but three of them have tendered their apologies for absence – two are sick and one is 'unavoidably detained' elsewhere. The first item on the Agenda is a consideration of some statistics which the Chairman, George Redknapp, has obtained from the Chief Accountant and the Sales Manager (see Table 36.1).

Table 36.1

	Last year (12 months)	This year (10 months to date)
Sales in £m.		
First Step Kits	83.5	70.4
Modello Kits	126.7	106.9
Exacto Kits	7.2	9.8
Advertising expenditure (£000)	81.3	62.3
Wages in £m.	48.7	44.6
Average work-force on pay-roll	8326	8487
Working days lost through absence	78364	75654
Workers leaving the firm (other than for retirement)	2564	2654

To what extent do you think these figures *should be disturbing to the Directors?*

The second item on the Agenda concerns the retirement of one of the existing members of the Board. Sam Miller was due for re-election at the next AGM but ill-health has forced him to retire. The Chairman has proposed an *ex gratia* payment of £40 000 in recognition of Sam's thirty-six years of service to the company – the last sixteen years as Sales Director.

The third item on the Agenda refers to a replacement for Sam on the Board of Directors. Three names are being put forward by the Board:

Alan Standford (aged 57) was appointed Sales Manager (immediately responsible to Sam Miller) two years ago. He joined the firm twenty-three years ago as a sales representative and was the London and Home Counties Area Manager for eleven years before getting his present appointment.

Sir Douglas Merridrew (aged 43) would function as a non-executive director (without departmental responsibilities). He is a director of three other companies, one of which is Glenco Stores Ltd – one of Redknapp's biggest customers. Glenco have recently acquired a controlling interest in a West German retailing chain.

Julian Redknapp (aged 31) is the son of the Chairman. Having obtained an economics degree at London University, he went on to Yale for a postgraduate course. Since returning to England a year ago, he has had spells in Accounts and Marketing (including three months selling 'in the field').

The task for the group

Play the role of the Board of Directors of this company and deal with the three items on the Agenda. Bear in mind that formal resolutions have to be proposed and passed by a simple majority of Directors present. This is the way the Board makes decisions. One of the group will be required to act as Secretary, keeping a record of the proceedings in the form of minutes. The Chairman will control the meeting.

CHAPTER 37

In-tray 1 – Marketing Department

You are personal assistant to Susan Bevis, the Marketing Manager at Liberty Freezers Ltd. The company have developed a new type of domestic refrigerator/freezer – Lady Luck – with the following features:
(i) it is noiseless, (ii) it has three separate inner cabinets to save a rise in temperature when the door is opened, and (iii) it uses a new insulating material which allows a much smaller and less expensive cooling unit to be installed.

Susan has just left for her three-week annual holiday and your instructions are to deal with routine queries yourself but refer any important matters to Alistair Forbes, the Managing Director. When you look at the morning's mail you find the following items that need attention.

Draft any replies and since Mr Forbes is heavily engaged in meetings for the next few days use memoranda to communicate with him.

BRITISH TELECOM
Tel. (77) 325 **Welcome Buildings,**
Nottingham

date

Mrs Susan Bevis,
Marketing Manager,
Liberty Freezers Ltd,
Liberty House,
Pemberton.

Ref. YP/36475/JW

Dear Mrs Bevis,

Thanking you for your letter of yesterday's date confirming your booking for a 6 cm × 6 cm. block in the next edition of the Yellow Pages for the Nottingham area. Would you let us know how you wish to utilize the advertising block.

If you draft the wording and indicate the nature of the artwork you have in mind we will pass on your ideas to our team of art editors who will carry out the detailed work.

We await your instructions.

Yours sincerely,

Janet Whalley

Janet Whalley
(Asst Area Manager)

K. KENNY (KITCHENS) Ltd
Leeds

date

Please quote in reply Ref. RK/PEM

Dear Mrs Bevis,

This company is planning to purchase a series of slots of advertising time on Yorkshire Television during the coming year. Our plans are by no means crystallised but we envisage the rather conventional approach of a catchy tune – with a couple of attractive housewives extolling the virtues of a Kenny Kitchen. 'Penny Saving Kenny' is the theme. Of course the costs of production are likely to be high for this sort of promotion – though the benefits are likely to be commensurate with the investment. We are toying with the idea of sharing the costs and benefits with one of our suppliers – and as you provide 90% of our basic kitchen equipment we naturally thought of you!

Would you be interested in this sort of joint venture? A London Agency (AVA) is looking after the project for us and if you joined us we would expect to feature your products prominently in the film – obviously after consultation and to your satisfaction. We have been given a deadline for providing essential details by the end of the month so we are hoping you could let us know within fourteen days whether you are interested.

Best Wishes,

Robert Kenny

Robert Kenny

Mrs Susan Bevis,
Marketing Manager,
Liberty Freezers Ltd,
Liberty House,
Pemberton.

Liberty Freezers Ltd

To Sue Bevis
Marketing Manager.

From Carol Bainton
Personal Assistant
to Managing Director

Mr Forbes has asked me to pass this letter on to you. No doubt you will contact the rep and let him know that Mr Forbes is not pleased about it.

CB

Brent Stores,
High Street,
Pemberton.

The Managing Director,
Liberty Freezers,
Pemberton.

date

Dear Sir,

I have always tried to support local firms and although I am only in a small way of business I have always kept a couple of your Penguin mini-freezers in stock ever since I opened three years ago. But the last two sales I made have been nothing but trouble.

Your rep Brian Lane got quite offensive when I told him about the complaints. Frankly if that is the way you do business I can take my custom elsewhere.

Yours faithfully,

George Webster

The Coppice,
High Reach,
Pemberton.
date

Dear Mrs Bevis,
I'm very sorry to have to tell you that my Brian will not be at work for some time. He's had a heart attack and is in Beddersley Infirmary. They say he'll pull through but he's very poorly.

Yours sincerely,

Alice Lane

Liberty Freezers Ltd
Internal Memorandum

To | From

These diagrams have just come through. Charles Forbes wants them for the Chairman's Annual Report. Pass them on to him with a few useful comments.

Sue.

**CAMELOT
ADVERTISING AGENCY
Sorenson House
Sorenson Square
Peebles.**

(76) 2309

Mrs Susan Bevis,
Marketing Manager,
Liberty Freezers Ltd,
Liberty House,
Pemberton.

date

Dear Susan,

*Proposed Advertising Campaign
Lady Luck Freezer Fridges*

I have now had the opportunity to carry out an initial examination of the proposals we discussed when we met last week. As I explained we will be happy to produce some sample tv material for your board to consider formally. However, we shall need to agree on the sort of approach to be adopted in order to avoid unnecessary expense in the development of material.

Assuming we are only looking for a single 25 second shot to be shown repetitively on ten consecutive evenings in the early spring, which was the maximum you envisaged as I understand, the following options are available:

Option one
The opening shot shows a young couple about to open the front door for important guests.
"Don't forget," the husband says, "If this evening goes off O.K. I'll get my promotion ..."
An older couple come in and the four of them are then seen eating around the table.
"Brussels sprouts in March?" the older lady says, "You must have a good freezer ..."
The final shot shows the younger (and very attractive) lady going to new fridge freezer. She is bringing out some colourful fresh fruit salads for sweet.

"Very nice," says the husband's boss, who comes behind her with an amorous twinkle in his eye.
Behind him suddenly looms his wife, "Yes isn't it," she says acidly, "You'll have to buy me one of these lovely Lady Luck freezer fridges won't you – darling."

Option Two
A young lad is sitting at the kitchen table studying a book on mathematics (in large writing). He looks across to his father – with a puzzled expression.
"Dad," he asks, "What do you reckon is the easiest job in the world?"
"Ah," says his father, "You're looking for a career for when you leave school are you son ...... It's a funny thing you should ask that .... The easiest job in the world ... Yes .... I reckon the easiest job in the world must be selling these new Lady Luck freezer fridges ...." He catalogues all the special features.
"And all that for £215...."

Option Three
A boffin (scientist) is demonstrating some of the wonders of Modern Technology. First, he points out – briefly – and with film snippets – the wonders of the micro chip. Then briefly he turns to communication satellites, followed by interplanetary space vehicles. Finally he introduces the viewers to the new Lady Luck freezer – pointing out all its special features.
"Aren't they all wonderful," he says, fading out to a picture split into four parts, one of which is the Liberty Refrigerator. The camera zooms in to the refrigerator on its own "A Wonder of Modern Technology" booms a resonant voice to the accompaniment of electronic music.

If you let me know which of these approaches interests you most I will make arrangements for some appropriate material to be developed. We can then bring the film to Pemberton and show it to your board for their consideration. We normally produce five or six alternative productions based on the option you select.
I look forward to hearing from you with your comments.

Yours sincerely,

Jeremy Hines

Jeremy Hines

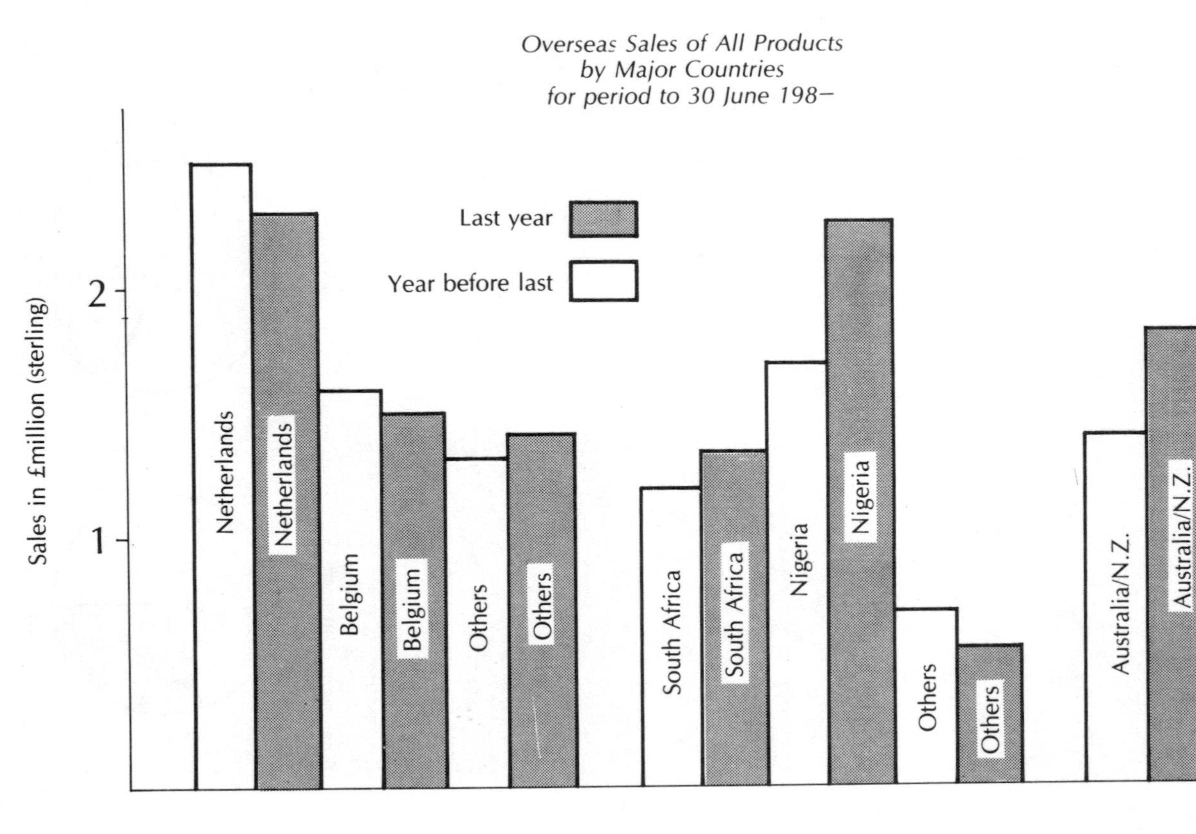
Overseas Sales of All Products
by Major Countries
for period to 30 June 198–
Last year
Year before last
Sales in £million (sterling)
2
1
Netherlands
Netherlands
Belgium
Belgium
Others
Others
South Africa
South Africa
Nigeria
Nigeria
Others
Others
Australia/N.Z.
Australia/N.Z.

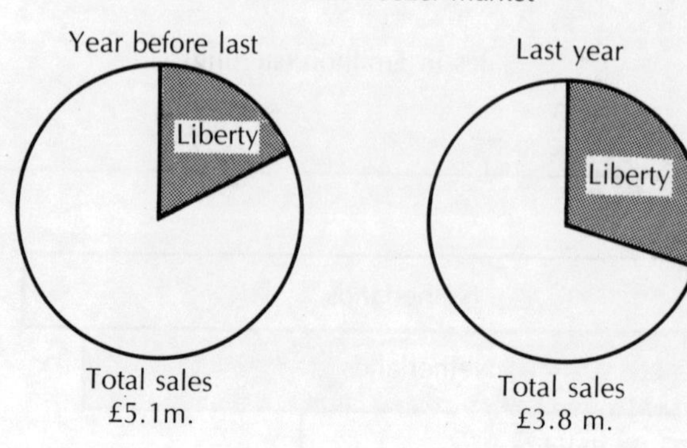
UK Mini-freezer market
Year before last
Liberty
Total sales
£5.1m.
Last year
Liberty
Total sales
£3.8 m.

CHAPTER 38

Wife-testing

Karl Kringle is one of the American directors of John Armitage (Industrial Machinery) Ltd, a British company based at Stockport. He has recently returned from a trip to the parent company in the USA. He has drafted a report to the rest of the Board of Directors of the British subsidiary in which he mentions the care taken by the parent company when selecting top executives. In some cases, when a candidate applies for a senior post, the selection process includes a full vetting of the candidate's wife. The wife is interviewed separately from her husband and is asked searching questions to discover her attitude on certain matters which the firm considers of importance. An attempt is made to discover whether she has any personality problems which might pose a threat to her husband's career.

Justification for this sort of action, according to Karl Kringle's report, comes under the following headings:

(i) the wife of a senior executive will have to attend a variety of functions, and will be associated with the company by the people who meet her;

(ii) if an executive's wife has serious personality problems, this is bound to affect his performance as an executive;

(iii) the stakes are high for the company, so that mistakes made by executives under stress will adversely affect the careers and livelihoods of all those who work for the company.

(iv) no one will be rejected as a candidate for a senior post simply on the assessment of the wife's suitability – this will be just one of the factors considered when a choice is made between candidates.

Kringle appreciates that these ideas will not be readily acceptable to British executives, but he points out that the parent company is considering a massive new development programme in Britain – through the Armitage subsidiary. He feels that introducing techniques like this would be a small price to pay for the benefits that would accrue to so many people. As he put it informally to his fellow directors, 'It is their money and as they see it they are simply protecting their investment every way they can.'

Table 38.1 Questionnaire

When a senior executive is being appointed to a key post, do you think the following factors should be taken into account? How important are they?		*Very important*	*Not very important*	*Of no importance*
(1) His wife is suing him for divorce	*Personal view*	☐	☐	☐
(2) His wife is receiving treatment for alcoholism	*Personal view*	☐	☐	☐
(3) His wife's father has useful connections (e.g. his company buys a lot of our products)	*Personal view*	☐	☐	☐
(4) His wife is attractive and has a pleasant personality	*Personal view*	☐	☐	☐
(5) His wife has expensive tastes	*Personal view*	☐	☐	☐
(6) His wife has spent time in a mental hospital in the recent past and is still receiving treatment	*Personal view*	☐	☐	☐
(7) His wife is actively involved in politics (she is a local councillor)	*Personal view*	☐	☐	☐
(8) His wife is heavily involved in voluntary work for charities	*Personal view*	☐	☐	☐
(9) He and his wife have seven children all under the age of 18	*Personal view*	☐	☐	☐
(10) The candidate has no wife (he is 45 and has never married)	*Personal view*	☐	☐	☐

Four tasks for the group

(1) Discuss the points raised in the questionnaire above (Table 38.1) which was circulated to the staff of John Armitage's head-

quarters. The staff were asked to tick the appropriate boxes to indicate their personal responses to the questions posed. How would the people in your group have responded to those questions? Find out how many people in your group would have ticked each box.

(2) Do you think the same considerations should apply if the candidate is a woman? Should her husband be vetted?

(3) Penultimately, consider together the implications of Karl Kringle's news that the parent company is planning to invest a large sum in Britain. Should this sort of investment be welcomed? Who would benefit? How would they benefit? What are the drawbacks, if any?

(4) Finally, in the light of the preceding discussions, draft a report (individually) to Karl Kringle explaining the reactions he can expect from the company's employees in Britain. You can write your report as if you are one of the senior executives who have been consulted on the matter.

CHAPTER 39

In-tray 2 – Gifford Electronics

John Gifford runs this business with his wife Anne. There are seven employees, five of whom are in the so-called workshop and two in the outer office. John runs the technical side of the business, which involves preparing software packages to order for one of the major firms of computer manufacturers. Anne looks after the paperwork.

Both John and Anne are out of town until Monday week. They are in London at the invitation of the computing company which gives them all their business. Pat Chadwick assists Anne in the office and generally runs it in her absence. The only other person in the office is a typist/telephonist who joined them two weeks ago.

Your task

You are asked to consider the items in Pat's in-tray on the first day of the Giffords's absence. How do you think they should be dealt with? Draft any correspondence you would have expected Pat to send out and make a note of any diary entries that should be recorded.

Flat 115, Deryk Court,
Walsall Road.
Leek.
date

Dear Sirs,
I hear you have some vacances for clerical jobs and would like to offer my services. For some years I was a copy-typist at Cadbury's Bourneville works and I have also worked for the civil service. I can give you good references and I am not afraid of a bit of work.

Yours sincerely, Emma Brylan

Barchester Bank
Sutton Park,
Birmingham

date

Mr J. Gifford,
Gifford Electronics,
Unit 5, Westland Industrial Estate,
Birmingham.

Dear Mr Gifford,
The cheque for £350 paid into your account last Wednesday, drawn by Unitex Technics has been returned "Refer to drawer. Please re-present." This usually means that there are uncleared effects on the account and I would suggest we re-present the cheque in a few days to see if the cheque is cleared then. I will retain the cheque until I hear from you.

Yours sincerley,

G. V. Crompton, Manager.

Flat 93, Deryk Court,
Walshall Road,
Leek.
date

Dear Mrs Gifford,
I thank you for your letter. I would be free to come for an interview any afternoon this week. You did mention that I would be able to have a holiday for two weeks with my family in July. I hope that is still possible because we want to book our holiday as soon as possible.

Yours sincerely, E. Singh

Pat,
Have a look at this letter about Alfred Brown's account for me. He was such a nice man. He went to pieces when his wife died, But I've checked the amount they owe us and it should be £5,976.75 not £5,876.75. And I'm sure his premises would be worth more than £15,000. How much do you think we will get out of the receiver by the time it's finished?

Anne

PS. Drop a line to our accountant, Griffith Pearson at Adderley Chambers, Sutton Park. He doesn't know anything about it yet but John agrees he should be told.

Pat, we have a Mrs Khan coming to be interviewed for a part-time job at the end of the week. Put her off until at least the Tuesday after I get back. You can make the arrangements though. She sounds useful.

Anne

PS. Our address in London in case of emergency:
Cavendish Hotel,
Squire's Gate

Gifford Electronics
Unit 5, Westlands Industrial Estate,
Birmingham

Pat, I think young Meera could do with a bit of guidance on how to deal with phone calls. Suggest you draw up a list of do's and don'ts for her. Be tactful because I think she's shaping up nicely.

John.

John Bane
Chartered Accountant,
Conroy Chambers,
London W1R 8LA

date

Dear Mr Gifford,

Re: Alfred Brown trading as Zeus Electrics

As you are one of the principal creditors of Mr Brown I thought you would appreciate an early intimation of the position with regard to the Receivership. I have now had an opportunity to draft an Interim Statement of Affairs. This will be produced for the Court's Approval, but it seems likely that the relevant figures from your point of view are as follows:

Assets (to be realised)		£17,985.98
less Amount due to Secured Creditors	2,654.75	
Administration and Legal Expenses (estimated)	800.00	3.454.75
Amount available to Unsecured Creditors		£14,531.23

The total debts outstanding to Unsecured Creditors amounts to £37,495.83 which sum includes the sum of £5,876.75 owed to your company. Included among the assets is the lease of the premises from which Mr Brown conducted his business. This is now on the market but the agents who are dealing with the sale have intimated that it will take time to find a purchaser if we are to achieve anything like the asking price of £15,000. I am sure you will agree that it is in our interest to obtain the highest possible price for the lease.

I will contact you again when material progress has been made.

Yours sincerely,

John Bane

John Bane FCA
Receiver

John Gifford,
Gifford Electronics,
Unit 5, Westland Industrial Estate,
Birmingham.

CHAPTER 40

The Royalty Grill

Frank Warren owned a confectioners/tobacconists shop in central Manchester and when his wife became ill he decided to move south to a warmer clime. He looked for a restaurant to purchase and eventually found one to his liking. It was called the *Royalty Grill* and was situated on one of the main routes into the holiday resort of Brighton. Frank visited the restaurant a couple of times – incognito – and was particularly impressed with the large number of customers who filled the place to capacity, and were free with their praises of the cuisine and the service.

The price being asked for the freehold of the restaurant was £60 000, and the business agency indicated that the net profit of approximately £12 000 a year enjoyed by the present proprietor gave a return of 20 per cent per annum, which was about what one could expect in this particular trade.

Frank decided to buy the restaurant. He negotiated a five-year loan for £20 000 with his bankers, which was secured by the deposit of the property deeds and the signature of his wife's brother as guarantor.

Things went well at the start, but after a few months the Warrens began to encounter staff problems. Mrs Warren had some disputes with the waitresses and there were soon none of the original staff left. Staff problems have continued to plague them. They just cannot find satisfactory staff to wait on the tables. There was one young lady whom Mrs Warren had felt sure was stealing money out of the till. When Mrs Warren accused her, she went red in the face and walked out without another word. Then there was Jill who had got tipsy at Christmas time. She had dropped a tray full of food. Some of it had splashed over a customer and that had been enough for Mrs Warren. Carol had been a chain smoker. Mrs Warren did not like cigarette smoke at any time, but when she found Carol smoking in the kitchen while food was being prepared, she sent her packing. Carol had been a good waitress otherwise, but she had been warned about her smoking many times.

The big blow for the Warrens came when the Italian chef, Nunzio, announced that he was going to work in one of Brighton's best hotels as Second Chef – with an extra £1000 a year salary.

It is now the end of their first year in the business and the accountant has produced the set of accounts you see in Table 40.1. Frank's brother-in-law is dismayed when he sees them.

Table 40.1
Profit and loss account for year ending ...

	£		£
Wages (including National Insurance, etc.)	15 591.37	Receipts	57 714.25
Supplies	32 733.17		
Bank charges	2 650.50		
Rates	1 236.15		
Electricity and gas	1 132.65		
Insurance	310.30		
Profit	4 060.11		
	£57 714.25		£57 714.25

Balance-sheet as at ...

		£		£
Capital	40 000.00		Premises at cost	60 000.00
Drawings	2 100.00		Equipment at cost	1 125.00
			Stocks and supplies	672.65
	37 900.00		Debtors	13.75
Profit	4 060.11		Cash	92.56
		41 960.11		
Creditors		1 622.24		
Bank loan		18 000.00		
Bank overdraft		321.61		
		£61 903.96		£61 903.96

Questions for the group

(1) What weaknesses are shown up in the balance-sheet?
(2) Why do you think the guarantor is so concerned?
(3) How much do you think Frank Warren would get if he sold the business now?
(4) With the benefit of hindsight, what do you think the Warrens could have done to avert the problems which have arisen?
(5) What would you advise Frank to do now?
(6) Do you think the staff who were dismissed might have any legal claims against the Warrens?

Written work

Draft a letter such as might have been written by Karen Austen, the Warrens's accountant, explaining the situation to them and giving recommendations as to the actions that might be taken.

CHAPTER 41

Trade Secrets

Spiro Cortex Ltd is a subsidiary of the International Metals Group. The main works are on the outskirts of Wigan, but there are two smaller units. One is the Head Office and administrative centre, which is in Burnley. The other unit is on the outskirts of Accrington, but it is planned to phase this out over the next few years. Spiro Cortex could be described as a technological path-finder. It is constantly producing new designs for industrial machinery. Large sums have been spent – and are continuing to be spent – on research, and it has a team of researchers and designers who are second to none in the world. The company's reputation is world-wide and that is where the problem starts. In spite of its long experience in protecting its interests, certain international competitors – and even some from Britain – have succeeded in outsmarting the company recently, specifically:

(1) When the company came to patent a revolutionary new power press – which had taken two and a half years to develop – they found that a West German firm had taken out international patents for a number of the vital new components. As a result the German firm was able to prohibit the sale of the press in Britain by Spiro Cortex. The Managing Director has undertaken some investigations and has found that the Chief Designer's personal secretary, Monica Schultz, who has recently left the firm, was married to an ex-employee of the German firm. Her staff records indicate that she was a first-class secretary who took an interest in everything that was going on.

(2) A project was started two years ago which involved using solar energy, both as a form of central heating and as a means of generating support power for certain light machinery within the same complex. The power was not sufficient to drive heavy machinery unaided, but it was capable of boosting existing power and thus substantially reducing costs. Just when an important breakthrough occurred, the key member of the research team was offered a post in a

rival American company – at double the salary he had been getting with Spiro Cortex.

(3) Six months ago a process was discovered which had the effect of delaying corrosion significantly. The technique was inexpensive and simply involved spraying a metal surface with a specially treated plastic film before painting. A rarely used chemical with restricted availability was a key ingredient. The first orders for the chemical were honoured by the American suppliers, but they have now raised the price to a prohibitive level. The explanation offered is that a French firm has contracted to purchase virtually the whole of the world supplies of this chemical for the next three years. This has resulted in a massive upsurge in the price of the remaining supplies. As a result of this development the whole of this research programme has had to be put into cold storage for the time being. The company had assigned a number of specialist staff to this project, and the Managing Director is having to think about making some of these workers redundant.

Questions for the group to discuss

(1) What changes in the organisation do you think the Managing Director of Spiro Cortex Ltd should make on this evidence? How do you think security might be improved in the company?
(2) What remedies are normally available to any employer whose staff have betrayed their trust? Do these remedies have any relevance to the present case?
(3) If redundancies are necessary, on what basis do you think these should take place? First in, last out? On an age basis? According to their competency in the job? Or some other basis? What rights do the employees have in these circumstances? Why does the government concern itself in these matters?
(4) Do you regard industrial espionage as an inevitable business hazard?

Report

When the discussion is completed, draft a report to the Managing Director, Nicholas Worthy, setting out your recommendations.

CHAPTER 42

Northfield United

Northfield United were in the First Division of the Football League once, but that was a long time ago, and for the past ten years they have been languishing near the foot of the Fourth Division. The supporters have been drifting off over the years, understandably preferring to air their vocal chords on the terraces of some of the more illustrious teams within reasonable travelling distance of Northfield. The average gates for home matches fell from 4000 to just over 3000 in the past season, though the capacity of the ground is over 30 000.

You represent the Board of Directors of the Northfield United Football Club Ltd who have been specially summoned to deal with a number of urgent problems, as indicated below:

(1) As a result of an altercation between officials and players which made headlines in the local newspaper, Daniel Marsden, the Chairman of the Board has resigned. He is also Managing Director of a brewery based in Northfield and is a local councillor. He has personally lent the club £50 000.

(2) The contract of Sam Goulden, the Player-Manager of the club for the past two seasons, has now run out. Sam has had a number of clashes with the Chairman since his appointment. A letter from Sam has been tabled which claims the club suffers through not having scouts to discover local players with talent. He aims to develop a more active Supporters' Club – the present Club is virtually defunct. And he claims the sole right to select the team each week – objecting to what he describes as 'occasional but damaging interference by certain members of the Board'.

It is common knowledge that there are two underlying causes of friction between Sam and Daniel Marsden. One of them is Sam's relationship with Daniel's married daughter. The other is Daniel's determination to sell the club's star striker. A well-known Second Division club has made inquiries and is prepared to offer £70 000 for him.

(3) The club's bankers have indicated that they are considering calling for a repayment of the £100 000 loan which was negotiated last

year and secured on the deeds of the ground. The ground is in the centre of the town. An offer of £500 000 was made for the ground recently by a property development company who want to build an office block and a covered market on the site. The bank is apparently concerned with the parlous state of the club's finances generally, and attention has been drawn to the latest balance-sheet, an abridged version of which is shown in Table 42.1.

Table 42.1

Balance-sheet as at 31 December

		£			£
Capital			*Fixed assets*		
Ordinary Stock			Equipment (at cost *less*		
(£1 units)		100 000	depreciation)		16 064
General reserves		6 000	Freehold property		
Balance on profit			(at cost)		243 000
and loss a/c		1 682			
		£107 682			£259 064
Loans		150 000			
Tax provision		2 000			
Current liabilities			*Current assets*		
Creditors	857		Loan to Supporters'		
Bank overdraft	45		Club	2 000	
Tax due	806		Debtors	326	
		1 708			2 326
		£261 390			£261 390

Questions for the group to consider

(1) What action do you think the club might take to solve its financial problems? Do you think an issue of new stocks or shares would help? What sort of stocks or shares would you suggest? How attractive do you think such an issue would be to investors?

(2) How do you think the personality clash between Daniel Marsden and Sam Goulden should be dealt with? Do you think Sam should be left to deal with team selection without interference from any members of the Board? What role do you think the Board (and its Chairman) should play?

(3) Do you think Sam's relationship with Daniel's daughter is of consequence to the club? Could Sam's behaviour damage morale generally? What action would you propose?

CHAPTER 43

Tropical Aquaria

As you may know, tropical fish-keeping is quite a popular hobby. The main requirements are:

(i) an aquarium of an adequate size according to the number and variety of fishes you intend to keep;
(ii) heating, aerating and cleaning equipment; and
(iii) a range of exotic tropical fish, together with sand and water plants.

A certain personable young man has approached Poltex Stafford, the well-known financier, with a business proposition. Although John Blunt is only in his mid-twenties, he has become quite an authority on tropical fish, particularly with regard to breeding certain rare species. He has written two books on the subject and has recently finished filming a television series for international release.

John Blunt proposes to market a new service to be known as 'Blunt's Commercial Aquaria'. The general aim is to provide aquaria for various institutions for use in their waiting-rooms, reception areas, and so on. The total effect is deemed to be aesthetically pleasant and psychologically soothing. The other selling points appear to be:

(i) the unusual and exotic fish, and the current television publicity, make the units very different from other products of a similar nature; and

(ii) there is no capital outlay for the customer – it is planned instead to charge a fixed rental, with three months' rental payable in advance.

John Blunt is suggesting that Poltex Stafford should provide the funds to enable the various items of equipment to be purchased. John would provide the expertise, as well as the fish and plant life. His proposal is that they should go into partnership together sharing profits in the ratio of 2 to 3 (in John's favour).

Poltex Stafford is an astute businessman and sees merit in the suggestion. He is giving the suggestion serious consideration.

The tasks for the group

(1) consider what sort of people and institutions would be interested in the service being offered.
(2) Discuss the sort of advertising programme which might be pursued.
(3) Reflect on the legal problems involved in this case. What are the dangers in the proposals from both Poltex Stafford's and John Blunt's viewpoints?
(4) What alternatives are there to a partnership?

Questionnaire
Who do you think would be the most likely customers? (Place them in order (i) to (vi).)

(i)
(ii)
(iii)
(iv)
(v)
(vi)

How do you think the new service could best be publicised?

(i)
(ii)
(iii)

Practical work

Draft a suitable half-page advertisement for inclusion in one of the Sunday colour supplements. Detailed artwork is not essential, but your ideas on artwork could be briefly explained. Work independently but compare efforts and decide which of the layouts produced in the group would be most effective.

Written work

Play the role of Poltex Stafford's personal assistant. He has asked you for your views on this project. Set them out in a formal report.

CHAPTER 44

The New Store Manager

Schumann's Stores sell almost everything – from ballpoint pens to bedroom furniture. They have branches all over the south of England. The firm appreciates the need to develop young talent and have devised a comprehensive management training scheme for graduates joining the company. One of the first young men to be trained under this scheme was Peter Shafer, who joined Schumann's four years ago after taking a business degree at a polytechnic. He has had a spell of six months as Assistant Manager at the Exeter branch and he has now been appointed manager-designate of the Bournemouth store, to take over when the present Manager, Tom Selhurst, retires next month.

When he arrives at his new branch Peter finds a number of problems looming up on the horizon:

(1) Many of the girl assistants – especially the younger ones – are arriving late in the mornings, and taking extended breaks during the day. Even when the situation is pointed out to Tom Selhurst, he does nothing about it.

(2) There is a general rule in Schumanns that female assistants wear navy-blue clothes (slacks are not allowed), while the men are exhorted to wear dark suits with collars and ties. Peter notices that this rule is being flouted openly, one small clique of girls appearing in quite garish outfits.

(3) Larger stocks than necessary seem to be carried in most lines. In the Ladies' Department many of the garments are old stock, while in the Radio and Television Department there seems to be a surplus of one particular make and a dearth of others, added to which the display is quite ineffective, in Peter's view.

(4) The Assistant Manager, Paul Bromfield, is ten years older than Peter (Peter is 28), and has been with the company six years longer. His resentment is already beginning to show.

How would you advise Peter to cope with each of these distinctive problems? Tom Selhurst has made it clear that he is going to stay in control of the store until the day of his retirement.

Other information available
For the past three years the profits of the branch have been 10–15 per cent above the targets set by Head Office.

There are fifty-three members of staff in all at the Bournemouth branch, including eight Departmental Managers and two Trainee Managers gaining experience under the special management training scheme.

When challenged about the time her garments take to sell, the Buyer in the Ladies' Department protested that her stock turned over at least four times a year, but Peter has produced some figures relating to a particular order for 1200 garments from one of the regular suppliers (see Table 44.1). (Do these figures give Peter an opportunity to refute the Buyer's arguments – or does he have to agree that she was right?)

Table 44.1 Asorted garments purchased from Ladylux

	Number of garments
Sold within 1 month of purchase	43
Sold by end of 2nd month	111
Sold by end of 3rd month	368
Sold by end of 4th month	656
Sold by end of 5th month	922
Sold by end of 6th month	1155
Sold between end of 6th month and end of 18th month*	1200

*There is a company rule which says that any stock unsold after twelve months has to be sold off at cost price.

When the Buyer in the Audio-visuals Department was challenged over the limited range of stocks, his contention was that it was more profitable to concentrate on a few makes. How do you think his view might be justified?

Your tasks

1. Draft a suitable memorandum on the subject of discipline such as Peter Shafer might circulate to the staff when he takes over the management of the Bournemouth store.

2. You have received a brief note from the Area Manager, Denise Hobart, expressing concern over the position of Paul Bromfield. 'I know he feels very disappointed at not getting the Bournemouth job,' she writes, 'I hope you will be able to get on together and make a success of it.' Write a reply to Mrs Hobart, explaining your views and intentions.
3. Produce a diagram/chart/graph to illustrate the statistics provided for the Ladylux range of clothes. The objective is to clarify the situation for all concerned.
4. Write a suitable memorandum such as Peter Shafer might have written to Don Cameron, the Buyer in the Audio-visuals Department, suggesting that a change of policy is required.

CHAPTER 45

The Bank Absentees

The Midchester Bank look after their staff very well. They receive above-average salaries for the sort of work they do and enjoy a variety of perks including low rates of interest on loans for cars and houses and a non-contributory pension scheme. Yet their Personnel Department are confronted by higher rates of absenteeism in the bank than in many institutions with far less favourable working environments. As a first step in finding a remedy or remedies they have compiled the following statistics to show the variation between rates of absenteeism last year in the different areas in which the bank operates (see Table 45.1).

Your task

You are asked to play the role of a group of trainee managers in the bank. The Personnel Manager, George Owen, has suggested you work in twos and threes to analyse these statistics to discover trends, etc. Draw up a list of points to be made such as 'The average male employee is absent nineteen days a year'.

You are then asked to discuss possible explanations for any variations which emerge and for the high incidence of absenteeism at the bank generally.

The bank is considering three proposals for improving the situation and you are asked to collectively weigh up the pros and cons of each of the alternatives.

(a) A system of flexible working hours to be introduced for staff in the larger branches (with more than fifty on the staff).

(b) A reduction in sick pay. At present when staff are away sick they receive pay in accordance with the following scale:

after six months' service –	full pay for one month
	half -pay for a further month
after five years' service –	full pay for three months
	half-pay for a further three months
after ten years' service –	full pay for six months
	half-pay for a further twelve months.

The proposal is that for new recruits the bank's sick-pay scheme only comes into operation after five years' service.

(c) Persistent offenders should be sent to Personnel Department for counselling.

Table 45.1

North-eastern region

Age groups	Numbers employed (average)		Days lost through absenteeism	
	Males	Females	Males	Females
under 25	765	1 157	24 327	33 726
26–35	735	885	18 742	24 072
36–45	660	601	12 211	12 441
46–55	586	343	5 804	6 689

North-western region

Age groups	Numbers employed (average)		Days lost through absenteeism	
	Males	Females	Males	Females
under 25	705	1 198	21 347	30 016
26–35	609	673	14 820	14 806
36–45	572	473	7 321	9 318
46–55	555	264	5 439	6 547

London and South-eastern region

Age groups	Numbers employed (average)		Days lost through absenteeism	
	Males	Females	Males	Females
under 25	1 148	2 882	40 183	87 613
26–35	1 057	2 019	29 490	42 399
36–45	991	1 027	9 812	21 567
46–55	936	511	8 519	10 231

Wales and South-western region

Age groups	Numbers employed (average)		Days lost through absenteeism	
	Males	Females	Males	Females
under 25	587	975	11 857	19 507
26–35	572	815	7 150	10 432
36–45	502	781	4 418	7 654
46–55	507	638	2 991	3 764

Written work

Prepare a report on absenteeism for the Personnel Manager and include some diagrammatic representation such as bar charts and pie-grams (300–400 words).

CHAPTER 46

The Credit Control Department

Canford Delicacies Ltd sell a wide variety of chocolates, biscuits and sweets to restaurants, shops and public houses in the North of England. Their factory in the Manchester suburbs has been expanded a number of times in recent years and they have now added a new office block to their buildings. One section of these new offices has been allocated to the Credit Control Department under the management of Alfred Cropper. Alfred's department has a straightforward function. It has to ensure that customers' accounts do not go beyond the credit limit which has been allocated to them and that the accounts are paid within a stipulated period.

Each account is given a classification along the following lines:

Class A. Unlimited credit available – up to six months to pay for any consignment.
Class B. Up to £500 allowed to be outstanding at any time, and up to three months allowed before consignment is paid for.
Class C. Up to £250 allowed to be outstanding at any time, and up to two months allowed before consignment is paid for.
Class D. Up to £125 allowed to be outstanding at any time, and up to one month allowed before consignment is paid for.
Class E. Cash transactions only allowed.

Before any order is passed through to the Dispatch Department in the factory, it is checked against the customer's account and his credit code. The salemen are not allowed to give customers credit when these limits would be exceeded without a special clearance from the Sales Manager or his deputy.

Your task

Your first task is to design an Excess Credit Form which would be suitable for attachment to orders exceeding the limits laid down by the credit-rating code. The form would give the signed approval of the Sales Manager (or his deputy) to either an extension of the time required for payment, or an increase in the amount allowed to be outstanding. At the end of a stipulated period the original limits would be reapplied. The form would be in triplicate. The top copy would be given to the salesman for attachment to the order. This would be retained by the Credit Control Department when it reached them. The second copy would be sent to the Computer Section on a daily basis. The third copy would be retained by the Sales Manager for reference.

What advantages do you think there are in having a credit-control system like this? What sort of problems might Alfred Cropper find in running the system?

Linda Frisby is only 23 years of age, but has just been appointed Deputy Manager of the Credit Control Department. She is very much aware that all eyes are on her, because she is the first female to be given this status. Alfred Cropper has been on holiday but a few days when two awkward orders come through to the department. One is for £600 worth of goods for a well-known local store (Class B). The other is for an order worth £250 received from Zachary Smith (an unclassified customer). Linda telephones the Sales Manager's office but neither he nor his deputy will be available for the next few days. Linda's superior – in the absence of Alfred Cropper – is the General Manager, but he is off sick at the present time. What do you think Linda should do in these circumstances?

The accounting entries

Suppose Zachary Smith takes delivery of the goods but fails to settle his account in due course? What entries would be passed in the books of Canford Delicacies? The account headings and the original entry in Smith's account are given in Table 46.1.

Three final questions for the group

(1) How long do you think a customer (like Zachary Smith) should be given to settle his account before action is taken against him? Be specific. What sort of action is possible?

(2) If, to everyone's surprise, Zachary eventually pays off his debt, what accounting entries will be required?

(3) There are certain agencies which keep a central record of 'bad risks', i.e. people who have defaulted in the payment of their accounts at some time. Subscribing firms are then able to refer to the agency's files before granting credit to would-be purchasers. What are the group's views on this sort of device?

Table 46.1

		Zachary Smith			
198–		£			
13 Jan	Goods	250.00			
		Bad debts			

CHAPTER 47

Funds for Expansion

Zeta Ltd has developed a new and cheap form of fibre-glass which is planned to be used in the building of a new form of sailing dinghy. A prototype has been on display at the National Boat Show and a large number of provisional orders have already been logged for the new craft. The Board of Directors have mapped out a marketing and construction programme for the new product and have calculated they will need extra finance in the sum of £300 000, plus a further £50 000 for each of the next five years.

The Directors estimate that this injection of capital will generate an inflow of cash as follows:

Year 1	*Year 2*	*Year 3*	*Year 4*	*Year 5*
£20 000	£60 000	£120 000	£150 000	£150 000

The balance-sheet as at 31 December last showed the situation displayed in Table 47.1 (with figures rounded to the nearest £10 000).

Other information available

(1) Profits over the past three years have averaged £202 000, and have not varied by more than £15 000 over the past six years.
(2) The Directors have established a policy over the years of distributing 80 per cent of available profits to shareholders.
(3) The company's bankers have expressed a willingness to grant a £100 000 five-year loan against the security of a second charge on the deeds of the factory.
(4) The prices of the shares quoted on the local stock exchange are:

Ordinary Stock units	70–90p
Preference Stock units	25–40p

These prices have remained fairly stable over the last two years.

(5) The Chairman of the Board owns 25 per cent of the Ordinary Stock. His immediate family and the remainder of the Board own a further 15 per cent of the Ordinaries.

Balance sheet of Zeta Ltd as at 31 December last
Table 47.1

	£	£
Fixed assets (at cost less depreciation)		
Factory and plant	1 000 000	
Machinery and equipment	200 000	
		1 200 000
Current assets		300 000
		£1 500 000
Share capital		
Ordinary Stock (50p units)	800 000	
8% Cumulative Preference Stock (50p units)	200 000	
		1 000 000
10½% Debenture Stock (secured by a mortage on the deeds of the factory – and redeemable in three years' time)		120 000
Reserves		200 000
Current liabilities		180 000
		£1 500 000

Your tasks

(1) Discuss the problem together and decide how the funds might best be raised, on the evidence available. Be as specific as possible. Consider alternatives. Try to reach a consensus.
(2) Looking at the situation from the differing view of (i) the company's employees; (ii) the shareholders; and (iii) the national economy generally, consider whether there is merit in ensuring that the existing Chairman and his family remain in control of Zeta. Also, consider how it is possible for the family to retain control over the affairs of the company with a minority of the voting shares.
(3) At the conclusion of the discussion, write a report to the Chairman of the company, Sir George Beaumont, indicating how you feel the necessary funds should be raised. Compare your reports at the end of the exercise.

CHAPTER 48

Executive Stock Options

If workers hold voting shares in the company which employs them, they have both a say in the making of decisions and a stake in the financial prosperity of the business. Various co-ownership schemes, as they are called, are operated in British industry. The purpose is always to break down the barriers which exist between those who provide the capital for industry and those who provide the labour. While management (representing the shareholders) and workers see their interests as diametrically opposed, the 'civil war' between them will continue, with catastrophic results for them both – and for society generally.

When a company is operating such a scheme it allocates a proportion of its profits for the year to a special fund. This fund is then used to purchase the company's shares in the names of the individual workers. The shares are allocated on an equitable basis – perhaps according to length of service – but more likely according to the amount of wages or salaries earned during the year in question. It is a bonus payment, with shares being passed over to the worker instead of cash. The value of such a scheme is lost, of course, to the extent that workers sell their shares. However, assuming the worker retains his share, in future years he will be able to attend shareholders' meetings and vote at such meetings – if he so desires. More importantly, perhaps, he will receive dividends on his stockholding so long as the company is making profits.

A variant of the co-ownership scheme is the so-called Executive Stock Option Scheme, which has become very popular in the USA. The purpose of this is to allow the executives and key staff of a firm, on whose efforts the firm's success so largely depends, a chance to buy shares in the future at the present price. The contract is an option which will become very valuable to the key employee – if the company does well. If the value of the company's shares does not appreciate, the option has no value. Obviously schemes vary, but a typical example follows.

International Marketing Agencies Ltd/John Dolby

John Dolby is offered by his employer an option to purchase 2000

Ordinary Stock units of £1 each in the company. There must be some consideration in order to make a contract legally enforceable, so John Dolby has to pay a nominal sum (say £1) for each £100 stock covered by the option.

By the terms of the contract John Dolby is able to exercise his option to buy the shares at any time after three years from the date of the option. The price of the shares is fixed at the middle price ruling on the Stock Exchange on the day of the contract. If the ruling price is 218p, but by the end of the three-year period the price has risen to 318p, the executive is able to buy shares in his company worth £6360 – for an expenditure of only £4360. He can sell the shares immediately and make a profit of approximately £2000; or he can sell sufficient of the stocks to enable him to take up the remaining stocks without resorting to other funds; or he can retain the stocks he has acquired in the hope that the company continues to prosper and the share prices continue to rise.

Of course if the price of the shares falls during the three-year period, the option has no value. There would be no point in John Dolby buying shares for 218p which he could buy in the open market for, say, 150p.

The options in John Dolby's case are not transferable. He is not given the right, in the contract, to sell or transfer the option to another person. Contracts such as this would normally terminate upon his death, or when he terminated his employment with the company. There would also be a terminal date for the exercise of the option – say ten years after the date of the contract. But each contract has to be read in order to establish the provisions which apply.

The Stock Option Schemes made a slower start in Britain than in the USA, no doubt because any gains made were taxable. But under Section 47 of the Companies Act, 1980, any benefits received by a Director or employee under any new and approved savings-related share option schemes are free of all taxes. And Section 46 of the same Act allows distributions of shares in normal profit-sharing schemes to be free of tax for any distributions up to £1000 in value for any tax year. Perhaps governmental support for co-ownership schemes such as these indicates at least some of the features which might be expected in a future industrial democracy?

Your task

The Board of Directors of International Marketing Agencies Ltd have been considering the possibility of introducing an Executive Stock Option Scheme on the lines above. You are asked to consider together the merits and demerits of such a scheme from the point of view of the company and also of the executives participating in the scheme (to do this complete Table 48.1)

Table 48.1

	For the executive
Merits	(1) (2) (3)
Demerits	(1) (2) (3)
	For the company
Merits	(1) (2) (3)
Demerits	(1) (2) (3)

When the discussion has been completed, prepare a brief report on your findings to the Chairman of the company, Sir Ralph Trevithick.

CHAPTER 49

Crypto Investment Projects

Crypto Ltd is a typical medium-sized manufacturing company. It has a work-force of approximately 3000 and makes quality glassware in the works at St Helens, and 45 per cent of sales are in overseas markets. The Board of Directors are currently meeting to discuss three potential investment projects which have each been proposed as a matter of urgency by senior executives in the company. The three projects put forward are all outside the capital budget which has been agreed upon within the last six months.

Proposal 1

This has been suggested by Peter Crabtree, the Personnel Manager. The existing canteen was built thirty years ago, and the kitchens are decidedly outdated. The plan put forward involves a complete rebuilding of the canteen (which is housed separately from the main works), the provision of modern kitchens, and the replacement of all existing canteen furniture and equipment. Special features of the new canteen include:

- (i) a covered way from the works to the dining-hall – workers have to cross in the open at present;
- (ii) a community dining-hall where employees of all grades (blue collar and white collar) would eat together – at the moment there are two separate rooms, one for staff and one for others;
- (iii) bar facilities where employees can enjoy drinks during the lunch hour (a licence would have to be applied for).

The Personnel Department feels that worker morale is adversely affected by the poor canteen facilities, and the Board is referred to a recent survey which was conducted and showed that 78 per cent of the 118 staff questioned regarded the canteen as 'very unsatisfactory'. The point is also made that visitors to the factory, even if they are entertained in the staff canteen, will not receive a favourable impression of the company.

The Personnel Department has produced a series of indices to monitor the level of morale in the organisation, and Peter Crabtree produces the latest figures to support his claim for a new canteen:

weekly index of absenteeism = 135 (last week)
base date 1980 (average) = 100
weekly index of productivity = 97 (last week)
base date 1980 (average) = 100
monthly index of labour turnover = 126 (last month)
base date 1980 (average) = 100

(*Note*: the group should try to think out how these indices would be compiled.)

Peter Crabtree has calculated that labour turnover is costing the company about £350 000 per annum, while absenteeism is costing about twice that sum. The cost of the canteen is calculated at £660 000.

Proposal 2

A new American glass-blowing machine has become available which would reduce the operating costs of the factory by approximately £100 000 per annum. The cost of the machine would be £600 000, but it could be paid in equal instalments over four years. Kevin Bright, the Works Manager, points out that it was while using one of the machines which would be replaced by this purchase that one of the operators received serious injuries. He has now recovered, but he has made a claim against Crypto, and this is still before the Courts.

Proposal 3

Don Appleby, the Marketing Manager, has planned an advertising campaign consisting of whole-page 'spreads' in a number of trade magazines overseas. He believes there are real opportunities for breaking into the emerging African and Middle Eastern markets, but the sustained campaign would cost in the region of £500 000 in a two-year period. Don's concern is that sales are falling. Not only have the value of the sales fallen by 5 per cent in the last twelve months compared with the previous twelve months, but Crypto's share of the market has fallen from 19 to 17 per cent in the same period. The Marketing Manager feels that no small part of the explanation lies in the fact that advertising expenditure has been severely curtailed in the recent past.

As he puts it to the Board, 'When sales are falling, you have got to spend on advertising'.

The Marketing Department has undertaken a modest amount of market research which indicates that it would be easier to break into new overseas markets than to concentrate effort on the home market.

Don Appleby has produced this scatter diagram to show the effect that advertising has had on sales over the past two years. The figures have been compared on a quarterly basis. 1 shows the figures for the first quarter, 2 for the second quarter and so on.

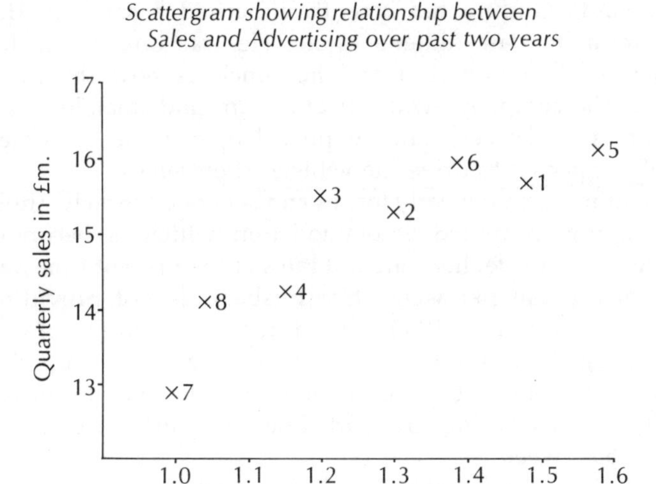

Figure 49.1

The tasks for the group

(1) Discuss the options and weigh up the pros and cons of each (on the evidence available).
(2) Break up into groups of two or three and, after studying the alternatives, prepare a report for the company's Chief Executive, John Evans, setting out recommendations. (This will be a joint effort.)
(3) Come together again when the reports have been completed. Compare the different reports critically. Revise the sub-group reports as considered necessary.

CHAPTER 50

RentaVan Ltd

Mrs Amanda Guthrie has recently inherited a small portfolio of stocks from her late father's estate. He was one of the founder members of RentaVan Ltd and her uncle is now the Managing Director. The company owns a fleet of vans and small lorries which they hire out. Drivers can be provided, but the customers are generally expected to drive the vehicles themselves.

Mrs Guthrie is in her early forties and separated from her husband. She is living in rented accommodation which is becoming increasingly expensive, her rent and rates at the present time amounting to nearly £40 per week. Her husband is not providing any financial support for either her or the two young sons of the marriage, aged 14 and 11. The boys are at a large comprehensive school and the older boy in particular looks destined for university. Mrs Guthrie is working as a part-time assistant in a London store earning £55 a week.

Mrs Guthrie now approaches Robert Simpson, the Manager of Midchester Bank, Bow branch, and poses two specific questions. She wants to know, first, whether he would advise her to sell the stocks and use the money towards buying a house. She has a particular house in mind. It is quite unpretentious and one of those at the lower end of the price range – on a new estate about forty miles outside London. She also wants to know what action he would recommend her to take when the option date for the convertible debentures arrive (see below).

The portfolio of stocks which represents the whole of Mrs Guthrie's wealth is as follows:

£5 000	3 per cent Redemption Stock 1986–96 (the current prices for this stock can be found in the majority of daily newspapers)
£40 000	Ordinary Stock (£1 units) in RentaVan Ltd
£60 000	8 per cent Convertible Debenture Stock (£1 units) in RentaVan Ltd.

There is some further information available which is provided in Table 50.1 and Figure 50.1. (Note that it has has been the policy of the Directors to distribute 50 per cent of profits to the shareholders.)

The holders of the Convertible Debentures have an option to convert their stock into Ordinary Stock units – on a one for one basis – in six months' time, the option lasting for a six-month period. Amanda's uncle has offered to buy the Ordinary Stock units from her at £1 each and the Convertible Debentures at 90p each. He owns £80 000 of the Ordinary Stock and the whole of the 7 per cent Preference Stock (which does not carry votes). His three co-directors own between them £40 000 Ordinary Stock. The remaining equity is owned by 23 different stockholders with holdings ranging from £1000 to £10 000.

Table 50.1
Balance sheet of RentaVan Ltd as at 31 December last

	£	£
Fixed assets		
Premises (at cost 1972)		100 000
Motor vehicles	295 000	
Less Provision for depreciation	95 000	
		200 000
Current assets		220 000
		520 000
Less Current liabilities		60 000
Net assets		£460 000
Represented by:		
Capital – authorised and issued		
Ordinary Stock (£1 units)		250 000
7% Preference Stock (£1 units)		50 000
		300 000
8% Convertible Debenture Stock (£1 units)		60 000
Reserves		100 000
		£460 000

Group work

Working in small groups, make the necessary calculations so that Mrs Guthrie can be properly advised. Exchange ideas and check the calculations with each other.

Also consider the merits and demerits of the convertible debenture stocks from the point of view of (i) the stockholders and (ii) the company.

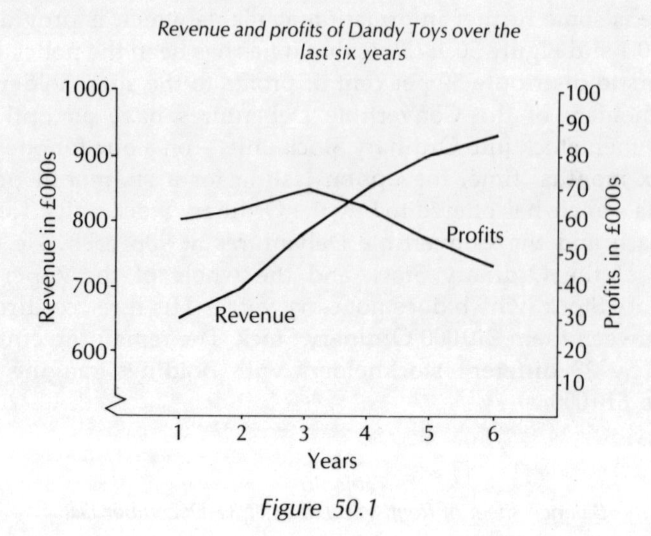

Figure 50.1

Written work

Write a letter to Mrs Guthrie as from the bank manager. Offer appropriate advice.

CHAPTER 51

Olympic Finances

Morganthwaite Bright & Associates operate a management consultancy business and they have recently been approached by a small group of businessmen who are looking for ways to support British athletes in future Olympic competitions. The athletes cannot receive payments, of course, but it is possible to improve their chances in almost all events by providing them with adequate training facilities and equipment, the best possible coaches and ample opportunity to compete against quality opposition both at home and abroad. It is recognised that all these things would cost a great deal of money and the consultants have agreed to look at various ways in which funds might be raised. The businessmen have already toyed with the idea of setting up some sort of national lottery, but before they pursue that notion any further they want to consider the alternatives.

Your task

You are asked to discuss this problem generally, and in particular produce answers to the following questions:

(1) How do you think funds might best be raised to support our athletes in their preparation for the Olympics?
(2) How do you think sums raised would be most effectively spent?
(3) On what grounds do you think businessmen might be persuaded to contribute funds to any of the projects you have in mind?

Written work

Write a report to Desmond Morganthwaite, the senior partner, setting out your recommendations in the light of the discussions you have had. Specifically cover the points of how funds might be raised and how they might be used most effectively. Explain how you think British businessmen might be persuaded to involve themselves in any of the proposed projects. How might they hope to benefit financially? Which firms would stand to benefit most? How do you think the government might be persuaded to become involved in the programme?

CHAPTER 52

In-tray 3 – The Registrar's Department

Grimswade Engineering plc supplies a variety of components to motor manufacturing firms in the Midlands and elsewhere. It employs a work-force of about 5000 including clerical staff and the capital structure is shown below:

£4 000 000 Ordinary Stock (units of £1 each)

£1 000 000 5 per cent Non-cumulative Preference Stock (units of £1 each).

Both stocks are quoted on the London Stock Exchange the range of prices over the past year being:

Ordinary Stock 375p – 450p
Preference Stock 45p –50p

Your task

You are to play the role of Personal Assistant to Stephen Meredith, the Company Registrar. He is going to be at an important meeting for most of the day and he has asked you to draft replies to the following items in his in-tray. He will sign the correspondence (hopefully) on his return to the office later in the day.

The Cottage,
Plender's Green,
Abbotsbury,
Wiltshire.
date

The Registrar
Grimswade Engineering
Coventry.

Dear Sir or Madam,
I own 600 ordinary shares in your company which were transferred to me on my father's death four years ago. I need money now to pay for repairs to the roof of my property damaged in the recent gales and so I would ask you to let me have the money for the shares as soon as possible. If you make out a cheque in my name I will pay it into my bank account.

Yours sincerely,
Thom. Sibley
Thomas Sibley

Grimswade Engineering plc
Memorandum

To Stephen Meredith, Registrar — From Patrick Cheeseman, Personnel Manager.

As you know a number of staff now own ordinary stock in the company and I am being asked what sort of dividends they might expect this year assuming the profits are the same as last year (£800,000 half of which was transferred to reserve). Can you let me know the answer so that I can give the enquirers some idea of what they might expect.

P. Cheeseman.

Grimswade Engineering plc
Memorandum

To All Department Heads From Joyce Howard, Secretary,
Works Safety Committee.

Office Safety Campaign

As you will know from the recent Management Conference on Safety we are now turning our attention to avoiding accidents in the offices. We are intending to produce a booklet on safety to be distributed to all of the company's employees and we are intending to devote a section of the booklet to office work. I am asking for ideas from all departments so that we can make sure that the major dangers are identified and eliminated as far as possible. The plan is to provide a list under the headings of (a) dangers and (b) remedies and I would welcome contributions from your staff. If every department can produce a dozen items for inclusion we should be able to produce a useful list of dangers and remedies. Please let me have your lists as soon as possible.

Joyce Howard

16, High Way,
West Park,
Bonham.
date

The Registrar,

Dear Sir,

I own 60 Preference shares in your company as you will no doubt see from your records. I was amazed to read in the Daily Telegraph yesterday that while my shares are only worth 45p each the Ordinary shares can be sold for 375p. How can this be? Since I bought my shares ten years ago the price of the Ordinaries have gone up and up while the preference go down and down. I just cannot understand it.

Yours faithfully,

Kathleen Wyatt

Kathleen Wyatt

Grimswade Engineering plc
Memorandum

To Stephen Meredith, Registrar.
From Patrick Cheesman, Personnel Manager.

One of your secretarial assistants, Pamela Phipps, has applied for the post of Assistant Personnel Officer and having interviewed all the candidates I am inclined to offer her the job. She tells me she has spoken to you and that you would have no objection to the transfer. She would be required in the post by the end of next month.

P. Cheeseman

PART 6

GUIDELINES

Guidelines

CHAPTER/CASE STUDY

5 Case study – Job Factors

It will be interesting to see whether patterns emerge in the rankings. For example, does everyone put 'a job with above-average pay' at the top of their list? One way of assessing the responses is to give 10 marks to each person's first choice in order of importance, 9 marks for their second, 8 for their third and so on. On this basis, which feature was deemed most important by the respondents?

6 Case study – The Staff Welfare Programme

Each of the proposals has obvious merits and demerits, but the choice is complicated by the monetary considerations. Essentially one is looking here for logical arguments.

Project 1
For this we have: (a) a sports ground is of little use *without* changing facilities; (b) the largest age group is that of the under–21s, and there are likely to be the ones with most spare time; (c) active games help to keep people fit, and encourage friendly rivalry.

Against this we have: (a) only a minority of staff will benefit, (b) the benefits largely accrue to the workers at Chadwell Heath – again a minority of the work-force.

Project 2
For this we have: (a) the long-servers and the sick benefit from the scheme; (b) it could prove to be a useful long-term investment.

Against this we have: (a) only a very small minority of the work-force can benefit, (b) there is bound to be some resentment among people who apply but get turned down.

Project 3

Why not tackle this project in stages, producing a fairly inexpensive news-sheet to start with and graduate to a full magazine *if* the news-sheet is a success?

For this we have: (a) all the work-force stand to get some benefit, and it could be used as a means for the Staff Social Committee to communicate with the workers throughout the organisation.

Against this we have (a) a free issue would make the magazine undervalued in the eyes of the work-force, while a payment to cover costs would be resented.

Project 4

For this we have: (a) a variety of interests can be catered for, e.g. weddings, social clubs, etc.; (b) the property might be a good long-term investment.

Against this we have: (a) the bulk of the benefits would accrue to the Chadwell Heath workers; (b) the club would be too near the works, and would not allow the workers to 'escape' from the work-place; (c) modernisation is required.

Project 5

For this: nearly the whole work-force would stand to benefit.

Against this: people would be obliged to listen whether they wanted to or not.

7 Case study – The Short List

This case study has three objectives. In the first place it gives students an opportunity to look at a constantly recurring business problem – choosing appropriate staff. They can think about the problem from the employer's point of view. At the same time they can reflect on the fact that they may one day be putting themselves forward as a candidate for a job. Finally, and by no means least, they can join other people in reaching an agreement as to which is the best of the four candidates for the job featured in the case study. In business we are often required to consult with others and reach a general agreement.

To what extent does appearance count in a job like the one being offered at the language school? What sort of appearance are we looking for? And how well-spoken should such a secretary be? Should she be able to speak foreign languages? How vital is that requirement? What sort of personality should we be looking for?

Are we at a disadvantage in that we cannot actually meet these young ladies? How might our opinions change if we met them personally?

What about the setting up of a filing system? Which of the candidates would be better suited to the methodical approach required for such an exercise? What sort of filing system would you envisage in this set up?

There could be some unpleasant things happening when her boss is travelling abroad. She might find herself taking orders from both the Administrative Officer and the Deputy for the Executive Director. Why could this be unpleasant? Could she equally find the situation has its advantages?

Supposing the Executive Director does not like her when he returns? Or vice versa? To what extent do you think the temperaments of people working together have to be compatible?

8 Case study – The Upgrading

Here are four members of staff with broadly similar claims for promotion, yet two of them have to be disappointed. Which two? It is not an uncommon problem for managers in many types of business. These young people are not only concerned with their absolute progress, they are also very much concerned with other people's progress. Perhaps, if they are equally deserving cases, the manager should seek to withhold the four promotions until they can be upgraded together? What would be the dangers of that course of action?

If a choice is to be made, it will presumably rest on factors such as length of service, ability, qualifications and age.

Should lateness be brought into account? And are balances on staff accounts an irrelevancy? Do they have any special significance when staff are handling large – sometimes very large – sums of money? Does it matter if a bank cashier is short of cash on his own account?

Should women be given equal opportunities? It is illegal to discriminate against someone simply because of their sex – but does discrimination take place? Why? Should family responsibilities be brought into account?

What do you think of the suggestion that the new manager should try to have a word with the previous manager if that is possible? Or perhaps he might leave it to his Assistant Manager to make the awkward decision. At least he is better acquainted with the members of staff in question. But is this an abdication of responsibility?

And, having reached a decision, how do you think the Manager should let his staff know that decision? Should he just let Head Office notify the favoured pair? Or should he have each of them into his office in turn, explaining the situation fully to them? Which would you prefer if you were in their shoes?

Banks have to pay careful attention to the problems of recruitment and staffing because of the large sums of money handled. Banks must inspire confidence in the public mind and they do this, partly at least, through the image created by their staffs.

9 Case study – Rewards for Loyalty

The discussion is likely to centre on the pros and cons of the different schemes, and a number of the possible arguments are set out below.

Luncheon vouchers
For these: the scheme benefits those who have been with the firm for a long time and is a reward for their loyalty.

Against these: there is no advantage for staff who have been with the firm for less than five years.

Holiday scheme
For this: it gives regular rewards for anyone staying with the firm, and means that staff are assured of a holiday at least every three years.

Against this: not everyone wants to go to a holiday camp, and what about families with more than two members, or workers without families?

Long-service bonus
For this: the benefits here are in cash, and reward good attenders as well as long servers.

Against this: there are no benefits for the first three years of service.

Staff shares
For these: staff could watch their stake in the business grow.

Against these: it takes a long time for the benefits to emerge.

Staff sickness scheme
For this: the workers are given a degree of security.

Against this: there are no rewards for those who keep healthy.

Badges
For these: if attractively designed, they could quickly become a prestige symbol.
Against these: they are possibly open to ridicule.

10 Group task – Fennex Switchgear

Some random thoughts on the problems

(1) How would you take a random sample of employees? Do you think a stratified sample would be more appropriate? How big would the sample be?
(2) Would it be wise to consult shop stewards, trade unions, works council? There would be distinct advantages in winning the co-operation of the work-force before circulating the questionnaire.
(3) If some staff are left out – as when a sample of views is taken – they may feel they are being ignored. Would it be better to send out the questionnaire to all staff? All the staff may wish to express their views.
(4) The survey would give the Personnel Department valuable insights into the attitudes of the work-people at Fennex. The workers will experience satisfaction in being able to make their views known, but they will be disgruntled if nothing is done to rectify their legitimate grievances.
(5) It may be advisable to leave a space at the foot of the questionnaire for 'other comments'.

You will find it helpful to form small groups in order to devise the questionnaire. One group can concentrate on the questions related to pay, while another group can formulate questions on the working environment. The group can come together to combine the various sections.

11 Case study – Pidgeon Savage Lewis

Communication within an organisation can never be perfect so long as idea-exchange between any two human beings is imperfect, but attempts to improve the situation might include any or all of the following:

1. *Joint Consultation*

Representatives of management and workers meet to discuss problems of common concern. Joint Consultation Committees are usually on an *ad hoc* basis (as and when required) but they meet on a regular basis. The unions are given a chance to make their views known to management and vice versa.

The unions could play a vital role in the communication process to the benefit of all concerned. If management are able to convince the union representatives that a particular innovation would be beneficial to the workers they can leave the union representatives to 'win over' their members to support the idea. The union might be seen as a second line of communication, providing a means of short-circuiting the overlong lines of communication in a typically large business unit.

2. *Works Councils*

These are normally set up with a formal constitution – a set of working rules and procedures. They are not obligatory in the UK as they are elsewhere in the European Economic Community. However, where they operate, duly elected representatives from the work-force meet with a team of managers periodically, perhaps once a month. The problems facing the business and the proposed courses of action can be explained by the managers, while workers are given the opportunity to express their viewpoints and air their grievances. The workers' representatives will take back the managers' explanations to their work-mates.

Typical topics on an agenda would be:

(a) Accident prevention
(b) Holiday rotas
(c) Social functions
(d) Canteen facilities
(e) Disciplinary problems such as absenteeism and lateness.

The matter of wages is usually excluded from the discussions being considered more appropriate to direct negotiations.

3. *Management meetings*

These may take a variety of forms. The so-called immediate command meeting occurs when a manager brings some or all of his immediate subordinates together. He may do this to give them instructions, or he might confer with them with regard to a problem situation. These get-togethers when they involve an exchange of ideas might be seen to be very similar to the case study sessions with which you are now becoming familiar. By contrast the extended command meeting takes place when the manager calls together not only his immediate subordinates but also their subordinates. Managers' meetings of all types allow the executives involved in the businesses to discuss problems and draw on a wider pool of knowledge and experience.

4. *Courses and seminars*
Many will be 'on job' (at the place of work). Procedures can be clarified, standardised and rectified where necessary. General communications training, however, is likely to be most effective when 'off job' (in colleges, etc.)

5. *Designing organisations and work-flows*

The more levels of management, the more opportunities for communication distortion. Flat structures are more effective than tall ones.

6. *Staff magazines*

These could be as valuable to the firm as the newspaper is to a government – consider *The Times*, or *Izvestia*.

12 Role play – Complaints Committee

Problems on the Agenda

(1) Compare cost of replacing/refunding with possible loss of revenue resulting from adverse publicity. Do you favour a cash refund, or a credit note, or replacement with a similarly-priced machine? Has the customer contributed to the breakdown of the machine? Is there any way in which one can tell whether he is telling the truth? Should we deal with Mr McAlister or his solicitor?

(2) Great care must be exercised here. Suppose we are generous and compensate her, and she has another, and worse, relapse. Perhaps this is a matter for our solicitors. If she has a genuine claim, she deserves compensation, but on the other hand ....

(3) This seems à genuine complaint, but it is not all that simple to dispose of. How much compensation do you intend to recommend? The holiday was 'spoiled'. But to what extent? An *ex gratia* payment perhaps. But how much? The full cost of the holiday? A

token payment? If compensation is in the form of goods from the store, it could be cost effective in the sense that £10 worth of goods would only cost us about £6.50.

(*Note*: It is intended that the group should act as a formally constituted committee set up by the Chief Executive expressly to give him the benefit of their advice. But the Chief Executive reserves the right to accept or reject that advice. An example of a resolution in these circumstances might be: 'It is recommended that Mr and Mrs Crampthorne be fully compensated for any financial losses they have incurred up to a limit of £50 each.')

13 Scenario – Motor-car Assembly Plant

The debate is essentially about values and each student will have personal views which can now be expressed. This is an eternal conflict between the rights of the individual and the will of the majority.

A student could toy with the following notion. A citizen might object to Britain joining the EEC or spending money on the development of a new supersonic bomber, but he has no immediate remedy. In a democracy his long-term safeguard is the right to vote against the government if it pursues policies of which he disapproves. However, if the majority of the populace supports the government, the dissenting individual has to accept the will of the majority. So long as the members of a union have the right to vote, they are part and parcel of a democratic institution. And democracy is the best form of government only if the 'electorate' are intelligent, perceptive – and active. If they are not, they will soon find themselves in the hands of demagogues.

Alternatively, consider a second line of thought. Can unions only influence wages in the short run? Are wages decided by the laws of demand and supply in the long run? If workers force up the price of their labour, the goods and services they produce become more costly. Because fewer people avail themselves of the more expensive goods and services, might not unemployment result? Or will entrepreneurs use more capital-intensive methods (automation) with a similar effect? Those who stay in employment benefit, but is it at the expense of those who are unemployed?

14 Case study – The Medicine Man

Thoughts on the financial incentives
How much do the workers get out of every £ million profit? Is that an exciting prospect? How much would a 'good attender' receive under the second scheme during the course of a year? How much would the company have to be earning to make the first scheme equally attractive?

Which do you think the workers would prefer: payment as every week goes by, or payment at a much later date?

Scheme 1 is for all workers, whereas Scheme 2 gives the rewards to the 'good attenders'.

Thoughts on the Worker Director
He could provide a communication link between the Board of Directors and the work-force. This link would be more direct and effective than communication through the normal channels. The Board would be able to explain management problems to him. He would be able to explain the workers' attitudes to them.

The appointment would be a conciliatory gesture, but it could be embarrassing when certain confidential matters come to be discussed, such as wage policies and negotiations, and possible plant closures and redundancies.

Would he mix easily with the existing Directors? Equally damaging, would he lose the support of his own side if he became too understanding of management's problems?

Would he be happy to function in the Board Room, where decisions are taken on a majority vote, and where he might too often find himself in a minority of one?

15 Case study – Glenfrew Construction

The following points might be made during the discussion:

Staff problems
(1) Many of the younger staff will have families and friends in Balham and will not be able/willing to move.
(2) Some senior staff will have children at school, as well as social ties.
(3) Married women on the staff present difficulties unless their husbands are also involved in the move.

(4) New staff will need to be recruited in the Bath area to make up for staff losses.
(5) Very senior staff, like Frank Flavell and George Crombie, are unlikely to welcome the move.

Open-office problems
(1) Executives will lose personal prestige if they lose their own office and various personal accoutrements.
(2) There will be a loss of privacy and secrecy, though by the same token supervision will be easier.
(3) Where will interviews be conducted with potential staff?
(4) How are noise and distractions to be dealt with?

Suggestions for overcoming problems
(1) Consult staff involved as soon as possible.
(2) Give the executives/staff an opportunity to see the area where they are going work.
(3) Involve the executives/staff in the planning of the new open-plan office.

16A Case study – The Holiday Rota

This case indicates the conflicting interests which exist among any group of people working together. In this case the conflicts are centred on the holiday rota. Holidays are highly prized – and so are statuses. This is no minor problem for those who are are involved personally. The task of the students is to try to imagine themselves in this situation. How would they feel if ...?

Before the rules can be drawn up it will be necessary to decide which of three factors should carry most weight: (i) responsibility, (ii) age, or (iii) length of service. When this has been established, how is the rule going to be applied in each of the departments? Should each department have its own separate rules? Why not? What would happen if someone was transferred to another department?

There is some information about the staff which is not disclosed. For example, we know there are twenty-two staff in the Accounts Department, but we do not know their ages or their grades. Is that relevant to our purpose?

When we draw up the rules we should try to make them as simple and as fair as possible. We should keep a note of the rules we suggest making and check up at the end to see whether we are complying with the manager's constraints.

It seems unfair that two out of nine staff in the Mailing Section might be allowed holidays at the same time (22 per cent), while only two out of twenty-two (9 per cent) will be allowed holidays at the same time in the fairly senior (?) Accounts Department.

To overcome the problem we might do the following:

(1) Combine the Accounts and Mailing Sections for the holiday rota, so that four out of thirty-one staff can go on holiday at the same time.

(2) Combine all departments and have eight staff on holiday at a time, shortfalls in any one department being made up by temporary transfers from other departments.

(3) Allow three to go on holiday from the Accounts Department but only one from the Mailing Section, transferring one person from that section to Accounts during the holiday period.

The manager's job would be made easier and he would have more options open to him if he practised job rotation in the office. In this way many staff would be able to switch jobs without difficulty at holiday times – and when there was a lot of sickness in the office. Quite apart from the value of job rotation for these purposes, it is also a method of training and developing staff for future promotion – and a way of alleviating boredom in some of the more routine jobs in the office.

16B Case study – The Liverpool Warehouse

Rewards

(1) Bonuses for good attenders:

- (i) some firms pay cash bonuses to workers who turn up for five days and are not late during the week;
- (ii) other firms have conducted a weekly draw for good attenders, who stand to win a prize, e.g. Premium Saving Bonds;
- (iii) free luncheon vouchers might be given; and
- (iv) extra holidays might be granted.

(2) Give pay increases and promotions to consistently good attenders?

(3) Badges could be worn to indicate a good record?

(4) Free tea might be arranged during the fifteen minutes up to the start of work?

Punishments
(1) Sort out the worst offenders – warn them – and if there is no improvement, dismiss them as a deterrent to others.
(2) Make deductions from pay for lateness.
(3) Give the persistent offenders the least pleasant jobs.
(4) Pin up the names of the persistent offenders on a 'shame' board.

Other ideas
(1) provide company transport.
(2) Introduce flexible working hours.

You might start the exercise by studying the statistics and deciding which groups are most troublesome. For example, if you find that young people tend to be late more often, then one way of overcoming the problem would be to employ older people where possible.

The results desired can be achieved by offering the staff a variety of rewards if they do the 'right' thing, or a varying degree of punishment if they do the 'wrong' thing.

16C Case study – Office Discipline

The report might take the following form:

Topex Finance Ltd
Romford Branch

To Mr D. McCulloch,
Group Chief Inspector,
Topex Group,
Head Office.

Mr David Rowan,
Manager.
date

Response to recent report on branch

Your report drew attention to four basic areas of concern at the Romford branch, viz.:

(a) staff dress (b) telephone service (c) staff relationship and (d) staff punctuality.

It is my intention to correct the deviations from acceptable behaviour as soon as possible and with this in mind I have acquainted my staff with the basic details of your report. My purpose in this has been twofold. I want them all to be aware of the nature of the problems confronting us here. Also it is my intention to encourage contributions from them which will help to solve our problems. Already certain solutions to our problems seem to be emerging.

(a)*Staff dress*
I am using your report as a challenge to the staff's egos. My approach has been along the lines of 'Let's make sure they find it right next time they come ...' At the same time I have indicated the type of clothing which I consider appropriate and the staff have discussed the issues together with me. It would be difficult to impose too many constraints in this day and age, but the staff have been made aware of the criticisms and encouraged to respond positively.

My approach includes making it clear to all members of staff that, in assessing their performance for recommending promotions and salary increases, I shall bring into account their personal appearance, bearing in mind the importance of this in our particular line of business.

(b) *Telephone service*
All staff have been reminded of the essentiality of being friendly and courteous to telephone callers at all times. A branch rule has been introduced to the effect that customers are not to be kept waiting for information. Wherever possible telephone numbers will be taken and the customer phoned back with the information required – unless the problem can be dealt with immediately. The telephonists have been entrusted with the task of ensuring that the follow-up procedures are complied with. Another measure I have taken is to delegate responsibility for signing some of the fairly routine mail to the more discriminating junior staff.

In this way recipients of the letters will be able to ask for the signatories and get more personal attention. First names as well as surnames will be used. The purpose of all this is to make the more junior staff feel more involved in our operations. Careful monitoring will be necessary – particulary in the early stages – but I am confident this step will have the double effect of improving the speed and quality of our responses to telephone inquiries as well as enriching in some small way the jobs of some of our more junior members of staff.

Of course it has also been necessary to evaluate our data-retrieval system to discover any technical faults in work-flows. The staff have been able to identify some of the problem areas and we should be able to introduce some useful changes to improve the overall situation.
Additionally, instruction on how to use the telephone will be included as part of the induction procedure for all new members of staff. And I shall be arranging a few test calls myself to see how much improvement has been achieved.

(c) *Staff relationships*
I have talked to the main offenders individually, pointing out the strengths and plus qualities of their opponents. I have also stressed to the whole staff the vital need for teamwork in this operation.

The main assault on this problem, however, has taken the form of what might be called a 'tutelage system'. The two senior female members of staff have been given responsibility for the welfare and development of a group of more junior members of staff. Discussions are still proceeding, but the intention is to encourage the seniors to take a positive and constructive interest in the juniors while offering the latter someone to whom they can refer on matters of routine or of a personal nature.
More drastic measures may be called for, but it is not my intention to recommend transferring any staff until the effectiveness of the new scheme can be judged.

(d) *Staff lateness*
My highly-valued Assistant Manager, John Travers, previously the Manager here, has been entrusted with responsibility for eradicating this problem. A red line will be drawn across the attendence book at 9.00 a.m. and anyone arriving after this time will have to offer a valid excuse to Mr Travers. I have made it clear that I shall have the attendance book at my side when making recommendations for promotions, salary increases and the allocation of jobs generally in the branch.

The staff have suggested that flexible working hours might work in our particular situation. I have pointed out that the introduction of such a system would need the approval of Head Office, but I would like to make the proposal to you now. The suggestion as it stands is that staff should be allowed to arrive at the office at any time between 9.00 and 9.45 a.m. and sign off at a matching time between 5.00 and 5.45 p.m. Obviously this is a watered-down version of the system, but we would like it to be known that flexible working hours would be welcomed at Romford branch.

I have made it clear to the staff generally that, in the present situation, arriving late for work is not a matte of personal choice. Some people make considerable sacrifices to get to work on time only to find that others are getting away with it. Discipline is necessary to ensure fair treatment for all.

Summary
I appreciate that the plans outlined here will receive the acid test when our performance is measured in the coming months. For my part, results will be carefully monitored and I shall take any further action deemed necessary to ensure the full efficiency of the branch.

Having acquainted my staff with the content of your report I am also advising them of the details of my response so that no one here is unaware of the seriousness of the problems and the nature of the remedies proposed. I am sure you will find the quality of my staff is such that their response will be positive and favourable.

Finally, I thank you for drawing my attention to these flaws at Romford, and trust you will find things much improved when you favour us with a return visit.

D. Rowan

David Rowan
Manager

17 Case study – Japanese Seaweed

Ideas to think about
As it is a local problem the local authority would be best equipped to deal with it. But the central government is likely to have more expertise. And an entrepreneur could solve the problem without expense to the community.

A land-reclamation scheme would reduce the amount of harbour area vulnerable to the weed. Land is valuable for farming or building purposes.

Offer a prize in the local press for ideas to deal with the problem. Obtain public support, including financial support in the same way as if the cathedral had got dry rot, or the death-watch beetle in its timbers.

Carry out a survey to find out the extent of the menace – the resources are presumably available to the Harbour Commissioners. Try to find out whether any similar waters have been affected elsewhere, and discover how the weed has been, or is being dealt with there.

Problems of the businessman's proposal

(1) Where would the factory be sited? Would it spoil the scenery?
(2) Where would the weed be stored prior to processing? Would it ensure clearing of the harbour, or cultivation of the weed?
(3) Would local farmers and gardeners benefit from cheap fertiliser, or would the benefits be more widespread?

18 Case study – Kelwyn Fireworks Plc

Thoughts on Problem 1

(1) Build factory in 'high-unemployment area'. This could give the company: (a) government grants (for development, etc.), and (b) plentiful supplies of workers.
(2) Existing workers (including executives) would like to move to a pleasant area, for reasons of climate and environment. The further from London the better perhaps – but that would mean a loss of existing social and family ties.
(3) Fire risks have to be considered. The site would presumably be better away from town centres and other buildings. A multi-storied building might, however, increase the dangers.
(4) There should be housing available in the immediate area of the new factory – preferably reasonably priced.
(5) The new factory should be optimally sited to be as close as possible to the principal markets.

Thoughts on Problem 2

(1) Communal firework shows could be organised and demonstrated by the company's own technicians.
(2) Research could be concentrated on safety factors.
(3) Encourage people to buy fireworks all the year round. For example, fireworks at the barbecue.

Thoughts on non-executive directors
Merits: (i) they bring a wider vision to the Board, beyond the confines of the company; (ii) they may bring an expertise to the Board which is not otherwise available (in the case of the firework company, a lawyer or research chemist might have particular value); (iii) they may have useful contacts and influence with important customers, suppliers or shareholders; (iv) they may have access to cash.

Demerit: the principal one would seem to be that they lack day-to-day contact with the business.

19 Case study – The New Product

The memo to the Production Manager:

By including a phrase such as 'if there are any problems I can help with please let me know', you would give the Production Manager the opportunity to come back at you. 'Mr Jessop is very concerned to get things moving' would be one way of forcing the pace without being offensive to a senior manager.

The memo to the boss:

See reasons for resistance to change (page 89 on) and apply them to the specific circumstances here. Additionally the Production Manager may fear that having set up the lines the new product may not take-off.

20 Case study – Small Cogs

Most points to be made are included in the narrative and have to be weighed up against each other, but further ideas could be mentioned:

(1) Large companies can achieve economies of scale – and may pass on some of the extra profits to workers. This is why large companies tend to be more 'generous'. Also, they need to attract a larger work-force. The incentives may have to be commensurate.

(2) There are some compensations when you can identify with a small unit even though this is part of a large organisation.

(3) Large organisations tend to operate in big buildings, often in town centres. This leads to commuting problems – but would it lead to better facilities generally?

(4) Some people would start off in a small company to gain experience and then move on to a large one.

(5) Large organisations might have a larger turnover of staff. This would damage the human relations in the working group. Staff moving from department to department would have the same effect.

Nepotism? Inevitable? Or evil? Is there any way you could stop 'preferment' of one sort or another?

Morale in a large organisation? Do economic factors tend to raise morale? Do socio-psychological factors tend to lower it?

21 Case study – Male Scent

To produce a name for the product it will be advisable to work in small groups of three or four. After an initial exchange of ideas the various offerings could be compared and the best name selected by consensus.

The choice of name will throw up one of the problems of international marketing. A name which is suitable in England may be offensive in France and vice versa.

The basic problem to overcome is that scent is regarded as essentially effeminate, so that there has to be an emphasis on masculinity in the publicity material. For this reason ultra-masculine names might be selected for the product such as 'Domination' or 'Mann'. Similarly, a television advertisement with a well-known 'masculine' actor or sports personality would probably be most effective.

In determining the price one would aim at maximising profit, but this is more difficult than it sounds. For example, if the price is set too low, it may be that the product is discredited. If Chanel perfume were to be the cheapest scent on the market, one wonders what would happen to its sales.

There is a continuous argument between those who say that marketing men are simply satisfying needs which exist in the population, and those who say they are creating demands which would not otherwise exist. The debate will no doubt continue for a long time.

22 Case study – The Television Production

This is basically an exercise in interaction. The participants will have to weigh up the merits and demerits of the alternatives offered by the advertising agency.

Film 1
In favour: young families, such as those in the film, will identify themselves with the family in the film.
Against: it could be confused with an advertisement for breakfast foods.

Film 2
In favour: a cartoon is likely to attract young families.
Against: the technical qualities of the product are likely to be submerged.

Film 3
In favour: the technical qualities will be emphasised.
Against: the film may not attract sufficient attention.

A general point
The film is wisely aimed at young families because it is in such families that the problem of kitchen space is likely to exist.

Naming the product and composing a jingle
For this purpose the group might well be divided into sub-groups of three of four. When they have conjured up ideas they could join forces again and compare findings.

23 Case study – Sunday Trading

There are obviously two sides to the argument, and the discussions may range about such points as:

Against Sunday opening
1. Staff in small shops forced to work longer hours?
2. Unsocial hours produce problems with husbands/wives, public transport, etc.

3. Sunday observance – many religious people offended.
4. More lighting and heating required.

For Sunday opening
1. Parking problems eased.
2. Better service to the public?
3. More jobs provided?
4. Traffic congestion eased generally?

24 Multiple Choice

1. C 2. C 3. B 4. C 5. A

25 Case study – Secretarial Duties

There is an immediate problem to contend with, and Polly is in an unenviable position. Here is an important customer, obviously, and Polly will have to do everything possible to placate him. At the same time she will have to try to contact Lawrence. Should Polly tell Mr Sundberg the truth? Or should she say she does not know where he is? Perhaps she could say she does not know what is keeping Mr Travers?

Should she bring him coffee and try to keep him in a good disposition? If she is with Mr Sundberg though, who is going to contact Lawrence? And how long should she keep the customer waiting?

How should she attempt to contact Lawrence? The golf club? Harry Pritchard? What if Lawrence has not arrived at the club yet?

Customers like Mr Sundberg are hard to come by. The income he provides for Travers and Bercholz helps to pay the wages and salaries of quite a few people associated with the firm. It probably took years to acquire such a valuable client, yet one small slip – two pages of a diary turned over together – and he might be lost to the firm for ever.

Secretaries like Polly should keep an eye on diaries particularly. They should also look ahead – keeping tomorrow's programme in mind as well as today's.

Is Lawrence absolved? Should he play golf in working hours anyway? Is it justification that he might make valuable contacts at the club? Does it matter so long as his work is under control? Does an efficient boss have an empty or a full desk?

How should routine letters be dealt with? Signed in Lawrence's absence? At what stage of the day? And how should the more important letters be dealt with?

26 Case study – The Glass Aviary

Questions such as the following might be considered:

(i) How is it that an increase in sales is accompanied by a decrease in profits?
(ii) What could be the explanation for a build-up of stock?
(iii) Why have the debtors increased by so much?
(iv) What is the danger in having a net outflow of capital?
(v) How are the £18 325 of creditors to be paid?

27 Case study – The Single Seater

Some thoughts on the problem

(1) *Attractive features*? Economy. Easy to park. Easy to drive. Safe speeds.
(2) *Unattractive features*? Single-seater. Slow acceleration. Fire risk.
(3) *Timing of campaign*? No point in arousing interest before product is available.
(4) *Publicity*? This could be centred on well-known affluent characters who prefer the new vehicle to the more opulent ones they would obviously be able to afford. The new car could provide a solution to the major national problem of overcrowded city centres. Instead of playing down the safety factor, it could be emphasised, i.e. the roads would surely be safer if small, modest-speed vehicles like these were in vogue. There would be a beneficial effect on the national economy in terms of fuel consumption – and hospital expenses. The project might be worth the support of the government.
(5) *Problems*? Demand could be so great that this company would not be able to cope. There would soon be serious competition. This would be intensified because the model would probably not be difficult to copy. Indeed, another company might be able to improve on the product which would make the car in question obsolete.

28A Case study – The Jumbo Jet

A variety of ideas should emerge from the discussion, and the following points should be covered:

(1) The programme will need to conform to what was included in the advertising brochures, e.g. a drink in an English pub, a visit to Windsor Castle.

(2) Hotels are likely to be cheaper outside London, i.e. better value for money. The group could stay in a hotel outside London and run trips into London.

(3) Americans will *expect* to see certain traditional things in England, e.g. Morris dancing, the Changing of the Guard, and so on.

(4) Parties might be split up into six or more sections to give the visitors alternative outings every day. In this case the options might have to be agreed by the visitors before they arrive. But is there sufficient time?

(5) There is a problem in providing evening entertainments as tastes are likely to vary so much. Some people would like to visit Soho while others would prefer to attend an orchestral concert.

(6) The last day could be left for the tourists to spend as they felt inclined. Shopping might become a priority (souvenirs, etc.).

(7) On the evening of the fifth day – or perhaps on the last day – a celebration dinner might be arranged to which local civic dignitaries are invited – a few speeches might be appropriate.

28B Case study – The Stately Home

It is important to be as specific as possible with the recommendations, and while students strive to be imaginative they should also be realistic. The best ideas will be those which involve little expenditure but promise to produce handsome returns.

Let us look at the proposals already made.

(1) *Developing the estate for American tourists*

(i) Specialisation would be possible, for example American tastes could be catered for and the ancient links between Britain and the USA could be featured, including railway history.

(ii) The Americans are likely to appreciate the possibility of telling their folks back home that they spent their holiday on a real live English Lord's estate.

(2) *Developing a railway museum*
(i) The railway line could be extended – possibly round the perimeter of the estate. There are plenty of railway enthusiasts around. To make this enterprise a little different it might use engines and carriages of the Victorian period – dresses and clothes of the period might be hired out, while photographic and film concessions might be negotiated.
(ii) If the track has to be confined to the Angerford estate the museum might have to be static, which makes it less attractive to the enthusiasts on whom the project depends.

(3) *Developing a leisure centre*
(i) The facilities would be in demand for the bulk of the year, whereas a centre for tourists would tend to be seasonal.
(ii) Being fairly close to London the centre would be readily accessible to a large number of Londoners.

Other suggestions might include:
(i) Convert the lodges into short-stay hotels for tourists.
(ii) Convert East Lodge into a restaurant/hotel with access to the Motorway. Hoardings could advertise the facilities offered.

28C Case study – The Holiday Camp

Advantages of the proposal
(1) All-the-year-round bookings are possible for retired people, which gives a lengthened holiday season.
(2) The camp could specialise in satisfying older people's tastes – for example, old-time dancing, brass bands, old-time music hall, bowls.
(3) Old folk's charity groups might be prepared to subsidise holidays in some cases.
(4) Coach trips might profitably be laid on.
(5) Car parks would be less essential and the land could be used for alternative purposes.

Disadvantages

(1) To the extent that older folk will tend to be infirm, they will require special transport facilities.
(2) Older retired people might have less money to spend than holiday-makers generally.
(3) Medical staff would have to be present at all times to cope with problems.

(4) Sea breezes are cold out of season – and central heating is expensive. Timber chalets are likely to be particularly cold for older folk.

Other points

(1) Flatlets could stay open in winter – with the chalets closed.
(2) If the cliffs are steep the steps to the beach could be dangerous.
(3) Mixed age groups might produce a happier atmosphere.

29 Case study – Capital Structures

Selected examples
How are the Ordinary dividend rates calculated (to complete the table)?

Consider first what dividend would be paid to Alpha Ltd Ordinary shareholders if the company made a distributable profit of £800 000: the whole of the distributable profit goes to the Preference stockholders (their dividend is 10 per cent of £80 000, i.e. £80 000), and so the Ordinary dividend = 0 per cent (at this level of profit).

Consider next what dividend would be paid to Beta Ltd Ordinary shareholders if the company made a distribution profit of £80 000: £40 000 will pass to the Preference stockholders (8 per cent of £500 000); £40 000 will then be available to the Ordinary stockholders. £40 000 has to be shared equally among the Ordinary units, i.e.

$$\frac{\text{£}40\,000}{\text{£}500\,000} \times 100 = 8 \text{ per cent Ordinary dividend.}$$

Similarly, the calculation for Gamma Ltd at £80 000 profit is:

$$\frac{\text{£}80\,000}{\text{£}1\,000\,000} \times 100 = 8 \text{ per cent Ordinary dividend.}$$

How do we estimate the prices which could be expected if investors were looking for a return of 8 per cent annum? *We use the table we have already prepared.* Consider, for example, Gamma Ltd at the level of £80 000 profit:

An 8 per cent Ordinary dividend would be payable and if an 8 per cent yield is required the price would be par, i.e.

$$\frac{\text{Actual yield}}{\text{Required yield}} = \frac{8\%}{8\%} \times 100 = 100\text{p (i.e. £1).}$$

or consider Alpha Ltd at the level of £160 000 profit:

An Ordinary dividend of 40 per cent would be payable and a yield of 14 per cent is required by investors, so the price would be:

$$\frac{40\%}{14\%} \times 100 = 286\text{p (i.e. £2.86).}$$

If the tutor agrees it would be possible to put the estimated prices alongside the existing figures, adding columns for 8 per cent and 14 per cent.

30 Case study – Reply If You Please

The problem here is to explain things simply and concisely without making it seem as if your client is unintelligent.

31 Assignment – Your Own Business

Some ideas on the sort of business that might be set up:

(a) A secretarial service for the small business? Phone in letters? Photocopying? A telephone answering service?

(b) A retail business? Are there any vacant shops in your area? How could it be used? What sort of competition would there be? Would there be enough trade? What would the outgoings be? What revenue could you expect? Make reasonable estimates.

(c) an exchange mart for discs, tapes and videos – coupled with a disc-jockey hire-service?

32 Case study – Grand Prix

First, calculate how much would have been transferred to London at the quoted exchange rates – ignoring any charges which would have been incurred.

Taking the yen, for example, at an exchange rate of 370 yen to the £ sterling, 46 478 yen would be worth

$$\frac{46\,478}{370} = £125.62.$$

You do the same sort of calculation for each of the other transactions and add them together. From the total you deduct the sum actually received by Stuart. The difference between the two figures will represent the banks' charges.

In order to see what would happen if the German Mark were to be devalued, take a hypothetical sum of 1000 Marks standing to Stuart's credit. Assume the exchange rate before devaluation is 4 Marks to the £. How much would the 1000 Marks be worth in sterling? Now consider a devaluation of the mark so that 5 Marks = £1. How much would the 1000 Marks be worth then? (You can apply the same sort of calculation to the Spanish pesetas when you are contemplating your holiday.)

From the point of view of a businessman concerned to minimise costs and maximise receipts, and with competition keeping profit margins low, a fluctuating exchange rate can convert an anticipated profit into an actual loss.

Think of the example of a British businessman who buys raw materials with comparatively expensive dollars ($1.50 to £) and then sells the goods he manufactured – bearing in mind the time-lag – for comparatively cheap dollars ($2.00 to £).

Assume that a bottle of whisky is selling in the USA for $10. How much is this worth in sterling? At $1.92 to £ a bottle is worth 10/1.92 = £5.21. When the pound sterling falls to $1.70 to £ a bottle is worth 10/1.70 = £5.88.

33 Case study 1

If insurance firms cut prices (premiums) they will tend to cut benefits. If they do not cut benefits they may find themselves in financial difficulties. This is presumably what has happened here.

One is inclined to assume that all insurance companies are 'safe' because of the nature of their business. Experience indicates otherwise.

Emil is one more creditor of the company and will have to wait until the Receiver has had an opportunity to sort out the claims on the company's assets. The Receiver will need to be very thorough, and it will take some time before the creditors can be paid out. If there are £1 million-worth of creditors and £100 000 of assets the creditors will receive 10p in the £. In those circumstances Emil, whose car had suffered £200 worth of damage, say, would receive £20 to cover the cost.

33 Case study 2

Remedies would include the following:

(1) Employment of store detectives
(2) Insurance (fire)
(3) A 'loss-of-profits' insurance policy, specifically guarding against this eventuality
(4) Advertising
(5) Life assurance
(6) Credit-control system
(7) Staff training
(8) Staff training
(9) Informal agreement with competitors
(10) Staff counselling

34 Business Organisations/Government Actions

1/E Sterling devaluation would make body-scanners cheaper to overseas hospitals, etc.
2/B Tax on petrol will increase the costs/reduce the profits of continental tour operators.
3/G Increased government spending on education would probably help educational book publishers.

35 Case study – Strubank Chinaware

Students may find themselves involved in a Works Council at some future date, and this exercise will give them an idea of what to expect.

Some thoughts for the discussion

(1) If a Canteen Committee is proposed, who would serve on it? Should management be represented? To what extent? Should the union be represented? Who would the Committee report to? The workers can have better meals, if they are prepared to pay for them. Would two services be possible (economy and quality) at different prices? Would there be separate dining-halls? How could you find out the staffs' views? How do you view management's 5 per cent interest charge?

(2) Consult the shop stewards? Draw lots? How long would spaces be allocated for? Allocate according to length of service? What about the possibility to allocating the spaces to departments *pro rata*? Leave them to select their own methods within each department? Work out a rota? On what basis? Should people have to apply for a space? What happens if someone is allocated a space but has no car? Is there a danger of a 'black market' developing? Would discs be required for use on cars?

(3) Music could be played when workers are becoming tired and bored. When would that be? How would you find out? What sort of music would you suggest? What about people who do not want music while they work? To what extent would you involve the staff in the programmes of music?

36 Case study – Boardroom Problems

In this exercise it might add to the atmosphere if desks could be formed into the shape of a boardroom table. The Chairperson should try to ensure that the decisions are made within the time allowed. Sometimes an undue length of time spent on the first item(s) at the expense of the remaining items. Time is of the essence in real-lfie board meetings. The Secretary will not only be expected to make sure resolutions are properly recorded. Minutes will also need to be made and this is a task which might be shared. Refer back to Chapter 12 if you have any doubt about how the Board of Directors would behave.

Taking each item on the Agenda in order:

(1) Your first step might well be to write up this year's figures by a fifth so that you are able to compare like with like, i.e. the figures for the two *twelve* months, one of which has to be projected. Thus, Modello sales per month = (£106.9/10) = £10.69m.; and sales per year = £10.69 × 12 = £128.28m. (adjusted). The results might be mislead-

ing where sales are seasonal as they might well be for this sort of product.

Sales of Modello Kits can be seen to be rising in value, but what about the effects of inflation? A high rate of inflation would produce a rising *value* of sales even though the *physical volume* of sales was actually falling.

You will need to perform the same calculations regarding the statistics shown for the First Step and Exacto Kits.

What has happened to wages? How does the change in wages compare to the change in sales? What is happening to the rates of absenteeism and labour turnover? What action would you propose on this evidence?

(2) What is the purpose of rewarding long-standing employees? Should directors be treated preferentially? Will there be adverse publicity? Could a less direct and less inflammatory method be found for rewarding Sam Miller?

(3) In choosing one of the candidates rather than another the discussion might centre on matters such as: (i) age; (ii) reward for loyalty; (iii) contacts; and (iv) qualifications.

37 In-tray 1 – The Marketing Department

Connection between Kenny's letter and Camelot's? Mutually exclusive? *Re* Lane: Sympathy to wife plus 'get well' to Lane? Apology to customer? Explanation to MD?

38 Case study – Wife-testing

Statistics?
Which questions produced the strongest reactions? Was there consistency in the responses? Can you learn anything about the group's attitudes by counting the total responses to all the questions under the following headings?

(i) very important;
(ii) not very important;
(iii) of no importance.

Foreign Investment?
Advantages: jobs are created – and this can be particularly valuable when there is unemployment in the home country. Most of the wealth generated by the investment will go to workers in the form of wages. Through this sort of investment, money tends to flow from the richer countries to the poorer. British investment in the American railroads in the nineteeth century was largely responsible for the opening up of the New World. The effect could be similar here in reverse.
Disadvantages: profits find their way back to the parent company, after being taxed by the British government, to the British taxpayers' advantage. Important decisions affecting the national economy are made abroad. Many top posts in the company will be reserved for overseas staff. (*But note* that an American company may have large numbers of British shareholders and vice versa.)

39 In-tray 2 – Gifford Electronics

Has there been a misunderstanding over the name of the lady asking for an interview? Does it matter?

The surname of the correspondent from Walsall Road, Leek is unreadable? Take a guess and explain in the letter? Or do not reply?

'Uncleared effects' are cheques which are still in the clearing system. They are normally converted into cash within a week.

40 Case study – the Royalty Grill

Here are brief comments on each of the questions posed, in order to start you thinking in the right direction:

(1) There is virtually no working capital and the Warrens are at the mercy of their bankers. The bank loan has only been reduced by £2000 and that is half of what the reductions should have been by now.

(2) If the bank cannot get full satisfaction from the Warrens it will be able to claim any outstanding debt from the brother.

(3) A business producing a net profit of £12 000 per annum was worth £60 000, so how much would a business producing a net profit of £4000 be worth?

(4) A business like the *'Royalty Grill'* depends for its success on

personal service, and Frank was impressed by the quality of the service when he made his early inspections. The human assets have been dissipated – with catastrophic results for the Warrens.

(5) If the Warrens sell now, they will make an enormous loss so they might be advised to try to build up the clientele again, having learned from previous mistakes. The trouble is that if the bank insisted on repayment of the loan now, they would be able to recover the whole of the loan. From its point of view, this might be a better course of action than trusting the Warrens to a recovery.

(6) The test is basically whether any misbehaviour was such as to affect the Warrens's business. There is a big question-mark over the incident at the till, particularly if there was a witness. There could be a claim for damages arising from slander as a result of an incident like this.

Under certain circumstances, workers alleging unfair dimissal may take their case to an Industrial Tribunal. If this decides the dismissal was unfair, it can either recommend reinstatement or award the ex-employee compensation. If any of the staff were part-time workers – or had not been working for the Warrens for a sufficient period – they would also lose protection. The Industrial Tribanals are composed of three members, only one of whom is a lawyer. They usually expect employers to give due warning before dismissing employees.

41 Case study – Trade Secrets

The following ideas could be considered:

(1) If research were concentrated at Accrington, it would be easier to enforce security. There would only be one building to look after.

(2) Vetting procedures could be produced so that all staff engaged in research, directly or indirectly, would be checked before being offered employment. Even the presence of such procedures could act as a deterrent.

(3) A senior executive in the Research Department could be given responsibility for security matters.

(4) A revision of the procedures for patenting new inventions might be called for. A Patent Agent might be employed, if one is not already being used. The majority of countries are party to an international convention and it is possible to patent rights overseas.

(5) The leakages of information could have occurred elsewhere in the organisation. The company is part of the International Metals

Group and the holding company would obviously have had access to much of the confidential details.

(6) The Managing Director could seek the aid of his colleagues in the holding company.

(7) It is now necessary for all contracts of employment to be evidenced in writing and so the company might make secrecy an express obligation of every contract by including an appropriate clause. There is an implied duty not to disclose confidential information but such a clause would strengthen the company's hand in dealing with any employee who betrayed the company. Any employee who is in breach of contract may be dismissed and sued for damages even after leaving the company.

Is Monica Schultz still in England? Would it be worth the expense of pursuing a claim?

General Comment

There is a danger that the discussion turns into a post-mortem and nothing else. What is required is a plan of action which will put an end to these damaging events. They are so damaging that some people are likely to lose their jobs.

42 Case study – Northfield United

A few of the pertinent suggestions which might be put forward are shown below:

(1) If the company sold the striker for £70 000 it would allow the club to pay off Daniel Marsden's loan, though it might well reduce future gate money. The remaining £20 000 could be used to pay off part of the £100 000 bank loan. This might reduce the financial pressure on the club and give them a chance to 'put their house in order'. It could think about selling *part* of the valuable ground, retaining enough to allow football to continue.

(2) The Manager should be allowed to manage, i.e. to select the team he wants to play from among those players he has been given as his squad (these are his resources). The Board of Directors determine the size and composition of the squad. In other words they decide the resources to be allocated to the Manager.

Thus team selection should be the Manager's prerogative, while the purchase and sale of players, and the wages they are to be paid, is rightly the responsibility of the Board of Directors.

There is an obvious need for consultation and harmony between the Manager and the Board of Directors, but 'damaging interference' implies that the Chairman has overruled the Manager's selections at times. This is bound to create friction, especially since the Manager is responsible for the results achieved.

(3) The personal affairs of the various officers of the club are of no relevance until the interests of the club are adversely affected. Bearing in mind the close working relationship called for between the company's Chairman and its Manager, it is apparent that one or other of them will have to leave the club – barring the possibility of reconciliation. The Board of Directors have to decide whether Daniel Marsden or Sam Goulden is more valuable to the Club.

43 Case study – Tropical Aquaria

The person at most risk here is Poltex Stafford. If he is deemed at law to be a partner, he will be fully liable for debts incurred in the business. A considerable amount of equipment is going to be purchased – possibly on credit. If the venture succeeds there is no problem, but if few people take up the service offered, the partners will have a lot of debts to pay and if John Blunt runs out of money, the creditors can turn to Poltex for full settlement. What makes the position doubly dangerous for this wealthy gentleman is the fact that there is no limit to the extent to which he can be committed by contracts entered into by his young partner.

A limited liability company would produce a much more satisfactory situation. Poltex Stafford would stand to lose the capital he had staked in the company through the purchase of shares, but he would not stand to lose more than this.

On the marketing problem generally:

(1) Hospitals and surgeries (dentists and doctors) might be useful targets.

(2) Old people's homes and children's homes might be provided the service by charity organisations.

(3) Larger commercial and industrial organisations might be interested (banking branches could be enhanced?).

(4) Wealthier private homes are promising – but businesses could charge the costs to revenue *before* tax is assessed, which makes it comparatively cheap for them.

Advertising

Perhaps this could be done through a display aquarium for public viewing at large seaside resorts, so that orders can be taken there.

This combines a straight commercial venture – with charges for admission – and advertising for the new product/service.

Magazines which circulate among top executives and high-income groups could carry attractive advertisements in luscious colours. A 'casual' mention of the new service/product/company could be made by John Blunt in the television programme – commonly called a 'plug'.

Problem
Conflict between the partners is almost inevitable at some time in the future, and a written agreement is imperative.

44 Case study – The New Store Manager

Taking the problems in order:

(1) Peter can do nothing for the time being, except observe and prepare his plans. He could introduce some sort of clocking-on system, or ensure reprimands for continual offenders. This problem could also call for more expansive thinking, perhaps, in terms of flexible working hours, good attendance bonuses, and the like. But it may not be necessary to go to these lengths initially. A show of discipline may be effective when the time comes for Peter to take over the helm.

(2) Again Peter must wait, but in due course he may choose to put a notice up on the Staff Notice Board, or call the principal offenders into his office for a tactful word or two. It would be advisable for Peter to explain *why* the rule is necessary – if he intends to enforce it.

What are the advantages and disadvantages of uniform clothing?

Pros: (a) Customers can identify staff easily (b) To avoid extreme styles (c) Can be attractive and prestigious.
Cons: (a) Can be rather dull (b) Limits freedom of choice and expression (c) Possibly expensive since staff's other clothes are available but cannot be worn.

(3) When you are calculating the average time taken to sell the Ladylux stock, you should bear in mind that of the forty-three garments sold in the first month some would have been sold in the first days of the month while others will be sold in the later weeks. The *average* date of sale will be ½ month. The same thinking will need to be applied to the remaining batches.

Large stocks give customers the benefit of a wide choice. In fashion goods they also leave a residue of out-of-date stock. Cut-price autumn sales necessary to clear out summer lines, etc.

Bulk-buying would give the store reduced costs in the Radio and Television Department, and it would no doubt give the store certain advantages when customers complained or sets were found to be faulty. Big buyers such as Schumanns can expect preferential treatment at such times and the benefits can be passed on to their customers.

(4) Peter would be wise to develop a spirit of mutual co-operation and understanding with his Assistant Manager. They will have to work as a team in future. Peter has the prime responsibility for setting the tone of this relationship.

45 Case study – The Bank Absentees

One explanation for different absentee rates between men and women might be that women will believe their chance of reaching managerial positions is limited. They will not therefore be so concerned to earn 'glowing reports'. Note the reduced number of women in the bank at the higher ages. Though this could be explained by a change in recruitment policy, the continuous trend seems to indicate a tendency for women to leave. A generous leaving gratuity would also reinforce the trend.

Many young men will be so far away from the managerial aspirations that they too will be less enthusiastic.

One explanation for the different rates between younger and older members of staff might be that the more interesting jobs and the more responsible positions go to the senior staff.

46 Case study – The Credit Control Department

Here are some background notes which should help you to understand the need for a Credit Control Department in the first place.

Few of the sales made by Canford will be paid for in cash. Their customers will not expect to pay for the goods until they have had a chance to sell them. That is the way business normally operates. By giving their customers, say, two months' credit, Canford are giving them ample time to sell the goods (which they will do for cash) and then settle their accounts.

Canford's suppliers – the people who provide them with the raw materials required for their confections – will in turn give Canford time to pay for their purchases. A considerable degree of interdependency is thus developed. If Canford's suppliers insisted on being paid in cash because they were afraid they were not going to get paid, Canfords would be in difficulties since their customers would still expect to have time to settle their accounts. Almost all of the business conducted between firms is on a credit basis and this is why credit control is of significance.

There is another aspect to bear in mind. If ten articles producing a 10 per cent profit margin for Canfords are sold – and eventually paid for – they will be exactly counterbalanced by one article which is sold – and not paid for. This is why it is important for businesses to be diligent when they are granting credit facilities.

47 Case study – Funds for Expansion

Dealing with the first two elements of your task, the following points can be made:

(1) Take a specific suggestion and work it through. Thus, if it is suggested we might issue some new Ordinary shares, we have to decide how many we should issue and at what price they should be issued.

If we decide to issue new Ordinaries at 65p each, the number required would be:

$$\frac{50}{65} \times 300\,000 \times 2,$$

$$\text{which is } \frac{\text{nominal value of shares}}{\text{issue price of shares}} \times \text{sum required} \times 2$$

(we multiply by 2 because the shares have a 50p nominal value so we need to issue twice as many)

Would it be preferable to make a Rights Issue? How many shares would you suggest issuing and at what price. Remember, of course, that with a Rights Issue you can be generous with the price because you are only benefiting your own shareholders.

(2) If a new Chairman and Board of Directors were appointed this would almost certainly herald new company policies. Would the employees and the shareholders benefit? Everything depends on the efficacy of the existing Board. Some takeovers have asset-stripping as their prime objective and that could be harmful to everyone currently associated with the company.

In many cases the people in control have long-standing connections with the company. They are faimiliar with its history, its present problems and its future possiblities. As the company grows, after its inception, the founding family issue more and more shares to the public, but usually remain as the self-perpetuating but firmly entrenched Board of Directors.

48 Case study – Executive Stock Options

Some random thoughts on the options:

(1) The options may make executives stay with the company for the wrong reasons. The executives may resent being bound to the company and losing opportunities for promotion elsewhere.

(2) They might cause jealousy among those executives who are not given the opportunity of joining the scheme.

(3) The value of the scheme is related to the price of the company's shares on the Stock Exchange. What control can the executive exercise over some of the short-term influences such as bad trade figures for the national economy, or a world trade recession?

(4) Generally, however, an executive is encouraged to work harder because he has a stake in the company. Among other things he may become more cost-conscious. He might take an interest in even minor expenses such as lighting and heating.

(5) An executive would probably prefer a straight cash payment, but on the other hand there is prestige attached to the contract.

(6) If the executive leaves the company, he loses his stake, which is one of the reasons for having the contract in the first place. It is one method of reducing labour turnover – among executives anyway.

(7) Perhaps it is the workers rather than the executives who need to feel identified with the company. This scheme does not cater for the rank and file.

(8) The exercise of the options could create problems where the principal shareholder(s) own a bare majority of the voting shares.

(9) From the company's point of view a fall in the price of its shares on the Stock Exchange negates the value of the scheme. Executives will lose motivation. Fluctuating prices could be particularly damaging.

(10) The scheme will tend to make executives less resistant to change, in those cases where they feel they are likely to benefit from the increased profits resulting from the change.

49 Case study – Crypto Investment Projects

Finances are scarce in this typical manufacturing concern, and that is a normal situation in business. Executives are constantly required to make difficult judgements such as those called for here. The technique to be applied is cost-benefit analysis. The costs and benefits are split into three groups, i.e.

(i) those that can be measured in money terms directly;
(ii) those that cannot be measured at all in monetary terms, for example the spoliation of a view by a new power-line; and
(iii) those that cannot be measured directly in terms of money but can be measured in some other unit initially, and then can be converted into money terms (e.g. a reduction in the accident rate would probably lead to lower labour turnover and less absenteeism – which could be costed).

The costs and benefits under (i) and (iii) are aggregated, bearing in mind that when there is a delay in payments or receipts one would need to discount them appropriately. (Which would you sooner have – £100 now or £100 next year?)

While many of the decisions that have to be made are based on estimates and hypotheses, it is better to base decisions on rational expectations rather than intuition, non-facts, or pressure from vested interests.

Since such decision-making operations are likely to be complex and open-ended, there is a particular value in using group discussion for the exchange of ideas and the identification of problem-areas.

Of course, in a real-life situation, as executives in the company, you would be steeped in the company's affairs, and much more information would be available to you than has been made available here. But you have to appreciate that more evidence would possibly make the problem even more difficult to solve!

50 Case study – RentaVan Ltd

To calculate the book value of the Ordinary shares now, deduct the Preference stock and the convertible Debenture stock from the net assets. Divide the result by the number of Ordinary stock units. Rework to find the effect if the Debentures were converted into Ordinary stock.

Consider the effect of the conversion of the Debentures on the control of the company. Would this be to Mrs Guthrie's advantage? How?

Although you do not have details of all her outgoings you could make some assumptions – likewise for the price of the house. You should also consider the possibility of her taking on a mortgage.

Table G.1 provides a summary of merits and demerits of Convertible Debentures to both the company and the stockholders.

Table G.1 Convertible Debentures

	Merits	Demerits
Stockholders	There is security if profits fall, and there are good dividends if profits rise	There is a delay before option can be exercised
Company	More attractive to investors	Over-generous to new stockholders

51 Case study – Olympic Finances

Ideas for raising funds

(1) Athletics meetings – with overseas competitors – proceeds to a National Olympics Fund.

(2) Televised variety shows, etc., with entertainers giving their services freely. They could benefit from the favourable publicity.

(3) Pressure for more government finance – by whipping up public interest and support (But how would you do this?)

(4) A National Olympics Week (entailing what?)

(5) Sales of badges, stickers, flags, T-shirts – with sponsoring companies' names added.

(6) Appearance of past medal winners in advertisements. (How do you think this would work?)

Use of funds

(1) Building stadiums. (Which groups might be interested in sharing the cost of such ventures, and why?)

(2) Donating funds to the bodies controlling the various sports (such as the Amateur Athletics Association), leaving them to spend the money as they see fit.

(3) Subsidising the manufacture of certain equipment which could then be bought by athletes more cheaply?

Reasons for businessmen to contribute

(1) Cheap form of advertising.
(2) Goodwill from public.
(3) Athletes might be persuaded to sign advertising contracts in the event of success.
(4) Possible overseas trading benefits.
(5) Benefits accruing from public interest arising out of the athletes' successes in a particular sport – stimulating demand for clothing, equipment and so on.

52 In-Tray 3 – The Registrar's Department

Letter 1 – refer to banker?
Memo 2 – calculate by deducting Preference dividend from share of profit to be distributed.
Memo 3 – for example, (a) danger? tripping over leads between plugs and electric typewriters? (b) remedy? move desks to avoid leads in gangways/walkways?
Letter 4 – need to explain politely – not easy by letter – bank manager or accountant to advise?
Memo 5 – replacement?

Select Bibliography

On the theme of people and communication at work

P. Armstrong and C. Dawson, *People in Organisations*, ELMs, 1981.
C. Baker and P. Caldwell, *Unions and Change since 1945*, Pan, 1981.
J. G. Capsey and N. R. Carr, *People and Work Organizations*, Holt, Rinehart & Winston, 1982.
J. Chilver, *People Communication and Organisation*, Pergamon, 1984.
A. G. Cowling and C. J. B. Mailer, *Managing Human Resources*, Edward Arnold, 1981.
J. E. Cronin, *Industrial Conflict in Modern Britain*, Croom-Helm, 1979.
T. L. Johnson, *Introduction to Industrial Relations*, Business Books, 1981.
Ernest J. McCormick and Daniel Ilgen, *Industrial Psychology*, George Allen & Unwin, 7th edn, 1981.
N. McDonald and M. Doyle, *The Stresses of Work*, Nelson, 1981.
N.M. Selwyn, *Law of Employment*, Butterworth, 4th edn, 1982.
Chris Webb, *People and Communication*, Macmillan, 1978.
Hugh Williamson, *The Trade Unions*, Heinemann, 6th edn, 1981.
L. A. Woolcott and W. Unwin, *Mastering Business Communication*, Macmillan, 1983.

On the structure of business

Barry Berman and Joel R. Evans, *Retail Management – A Strategic Approach*, Collier-Macmillan, 1979.
Paul Bailey, *Mastering Office Practice*, Macmillan, 1982.
Tom Cannon, *Basic Marketing*, Holt, Rinehart & Winston, 1980.
J. Chilver, *Numeracy and Accounting*, Macmillan, 1984.
B. Chiplin and B. Sturgess, *Economics of Advertising*, Holt, Rinehart & Winston with the Advertising Association, 1981.
D. Eva and R. Oswald, *Health and Safety at Work*, Pan, 1981.
E. C. Eyre, *Mastering Basic Management*, Macmillan, 1982.
D. Foster, *Mastering Marketing*, Macmillan, 1982.
J. Halloram, *Supervision: The Art of Management*, Prentice-Hall, 1981.
John Hibbs, *Transport Without Politics*, Institute of Economic Affairs, 1982.
G. A. Lee, *Modern Financial Accounting*, Nelson, 3rd edn, 1981.
Eleanor Macdonald and Julia Little, *The Successful Secretary*, Macdonald & Evans, 1980.
Joan Moncrieff and Doreen Sharp, *The P. A.'s Handbook*, Macmillan, 2nd edn, 1983.
Stanley Nicholls, *Workbook on Office Safety and Organisation*, Cassell, 1975.
D. Pitt Francis, *Accounting Concepts and Methods*, Holt, 1982.

K. Roman and J. Maas, *How to Advertise*, Kogan Page, 1979.
A. D. Smith, *Filing, Retrieval and Control Systems*, Business Equipment Trade Association, 1980.
C. Woodcock (ed.), *The Guardian Guide to Running Small Businesses*, Kogan Page, 2nd edn, 1981.

On the theme of money

Central Office of Information, Reference Pamphlet 133, *Insurance in Britain*, HMSO, 1979.
J. Chilver, *Investment: A Student-centred Approach*, Macmillan, 1982.
D. Cox, *Success in Elements of Banking*, John Murray, 1979.
Michael Davey, *Everyday Economics*, Macmillan, 1983.
A. M. El-Agraa (ed.), *The Economics of the European Community*, Philip Allan, 1980.
J. Harvey, *Intermediate Economics*, Macmillan, 4th edn, 1983.
C. Hood and M. Wright (eds), *Big Government in Hard Times*, Martin Robertson, 1981.
Dudley Jackson, *Introduction to Economics: Theory and Data*, Macmillan, 1982.
E. V. Morgan, R. A. Brealey, B. S. Yamey and P. Bareau, *City Lights: Essays on Financial Institutions and Markets in the City of London*, Institute of Economic Affairs, 1979.

Cross-modular studies

H. A. V. Bulleid, *Brief Cases*, Mechanical Engineering Publications, 1977.
J. Chilver, *Business Decisions – A Cross-modular Case-study Approach*, Macmillan, 1983.
Geoff Easton, *Learning from Case Studies*, Prentice-Hall, 1982.
Peter Fearns, *Business Studies: An Integrated Approach*, Hodder & Stoughton, 1980.
E. R. Hardy Ivamy, *Principles of the Law of Partnership*, Butterworth, 11th edn, 1981.
S. B. Marsh and J. Soulsby, *Business Law*, McGraw-Hill, 2nd edn, 1981.
M. C. Oliver, *Company Law*, Macdonald & Evans, 8th edn, 1981.

Index